Family &Tree Guide Book
to Europe

The Family & Tree Guide Book
to Europe

your passport to tracing your genealogy across Europe

FROM ERIN NEVIUS AND THE EDITORS OF FAMILY TREE MAGAZINE

BETTERWAY BOOKS
CINCINNATI, OHIO

The Family Tree Guide Book to Europe © 2003 F&W Publications, Inc.
Manufactured in the United States of America. All rights reserved. No part of this
book may be reproduced in any form or by any electronic or mechanical means
including information storage and retrieval systems without permission in writing
from the publisher, except by a reviewer, who may quote brief passages in a
review. Published by Betterway Books, an imprint of F&W Publications, Inc.,
4700 East Galbraith Road, Cincinnati, OH 45236. (800) 289-0963.
First edition.

Other fine Betterway Books are available from your local bookstore or on our
Web site at www.familytreemagazine.com

07 06 05 04 03   5 4 3 2 1

Library of Congress Cataloging-in-Publication Data

The family tree guide book to Europe : your passport to tracing your
genealogy across Europe / Erin Nevius and the editors of Family Tree Magazine.
      p. cm.
   Includes bibliographical references and index.
   ISBN 1-55870-675-5 (alk. Paper)
      1. Europe—Genealogy—Handbooks, manuals, etc. 2. European
Americans—Genealogy—Handbooks, manuals, etc. I. Family tree magazine.

   CS403.F36 2003
   929'.1'07204—dc22

                                                    2003060086
                                                    CIP

Editors: Erin Nevius, Lauren Mosko, Sharon DeBartolo Carmack, CG
Production coordinator: Sara Dumford
Cover design: Stephanie Strang
Interior design: Clare Finney and Camille DeRhodes

Contents

London Skyline—
The Thames, House
of Commons, House
of Lords, Parliment,
Big Ben

SCOTLAND

Scottish descendants have easy access to more resources and records than ever before. Here's how to look past the plaid and get started finding your real Scottish ancestors.

SCANDINAVIA

Did your ancestors hail from Denmark, Finland, Iceland, Norway, or Sweden? Trace your roots back to the Viking in your past.

FRANCE

Vive la French roots! If you have ancestors who came from France, follow these six steps to get started tracing them and discovering your French heritage.

Abbey of Senanque, Gordes, Provence, France

Parliment, Budapest, Hungary

Venice waterway

Foreword

BY RHONDA R. McCLURE

Researching your European family history is a fascinating and rewarding project. It stirs your mind as you try to uncover the origins and follow the journeys of each generation of your ancestors. Like the constant—or constantly changing—paths of those you are tracing, your research is a continual adventure. For each predecessor you find, you encounter two new trails to follow to identify their parents. In this way, studying genealogy is a lifelong process. Those who take up the challenge receive the rich history of their forefathers and a heightened sense of, and deep appreciation for, their own roots, identity, and culture.

Genealogy is more than just names and dates; it's the story of your past.

SLEUTHS WANTED

It's not uncommon for those studying genealogy to share similar non-genealogical interests, such as solving word puzzles or reading mysteries. Those who are fascinated by family history typically love to analyze things and then see if their hypotheses are correct. Compiling your family tree is a similar sort of game. As you analyze what you already know about your family and collect new clues about their past, you begin to see how their lives fit into the broader scope of European history. You begin to wonder why they married the people they did and settled in the communities they chose. As you piece together the stories, a clearer picture of the finished puzzle forms.

IN TOUCH WITH THE PAST

Just as many genealogists love a good mystery, their searches for the roots of their family trees often spark an interest in a time long gone. Even if they admit to sleeping through history class as students, many now confess that they are fascinated when they discover an ancestor who was a soldier in a war that previously meant nothing more than a series of dates and places in a textbook. In the context of a genealogical search, everything from battles and empires to natural disasters and passenger-ship routes takes on a personal significance. So often, those events in history are what forced our ancestors to make the decisions they did. Once you begin to realize how much the tides of history have affected your family, you will find yourself reveling in eras that you may once have considered boring. (You may even want to write a letter to your old history teacher and apologize for those naps during the lectures.)

HEADING FOR THE GREAT UNKNOWN

For some, the idea of researching family history becomes a daunting task. Oftentimes ancestors, even those just a few generations removed, originated in a different country. Some may fear a struggle with the difference in language and haven't any idea what records they may need to access. As a result, it's easy to give up before the real adventure has begun—the adventure that brings these almost-forgotten individuals back to life, at least in memory.

The differences in records in many of the European countries are not as startling as you may have imagined. In fact, civil registration records, particularly in Italy, the Benelux region, and Scandinavia, offer so much to truly help your research that once you begin it's hard to imagine why you were ever afraid. Of course, fear of the great unknown is natural, but once you finally decide to set out on your quest, you'll find that it's a lot of fun and well worth the minor struggle involved in mastering at least the basics of the countries' languages.

POINT ME IN THE RIGHT DIRECTION

There are so many great resources, Web sites, and other aids to help you with your European research that today's family historian is at a distinct advantage. There are more electronic translators, online databases, and genealogy-focused message boards than you can imagine, not to mention the impressive records and microfilm collections available through the Family History Library and its worldwide Family History Centers. Today's family historian has an almost overwhelming amount of available material, which is why this guide serves as such a useful map and toolbox as you begin your European adventure.

Each chapter in this book is devoted to a different region or country and is written by those genealogists who are familiar with that specific region or country and its records. As you are introduced to each area, the respective author(s) will provide you with an overview and a list of the more popular records in order to help jump-start your search. You will also find a little history, especially as it may affect some of the records (or the location of the records) you may require.

Soon, you will no longer be looking into the great unknown but instead embarking on the first branch of exploration into the roots of your family tree. Enjoy the real adventure as you get to know your ancestors, and be assured that The Family Tree Guide Book to Europe is always here to give you information about the many countries your ancestors called home.

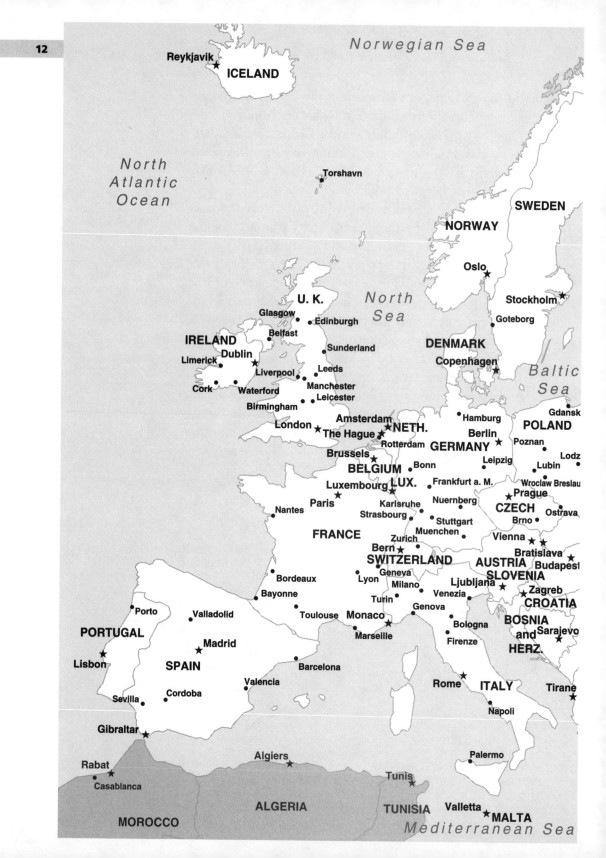

Norwegian Sea

Reykjavik ★
ICELAND

North
Atlantic
Ocean

Torshavn •

SWEDEN

NORWAY

Oslo •

North
Sea

Stockholm ★
Goteborg •

U. K.

Glasgow •
Edinburgh •
Belfast •

DENMARK
Copenhagen ★

Baltic
Sea

IRELAND
Limerick •
Dublin ★
Cork •
Waterford •
Liverpool •
Birmingham •

Sunderland •

Leeds •
Manchester •
Leicester •

London ★

Amsterdam ★
The Hague ★
Rotterdam •

NETH.

Hamburg •
Berlin ★

Gdansk •
POLAND
Poznan •

GERMANY
Bonn •
Leipzig •

Lodz •
Lubin •

Brussels ★
BELGIUM
Luxembourg ★ LUX.

Paris ★

Frankfurt a. M. •

Wroclaw Breslau •
Prague ★

Nantes •

Karlsruhe •
Strasbourg •

Nuernberg •

CZECH
Brno •

Ostrava •

FRANCE

Stuttgart •
Zurich •
Bern ★
SWITZERLAND

Muenchen •
Vienna ★
AUSTRIA

Bratislava ★
Budapest ★

Bordeaux •
Bayonne •

Geneva •
Lyon •
Milano •

SLOVENIA
Ljubljana ★
Venezia •

Zagreb ★
CROATIA

Porto •
Valladolid •

Toulouse •
Monaco ★

Turin •
Genova •

Bologna •
Firenze •

BOSNIA
and Sarajevo ★
HERZ.

PORTUGAL
Lisbon ★

Madrid ★
SPAIN

Marseille •

Barcelona •

Rome ★
ITALY

Tirane ★

Sevilla •
Cordoba •

Valencia •

Napoli •

Gibraltar ★

Algiers ★

Palermo •

Rabat •
Casablanca •

Tunis •

Valletta ★ MALTA

MOROCCO

ALGERIA

TUNISIA

Mediterranean Sea

FINLAND

Helsinki
Tallinn
ESTONIA

St. Petersburg

Perm
Sverdlovsk
Chelyabinsk
Izevsk
Ufa

Jaroslavl
Rostov
Gorkiy
Kazan

Riga ★LATVIA

Moscow

Tol Yatti
Kuybyshev

LITHUANIA
Vilnius

Saratov

Minsk
BELARUS

Warsaw

Kiev
Kharkov

Volgograd

Krakow
Lviv
UKRAINE
Donetsk
Krivoy Rog
Zaporozhye
RUSSIA

SLOVAKIA
Frunze

HUNGARY
Chisinau
Cluj
MOLDOVA Odessa
Krasnodar

Timisoara
ROMANIA
GEORGIA
Baku

Bucharest
Black Sea
Tbilisi ★ AZERBAIJAN
Belgrade
Constanta
ARMENIA

YUGOSLAVIA
Varna
Yerevan
Sofia
Burgas

Skopje
BULGARIA
Tabriz

MACEDONIA
Istanbul
Thessaloniki
Ankara

ALBANIA
Bursa
TURKEY

GREECE
Al Mawsil
Agrinion
Izmir
Adana

Athens
Halab

Baghdad
NORTH CYPRUS
SYRIA
IRAQ

CYPRUS
Beirut ★ Damascus

Ireland

REGIONAL GUIDE

DWIGHT A. RADFORD AND KYLE J. BETIT

What does Irish mean? The answer isn't as simple as you might think. This can be an emotional subject—and a confusing one. Many people have the perception that Irish means both Gaelic and Catholic, thus eliminating anyone who doesn't fit into those categories. But when we visit Irish festivals and genealogy gatherings around the world, we find that at least half of the people have ancestors from Ireland who were Protestants rather than Catholics. We also find that many Irish Catholics and their children left the church in the country to which they emigrated. Does that mean they are no longer Irish?

In our search for Irish ancestry, we have realized just how complicated the term "Irish" is. We also have found that historians, for the sake of weaving together this complex history, have sometimes unknowingly contributed to its oversimplification. So we'll begin by dispelling a few myths and sharing some observations that have affected our genealogical research:

- Not all Irish emigrants were the poor, starving, illiterate peasants that many books and movies would have us believe. The Irish of all social classes settled just about everywhere. You need to do your Canadian, Australian, English—wherever your ancestor settled—research before even considering Irish records. Always start with yourself and trace backwards one generation at a time.

- On the subject of religion, people tend to assume that their ancestors always did what they themselves would have done. To be frank, they didn't. We've found that many Irish Catholics either left the church or married into non-Catholic families. In reverse, we find that Protestant Irish families mar-

ried into Catholic families and raised their families as Catholics. The Irish were among the founders or earliest members of nontraditional churches such as the Church of Jesus Christ of Latter-day Saints, the Church of the New Jerusalem (Swedenborg), the Shakers, and other experimental or communal groups of the nineteenth century.

- The Irish were members of many fraternal, benevolent, secret, and social societies. While this was not unique to the Irish, the anomalies are interesting. For example, Irish Catholics are documented in Freemasons' records, even though membership in such organizations would have been against the wishes of their church.

But the question remains: Who are the Irish? Many thousands of Presbyterians from the lowlands of Scotland settled in Ulster (the northern province of Ireland) in the 1600s, and their descendants emigrated in great numbers, starting in 1718. There were both "Old English" (Normans who were Catholic) and "New English" (Protestants who came after the Reformation) families who settled in Ireland, as well. Irish residents of English origin were often called the Anglo-Irish. The more prominent Anglo-Irish residents comprised the Protestant Ascendancy, which ruled Ireland for several centuries.

We can't use religion as a guideline to what Irish means because religion is so intermixed among families in Ireland. (Mixed marriages are more common than anyone wants to admit.) And, of course, we have to consider the political division between the Republic of Ireland and Northern Ireland. So for our purposes, we'll say that Irish means simply "from the island of Ireland."

STARTING AT HOME

To begin researching your Irish roots, you don't even have to leave home. In fact, you can access many Irish records right from your living room with the FamilySearch Web site, <www.familysearch.org>. The site details the records of the Family History Library (FHL) in Salt Lake City, Utah, which houses the largest collection of Irish records outside of Ireland. The library is operated by the Church of Jesus Christ of Latter-day Saints (LDS), but it's free for all to use.

But you don't have to travel to Utah to access these records. The library has more than 3,700 branches, called Family History Centers (FHCs for short), worldwide, so chances are there's one close to you. By visiting an FHC, you can order the microfilmed records held at the FHL for the cost of the postage. To find the FHC nearest you, see Appendix A or visit the FamilySearch Web site at <www.familysearch.org/eng/Library/FHC/frameset _fhc. asp>.

From one perspective, doing Irish research is easier in Salt Lake City or on the Web than it is in Ireland. That's because the FHL has

Windmill, Wicklow

microfilm from multiple Irish repositories. Among the FHL's holdings are cemetery, census, church, estate, land, military, occupational, and taxation records; directories; genealogies; and wills. For a research outline, historical background, and a guide to FHL holdings, click on the FamilySearch Research Help for Ireland <www.familysearch.org/Eng/Search/RG/frameset_ rhelps.asp>.

Other valuable repositories in the U.S. that can be accessed online are the Allen County Public Library <www.acpl.lib. in.us/genealogy> in Fort Wayne, Indiana, and the New England Historic Genealogical Society <www.newenglandancestors.org> in Boston, Massachusetts. The library of the Irish Genealogical Society International <www.rootsweb.com/~irish> in St. Paul,

Minnesota, is especially worth mentioning because it collects a large number of Irish books and journals, including many that are out of print or of limited circulation.

THE TWO Ws: WHO AND WHERE

To successfully trace your Irish ancestors, you'll need to understand a certain complexity to Irish names. Your ancestor may have used several given names during his or her life. Church records and civil registrations often record nicknames rather than formal given names. Many nicknames, such as Kate for Catherine or Con for Cornelius, are easy to spot, while others, such as Delia for Bridget or Sarah for Cecilia, are not. We recommend two books that list nicknames: *Irish Christian Names: An A-Z of First Names* by Ronan Coghlan (London: Johnston and Bacon, 1979) and, for Scots-Irish, *Scottish Christian Names: An A-Z of First Names* by Leslie Alan Dunkling (London: Johnston and Bacon, 1978). Many Irish Catholic parish registers are recorded in Latin, so it helps to have a basic understanding of Latin names. *The Record Interpreter: A Collection of Abbreviations, Latin Words and Names Used in English Historical Manuscripts and Records* by Charles T. Martin (London: Stevens and Sons, 1910) includes a helpful list of Latin names and their English equivalents.

Irish surnames are just as complex. Variations in both form and spelling are common problems. One of the most common variations you'll find is the adding and dropping of O' and Mc before Irish family names. You may see a family listed as both Connor and O'Connor in a church register. The Irish often dropped or added the prefix in their name, but there's no hard-and-fast rule about this principle. One of the most useful guides regarding the complexity of Irish surnames is *Varieties and Synonyms of Surnames and Christian Names in Ireland* by Robert E. Matheson (Bowie, Md.: Heritage Books, 1995).

If you don't know where in Ireland your ancestor lived, usually you'll need to concentrate on sources in the country where your immigrant family settled. We don't recommend that you try to use Irish records before you know the family's Irish origins.

It's impossible to know in advance which sources will tell you where in Ireland your ancestor was born; however, you will find many sources useful regardless of whether they state a specific birthplace. As far as finding an Irish place of origin, some of the most useful sources include obituaries, death certificates, and tombstones. Local histories and census, marriage, and church records also are important potential sources. Trace the immigrant ancestor back in time step by step to compile documents from arrival in the adoptive country until death and burial. Besides finding the actual birthplace in Ireland, you'll want to look for other important clues, such as birth date and parents' names, especially the mother's maiden name. And don't forget to research the extended family, friends, and neighbors. Immigrants from the same community in Ireland often emigrated together and settled together abroad.

Dunbrody Abbey, Waterford

ON TO IRELAND

Why go to Dublin or Belfast for your Irish research? Isn't everything available through the Family History Library Web site anyway? The truth is that many Irish genealogy sources are available through the FHL, but many original records of your Irish ancestors are available only in Ireland. Some main Dublin repositories include the National Archives of Ireland, National Library of Ireland, and the Representative Church Body Library; the largest archive in Belfast is the Public Record Office of Northern Ireland. Remember that the island of Ireland is politically divided; Belfast has its own repositories covering Northern Ireland. For a good guide to libraries and archives throughout the island, read *Directory of Irish Archives*, edited by Seamus Helferty and Raymond Refausse (Dublin: Irish Academic Press, 1993).

You may have heard someone say that Irish research is impossible because "all the Irish records were destroyed." This is a common oversimplification of what has happened to Irish records. During the 1922 Irish Civil War, the Public Record Office of Ireland at Four Courts in Dublin was destroyed by fire, and a number of records, including pre-1858 wills and administrations, 1821 to 1851 census records, and more than half of the Church of Ireland parish registers, were destroyed. But this is by no means a reason to avoid Irish records; a wide variety of sources are still available for your research.

Geography: The key to your success

Understanding the lay of the land and its divisions is the key to successful research. Ireland is divided into provinces, which in turn are divided into counties, which in turn are divided into civil parishes (not the same as church parishes, mind you). Civil parishes are divided into townlands, each of which is a surveyed area of land with a certain acreage and set of boundaries. As if this were not enough, Irish records are also arranged by poor-law unions, superintendent registrar's districts, and baronies, which were all created to meet the government's needs to serve its growing population.

These administrative units often overlap, which means you

must think in a more abstract way than you would in other types of genealogical research. If you have an Irish place name and you're not sure what or where it is, we suggest the 1851, 1871, and 1901 General Alphabetical Index to the Townlands and Towns, Parishes, and Baronies of Ireland to find the official spelling and location of each townland in Ireland. The 1871 and 1901 indexes are available on microfilm; the 1851 edition has been reprinted by the Genealogical Publishing Co.

On the records

Once you've located your ancestor's place of origin, you can begin searching Irish records. Here's a look at what's available:

Censuses and name lists: The earliest surviving census for Ireland is 1901. Nearly all Irish census returns for 1821 through 1851 were destroyed in the Dublin Four Courts fire of 1922; the returns for 1861 through 1891 were pulped after the statistical information was compiled. Nonetheless, both the 1901 and 1911 censuses have been microfilmed and released to the public; you can access them through the FHL.

Because many of the records have been destroyed, researchers often use "census substitutes"—partial name lists recorded for a variety of reasons, such as taxation or voter registration. Fortunately, many researchers have put together lists of what they consider useful census fragments and name lists. You can find the FHL's list of its holdings in the guide *Register of Irish Census and Census Substitutes*.

Church records: Roman Catholics make up the majority of Ireland's population. The second-largest denomination is the Church of Ireland, followed by the Presbyterian and Methodist churches. Minority faiths include the United Brethren (Moravian), Church of Jesus Christ of Latter-day Saints (Mormon), Society of Friends (Quaker), and Baptist. For a guide to the records of most faiths represented in Ireland, consult *Irish Church Records*, edited by James G. Ryan (Dublin: Flyleaf Press, 2001).

Regardless of an ancestor's faith, don't overlook the Church of Ireland's records. Roman Catholics and nonconformists were often buried in Church of Ireland cemeteries. If a Catholic or

Presbyterian family had real estate, members of the family might have had a Church of Ireland marriage ceremony to make the union legal and preserve their property rights.

If you know the county where your ancestor lived, you can contact the appropriate heritage center that has indexed the church records for that county. (For information about most heritage centers, visit the Irish Family History Foundation site at <www.irishroots.net>.) If you know a specific town or townland where your ancestor lived, you can find out what churches of your ancestor's denomination served that place. An easy way to do this is to use *The Irish Times* Irish Ancestors Web site <www.ireland.com/ancestor>. (Note that it charges a subscription fee.)

Civil registrations: Ireland didn't begin recording all births, deaths, and marriages until January 1864. (Registration of non-Catholic marriages began in April 1845.) But it's relatively easy to find an Irish civil registration entry if one was recorded for your ancestor. That's because there are yearly indexes for 1845 to 1877 and quarterly indexes starting in 1878 that cover the whole island. Mind you, there are some limitations; for example, the birth indexes don't give parents' names.

The Republic of Ireland and Northern Ireland have kept separate civil registrations since 1921. The original records of 1845

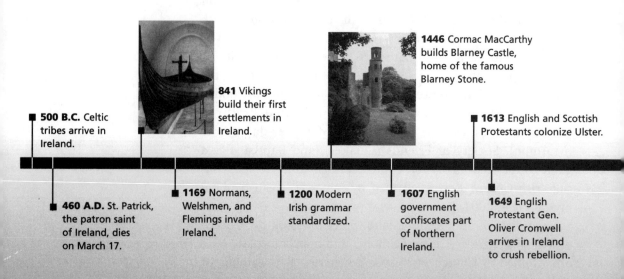

500 B.C. Celtic tribes arrive in Ireland.

841 Vikings build their first settlements in Ireland.

1446 Cormac MacCarthy builds Blarney Castle, home of the famous Blarney Stone.

1613 English and Scottish Protestants colonize Ulster.

460 A.D. St. Patrick, the patron saint of Ireland, dies on March 17.

1169 Normans, Welshmen, and Flemings invade Ireland.

1200 Modern Irish grammar standardized.

1607 English government confiscates part of Northern Ireland.

1649 English Protestant Gen. Oliver Cromwell arrives in Ireland to crush rebellion.

to 1921 for all of Ireland are at the General Register Office at Joyce House in Dublin. Those from 1921 to the present day for the Republic of Ireland are at Joyce House, and those for Northern Ireland are at the General Register Office at Oxford House in Belfast. The indexes at Joyce House are open to the public, and you can search them in person or through the mail for a fee. You can also get microfilm copies of the indexes to civil registration from 1845 through 1958 from the FHL.

Land records: Many of our Irish ancestors were tenant farmers who leased or rented their land directly from a landowner or indirectly from a middleman. Only a small percentage of people in Ireland owned their land outright, or "in fee." Several layers of subleasing might separate the actual landowner and your ancestor.

Beginning in 1708, the Irish registered land transactions with the Registry of Deeds in Dublin, although registration wasn't mandatory. In the Registry of Deeds, you can find deeds of sale, lease agreements, marriage settlements, and wills. Don't assume that just because your ancestor wasn't rich or prominent, you won't find information about him or her in the Registry of Deeds. One of the most valuable finds is a deed with a list of tenants.

You can find two useful indexes to the Registry of Deeds. The Surname Index is a personal-name index to the sellers (grantors)

1690 English King William defeats the exiled English King James II at the Battle of the Boyne.

1759 Arthur Guinness starts brewing his famous dark beer at St. James' Gate.

1791 Society of United Irishmen is formed to fight for political, economic, and social rights for all Irish.

1800 Dublin Parliament dissolves itself; England and Ireland unite as one country.

1900 Nationalists demand freedom from British rule.

1695 Law forbids Irish Catholics from voting or joining the armed forces.

1780 Irish nationalist leader Henry Grattan calls for home rule.

1793 Catholics can vote.

1845 Potato famine drives 1.6 million Irish to migrate to the United States between 1847 and 1854.

of land; not until 1833 does it include the buyers (grantees) or identify where the property was located. The Lands Index or County Index is arranged geographically by the first letter of the townland name in the transaction. This index can also list streets within towns and cities. The huge collection of Registry of Deeds records from 1708 to 1929 and the corresponding Surname Index and Lands Index are available on microfilm from the FHL.

Military records: The Irish made up a large percentage of the British Army. Not only were well-educated young men attracted to the army, but many poor young men also would enlist to improve their status in life. The army was often a family tradition. Use the records generated about these men and their families to reconstruct what your ancestor did with his life. And if you're still looking for your army ancestor's birthplace, his military records might reveal it.

We recommend a couple of research guides for army records: *My Ancestor Was in the British Army: How Can I Find Out More About Him?* by Michael J. Watts and Christopher T. Watts (London: Society of Genealogists, 1986) and *Army Records for Family Historians* by Simon Fowler and William Spencer (London: PRO Publications, 1992). Most British military records are in the Public Record Office outside of London. You can also access large collections on microfilm at the Family History Library.

1997 Frank McCourt wins the Pulitzer Prize for *Angela's Ashes*.

1914 Home rule bill becomes a law but is delayed until the end of World War I.

1921 Southern Ireland becomes a free state; six northern counties remain part of the United Kingdom.

1972 British troops fire on crowd of civil rights protesters on Bloody Sunday; protesters destroy British embassy three days later.

1916 Hundreds of Irish rebels die in unsuccessful Easter Rising.

1923 Poet and playwright William Butler Yeats wins Nobel Prize.

1993 Prime ministers of Great Britain and Ireland sign declaration promising peace to Northern Ireland.

Taxation records: In tracing just about any ancestor in nineteenth- or twentieth-century Ireland, you'll find tax records to be an indispensable resource. The major tax sources most people use in their research are the *Tithe Applotment Composition Books* (1823 to 1837) and *Griffith's Valuation of Ireland* (1847 to 1864). Tax records are particularly important because the nineteenth-century censuses were destroyed, and they record not only landowners but also renters, leaseholders, and sometimes even squatters.

The tithe was a tax based on how much land a person occupied, and rural inhabitants paid it to support clergy of the Church of Ireland. People of all denominations were required to pay the tithe because the Church of Ireland was the established church until 1871. The Tithe Applotment Books were first compiled in 1823—long after the Irish had begun paying taxes—when the Tithe Composition Act of 1823 allowed the Irish to pay taxes in cash rather than "in kind" (by giving a portion of their crops or herd). The Tithe Applotment Books record how much each tithe-payer had to give the Church of Ireland. Microfilm copies of the books for all counties are available at the FHL. *Griffith's Valuation of Rateable Property* (commonly called "Griffith's Primary Valuation") was a valuation of land and building holdings arranged by poor-law union, barony, civil parish, and townland. Griffith's is an important source because it lists a greater percentage of land occupants than the Tithe Applotment Books do. It includes landowners, landlords, tenants with leases, and renters. If your ancestors were in Ireland in the nineteenth century, there's a good chance that they are listed in Griffith's.

You can use Griffith's Valuation to find an ancestor's home or the site of a former home on a map. Each property listed in Griffith's was assigned a "map reference number," which corresponds to a set of Griffith's Valuation maps. Collections of Griffith's Valuation are available on microfilm, microfiche, and CD-ROM. You can now access Griffith's online via the subscription Otherdays.com Web site <www.otherdays.com>.

Origins.net <www.origins.net> and Eneclann <www.eneclann.ie>, in association with the National Library of Ireland, are also working to digitize these valuable records.

Now that you have the know-how to trace your Irish roots, are you eager to get back to the *auld sod*? Don't plan a trip to Ireland just yet. At some point, you may want to have the exciting experience of researching in your ancestors' homeland, but don't go to Ireland unprepared. Do what work is possible at home. Then you can hop a plane to the Emerald Isle.

To continue with your homework, the revision books generated after Griffith's Primary Valuation can be a prime source. These books document the changes in land occupancy and have been microfilmed by the Family History Library. Records for the counties of the Republic of Ireland often date into the 1930s, with records for some areas continuing into the 1960s. The revision books for the counties in Northern Ireland are at the Public Record Office in Belfast.

CENSUS

Government censuses of the population are particularly valuable because they list nearly all the population at a given time. The Irish government took a census in 1813 (which no longer exists), then every ten years from 1821 through 1911. Due to the Irish Civil War of 1921–22, another census was not taken until 1926. The next census was taken in 1936. Starting in 1946, censuses were taken every five years through 1971. Since 1971, censuses have been taken every ten years.

Only parts of the early censuses survive. The censuses from 1821 through 1851 were mostly destroyed in the 1922 fire at the Public Record Office in Dublin. The censuses from 1861 through 1891 were destroyed by the government after statistics had been compiled from them.

The 1901 census is the first complete census available for Ireland. The 1901 and 1911 censuses are available to the public, but all censuses taken since 1911 are not.

The 1821 to 1851 censuses are divided by county, barony, civil parish, and townland. The 1901 and 1911 censuses are divided by county, electoral division, and townland.

You will find the following information in the 1901 and 1911 censuses:

1901: The 1901 census lists each member of the household's name, age, sex, relationship to the head of the household, religion, occupation, marital status, county of birth (except for foreign births, which give country only), whether the individual spoke Irish, and whether the individual could read or write.

1911: The 1911 census lists the same information as the 1901 census and adds for each married woman the number of years she had been married to her current husband, the number of children that had been born to them, and the number of their children who were still alive.

RESOURCES

ORGANIZATIONS AND ARCHIVES

British Library, Department of Western Manuscripts
Great Russell St.
London WCIB 3DG
England

British Library, India Office Library and Records
197 Blackfriars Rd.
London SEI 8NG
England

British Library, Newspaper Library
Colindale Ave.
London NW9 5HE
England

Genealogical Office
2 Kildare St.
Dublin 2, Ireland

General Register Office (Ireland)
Joyce House
8-11 Lombard St. E.
Dublin 2, Ireland
Tel: +353 (1) 635-4000
<www.groireland.ie>

General Register Office (Northern Ireland)
Oxford House
49-55 Chichester St.
Belfast, Northern Ireland
Tel: +44 (028 90) 252000
<www.groni.gov.uk>

Linen Hall Library
17 Donegall Square North
Belfast BT1 5GD
Northern Ireland

National Archives of Ireland
Bishop St.
Dublin 8, Ireland
Tel: +353 (1) 407-2300
<www.nationalarchives.ie>

National Library of Ireland
Kildare St.
Dublin 2, Ireland
Tel: +353 (1) 603-0200
<www.nli.ie>

Public Record Office
Ruskin Ave., Kew
Richmond, Surrey TW9 4DU
England
Tel: +44 (020 88) 763444
<www.pro.gov.uk>

Public Record Office of Northern Ireland
66 Balmoral Ave.
Belfast BT9 6NY

Northern Ireland
Tel: +44 (028 90) 255905
<proni.nics.gov.uk>

Registry of Deeds
Chancery St.
Dublin 7, Ireland
Tel: +353 (1) 670-7500
<www.irlgov.ie/landreg>

Representative Church Body Library
Braemor Park, Churchtown
Dublin 14, Ireland
Tel: +353 (1) 492-3979
<www.ireland.anglican.org/library>

Trinity College Library
College St.
Dublin 2, Ireland

Valuation Office
6 Ely Place
Dublin 2, Ireland

BOOKS

British Archives: A Guide to Archive Resources in the United Kingdom
By Janet Foster and Julia Sheppard, 3rd ed. (New York: Macmillan Publishers, 1995)

Directory of Irish Archives
By Seamus Helferty and
Raymond Refausse, eds.
2nd ed. (Blackrock, Ireland:
Irish Academic Press, 1993)

*A Genealogist's Guide to
Discovering Your Irish
Ancestors*
By Dwight A. Radford and
Kyle J. Betit (Cincinnati,
Ohio: Betterway Books,
2001)

*Irish Records: Sources for
Family and Local History*
By James G. Ryan, Rev. ed.
(Salt Lake City, Utah:
Ancestry, 1997)

The Irish Roots Guide
By Tony McCarthy (Dublin:
Lilliput, 1991)

*Manuscript Sources for the
History of Irish Civilisation*
By Richard J. Hayes, 11 vols.
(Boston: G.K. Hall & Co.,
1965)

*Sources for the History of
Irish Civilisation: Articles in
Irish Periodicals*
By Richard J. Hayes, 9 vols.
(Boston: G.K. Hall and Co.,
1970)

*Tracing Your Irish Ancestors:
The Complete Guide*
By John Grenham, 2nd ed.
(Dublin: Gill & Macmillan,
1999)

CD-ROMS

RICK CRUME
Find the end of the rainbow
with these Irish CD-ROM
databases, which include

indexes to birth and mar-
riage records, census
records, wills, passenger lists,
and gravestone transcrip-
tions. You can access many
of them online through subscription services, too.

**The 1851 Dublin City
Census:** Before the unfortu-
nate destruction of the 1851
census of Ireland, the Public
Record Office created this
invaluable list of the names
and addresses of more than
60,000 heads of household
in the city of Dublin.
Windows, $42.95, Eneclann

**Grenham's Irish
Recordfinder:** Enter information about where your
ancestors lived, and the
Recordfinder will tell you
what records are available
for that place. Includes maps
and Griffith's Valuation
household survey (1848 to
1864). Windows, about
$629, John Grenham

**Heritage Books Archives:
Ireland Volume 1:** This collection of five digitized Irish
history and genealogy books
includes the Index to the
Prerogative Wills of Ireland,
1536–1810, and many mar-
riage records. Mac or
Windows, $37, Heritage
Books

**Index of Irish Wills
1484–1858:** An index to
records in the National
Archives of Ireland, this CD
includes more than 100,000
names. Windows, $39.95,
Eneclann

**Index to Griffith's Valuation
of Ireland, 1848–1864:** This
survey of landholders and
householders can help you
identify an immigrant ancestor's exact place of origin.
Mac or Windows, $59.99,
Genealogy.com; online,
International & Passenger
Records Collection

Indexes to Irish Wills: View
page images of indexes to
wills probated before 1800
(from five volumes edited by
W.P.W. Phillimore). Mac or
Windows, $29.95, Quintin
Publications

**From Genealogy.com
<www.genealogy.com>:**
   **1. Irish Immigrants to
North America, 1803–1871:**
Data on 46,000 Irish immigrants to the United States
and Canada; $39.99
   **2. Irish to America,
1846–1865 Passenger and
Immigration Lists:** Records
for 1.5 million Irish immigrants arriving in Boston
(1846 to 1851) and New York
(1846 to 1865); $59.99
   **3. Irish to America
Passenger and Immigration
Lists Vol. 2, 1846–1886:** Data
on 1.5 million immigrants
arriving in Boston (1846 to
1851) and New York (1866 to
1886); $59.99

**Irish Flax Grower's List, 1796
International Land Records:**
Each of the 60,000 people
on this list received an
award for planting between
one and five acres of flax:
four spinning wheels for one
acre or a loom for five.

Entries give the parish of residence, and most counties are covered. Mac or Windows, $29.99, Genealogy.com; online, International & Passenger Records Collection

Irish Parish Records: Antrim, Down, Louth: Despite the CD-ROM's name, most of the 435,008 records in this database came from gravestone transcriptions. Windows, $39.95, Ancestry.com; online, UK & Ireland Records Collection

Irish Source Records, 1500s–1800s: This collection of digitized books includes about 190,000 names from marriage records, 1841 and 1851 census records, and indexes to Irish wills. Mac or Windows, $39.99, Genealogy.com; online, International & Passenger Records Collection

Memorials of the Dead: This product has gravestone transcriptions from 128 cemeteries in the western Irish counties of Galway and Mayo. Of the 8,000 names, 3,000 date from before 1901, and many of the gravestones were erected by American relatives. Windows, $29.95, Eneclann

The Search for Missing Friends: Irish Immigrant Advertisements Placed in The Boston Pilot 1831–1920: These ads refer to Irish immigrants across the United States and often cite places

of origin and dates and places of arrival in North America. Mac or Windows, $69.99, New England Historic Genealogical Society; online, NEHGS

Tithe Applotment Books of Ireland, 1823–1838 International Land Records: Like a census, this survey names landholders in the six counties of present-day Northern Ireland. Each entry lists the full name, county, civil parish, townland, and year of the tithe book. Mac or Windows, $49.99, Genealogy.com

Vital Records Index: British Isles, 2nd edition: This set of CDs includes Irish birth, baptism, and marriage records from 1538 to 1906. Windows, $20, FamilySearch

The William Smith O'Brien Petition, 1848–1849: After the Irish rebel leader William Smith O'Brien was sentenced to death, 80,000 people signed a petition to gain his clemency. Entries include the signers' names, addresses, and occupations. Windows, $39.95, Eneclann CD-ROM

Publishers and Online Subscriptions

Ancestry.com
<www.ancestry.com>
Tel: (800) 262-3787

Eneclann
<www.eneclann.ie>
Tel: +353 (1) 671-0338

FamilySearch
<www.familysearch.org>
Tel: (800) 537-5971

Genealogy.com
<www.genealogy.com>
Tel: (800) 548-1806

Heritage Books
<www.heritagebooks.com>
Tel: (800) 398-7709

Heritage Quest
<www.heritagequest.com>
Tel: (800) 760-2455

International & Passenger Records Collection
<www.genealogy.com/genealogy/8100252_pili_html_email.html>
Online subscription, $14.99 per month or $79.99 per year

John Grenham: Irish Record Finder
<indigo.ie/~rfinder>
Tel: +353 (1) 837-9290

New England Historic Genealogical Society
<www.newenglandancestors.org>
Tel: (888) 296-3447

Otherdays.com
<www.otherdays.com>
Subscriptions range from $8 for 72 hours to $44 per year

Quintin Publications
<www.quintinpublications.com>
Tel: (800) 747-6687

UK & Ireland Records Collection
<www.ancestry.com/search/rectype/vital/epr/main.htm>

Online subscription, $39.95 per quarter or $99.95 per year

PERIODICALS

The Irish Ancestor
1969–1981. Published by the Irish Ancestor, the Glebe House, Fethard, County Tipperary, Ireland. This journal published copies of will abstracts, church records, gravestone inscriptions, family Bible entries, and any other previously unpublished genealogical source.

The Irish At Home and Abroad
1993–1999. This journal contained articles on how to do Irish research, as well as tracing Irish immigrants. Back issues available at major libraries with Irish collections.

Irish Family History
1985–. Published by the Irish Family History Society, P.O. Box 36, Naas, County Kildare, Eire. This journal contains articles on and extracts from Irish records.

The Irish Genealogist
1937–. Published by the Irish Genealogical Research Society, Challoner Club, 59/61 Pont Street, London SW1X OBG, England. This journal contains record extracts as well as documented articles on families, repositories, and records.

The Irish Link
1984. Published by the Irish Link, P.O. Box 135, South Melbourne, Victoria 3205, Australia.

Irish Roots
1992–. Published by Belgrave Publications, Cork, Ireland. This journal contains articles on many topics, including surnames and new developments in Irish genealogy.

WEB SITES

A to Z of Irish Genealogy
<www.irish-insight.com/a2z-genealogy>

All things Irish: Genealogy, Books, Classes & Travel
<www.irishgenealogy.com>

Browse Ireland
<www.browseireland.com/genealogy>

Celtic Origins
<www.genealogy.ie>

The Church of Ireland: Genealogy and Family History
<www.ireland.anglican.org/library/libroots.html>

Cyndi's List: Ireland & Northern Ireland
<www.cyndislist.com/ireland.htm>

Directory of Irish Genealogy
<homepage.tinet.ie/~seanjmurphy/dir>

Genealogy: GoIreland.com
<www.goireland.com/Genealogy/Genealogy.htm>

Genealogy Resources on the Internet
<www-personal.umich.edu/~cgaunt/irish.html>

GENUKI UK & Ireland Genealogy
<www.genuki.org.uk>

Ireland Genealogy Information
<www.ireland-information.com/heraldichall/irishcoatsofarms.htm>

Irish Ancestors
<www.ireland.com/ancestor>

Irish Ancestors
<www.irish-ancestors.com>

Irish Ancestors.net
<freepages.genealogy.rootsweb.com/~irishancestors>

Irish Family History Foundation
<www.irishroots.net>

Irish Genealogical Research Society
<www.igrsoc.org>

Irish Genealogical Society Int'l.
<www.rootsweb.com/~irish/>

Irish Genealogy: Andrew J. Morris Genealogy
<www.ajmorris.com/roots/>

Irish Genealogy Bridge
<www.geocities.com/Silicon Valley/Haven/1538/irish.html>

Irish Genealogy Guide
<www.irishabroad.com/
yourroots>

Irish Genealogy Limited
<www.irishgenealogy.ie>

Irish Genealogy Pages
<www.scotlandsclans.com/
ireland.htm>

Irish Genealogy Resources
<www.distantcousin.com/
Links/Ethnic/Irish>

**Irish Genealogy Search Tools
and Articles**
<www.daddezio.com/
irshgen.html>

**Irish Genealogy,
Surnames, and Coat of Arms
Resource**
<www.youririshroots.com>

**Irish History:
Genealogical Research**
<www.vms.utexas.edu/~
jdana/history/genealogy.
html>

Irish in America
<www.pbs.org/wgbh/pages/
irish/genealogy.html>

Irish Origins
<www.irishorigins.com>

Local Ireland Genealogy
<www.local.ie/genealogy>

National Archives of Ireland
<www.nationalarchives.ie/
genealogy.html>

**O'Lochlainns Irish Family
Journal/Irish Genealogical
Foundation**
<www.irishroots.com>

**Professional Irish Genealogy
Research**
<www.ireland.
progenealogists.com>

**Sources for Research
in Irish Genealogy**
<www.loc.gov/rr/
genealogy/bib_guid/
ireland.html>

England and Wales

REGIONAL GUIDE
PAUL MILNER AND LINDA JONAS

N o matter who you are or where you live, you can find your English ancestors. You don't even have to travel to England. In fact, it's often just as easy to trace your English ancestors from outside of England than inside of it, and that's good news for those of you whose ancestors crossed the ocean to the American colonies or the English Channel to France.

Some people begin their genealogy research looking for famous ancestors or, especially in the case of English roots, hoping to find royal lines. Luckily, time heals all class divisions, and both your noble and surf English ancestors can be found in the multitude of English records.

A MATTER OF RECORDS
To start finding your English ancestors and discovering their stories, you need to begin with English records such as civil registrations, census returns, parish registers, and probate records. English records are remarkably complete and, in many cases, go back centuries. But because of the way the records are organized and stored, it can actually be easier to do research outside of England itself, a major help to those whose predecessors emigrated to a different country. Hands-on research in England involves traveling to many different record offices; whether you're searching from England, Ireland, or Sweden, it's much more convenient to access them via the Internet.

Because of the microfilming efforts of the Church of Jesus

Big Ben, London

Windsor Castle,
Windsor

Christ of Latter-day Saints (LDS), almost all of the original records you need to begin your research are available from the church's Family History Library, located in Salt Lake City, Utah. To learn more about the records held in the Family History Library, visit the FamilySearch Web site <www.familysearch.org/Search/searchfhc2.asp>.

Many genealogists have made the mistake, when learning that an ancestor was born in England, of finding someone by the same name there and assuming they've found their ancestor. A mistake like this can lead to years of tracing an incorrect family line. It's essential that you have enough information about your ancestor to distinguish him from the many others of the same name in England. Find out anything and everything you can about your ancestor. It's helpful to know your ancestor's full name; place of birth; dates of birth, marriage, and death; name of spouse; children's names; names of parents; date of immigration; occupation; religion; and names of cousins, friends, and associates. Of course, you don't have to know all of that before commencing English research, but the more information you have, the easier it will be to identify your ancestor in English records.

It's important to try to examine the original records (or microfilm of the originals) rather than merely relying on transcripts or online databases. Let's look at an example from the 1881 census of England to see why:

Say you have an ancestor named Henry Goddard, who is listed in the 1881 census transcript as living in London, St. Pancras, occupation "Door Keeper H+." The "+" sign means that the occupation stated on the census record was too long to fit in the database. He is living next to a man named Karl Wass, an "Author Politi+." A doorkeeper with an unknown author living next door might not seem interesting, but the original census tells a different story: Goddard's occupation in full is "Door Keeper—House of Lords." His neighbor turns out to be a German "Author, Political Economy," whose mistranscribed name is actually Karl Marx. Yes, that Karl Marx. The moral? Always go to the source.

Certain British given names can also cause problems when consulting the records. Some names get abbreviated (William to Wm.), some can be interchangeable in England (Elizabeth and Isobel or Edward and Edmond), and sometimes nicknames were used (Will, Dick, Betty, or Molly).

PLACING YOUR ANCESTORS

Even the term "England" can be confusing. In 1536, King Henry VIII united England and Wales under the same system of laws and government. In 1707, Great Britain was formed when the Parliaments of the Kingdom of England and Wales and of the Kingdom of Scotland passed the Act of Union. In 1801, Ireland was united politically with Great Britain to form the United Kingdom of Great Britain and Ireland. In 1921, most of Ireland separated from the United Kingdom. So today, Great Britain refers to England, Wales, and Scotland, while United Kingdom refers to all of the above plus Northern Ireland.

Windsor Castle, Windsor

Telephone booth,
London

As in all research, it's important to locate the places where events occurred in the lives of your ancestors. Begin by locating the county. In England, the county boundaries changed in 1974, so you will need the pre-1974 maps. For family historians, all pre-1974 counties have been given standardized three-letter codes known as Chapman Codes. (See list on page 40.) The three letters make them easy to use when recording the name of the county and entering information into a computer.

In England, however, it's not enough to know the name of the county where an ancestor lived. You need to know your ancestor's parish. The Church of England is the official church, and the parish is the fundamental unit of the Church of England. You will find many records of your ancestors in the Church of England parish records, even if they were Catholics or "nonconformists" (those who did not follow the beliefs of the Church of England). Having your baptism, marriage, and burial recorded in the Church of England was necessary to prove your right to inherit, to hold public office, or to get welfare relief.

IT'S LATIN TO ME

You may run into problems with old handwriting. Both the "secretary" style, which petered out around 1700, and the newer "italic" style can seem very hard to read at first. Luckily, a bit of practice with copybooks should make the process easier.

1536 King Henry VIII unites England and Wales.

1600 Shakespeare's Hamlet premieres (est.).

1634 Lord Baltimore founds Maryland as a haven for English Catholics.

1649 King Charles I beheaded.

1538 Parish registers begin.

1607 Jamestown, Va., founded.

1620 Mayflower lands in Massachusetts.

1642 Civil war begins as Oliver Cromwell seeks to overthrow the monarchy; record keeping from here until the end of the Commonwealth period (1660) is irregular.

London Skyline, with the Thames, House of Commons, House of Lords, Parliament, Big Ben

1707 Act of Union forms Great Britain from the Kingdom of England and Wales and the Kingdom of Scotland.

1733 Parish registers switch from Latin to English.

1754 Lord Hardwicke's Act outlaws marriages outside the Church of England except for Quakers and Jews.

1660 Monarchy is restored under Charles II, who officially discourages emigration.

1752 Gregorian calendar adopted.

1768 First edition of the Encyclopedia Britannica published.

Dover Castle, Dover

Remember that words won't always be spelled the same as they are today and that their spelling might vary even within a given document.

Most legal documents before 1733 were written in Latin. To decipher these, however, fluency isn't important and there are books available to translate key words. When you do encounter Latin records, treat them as a sign that you have completed a significant amount of research.

Another unexpected difficulty in English records is in date keeping. Prior to 1752, England used the Julian calendar, in which the new year started on March 25, the day it was believed Christ was conceived. By 1752, however, the calendar was eleven days off from the actual seasons and solstices. So September 3–13 of that year were simply skipped, a leap year was instituted, New Year's Day was changed to January 1, and

1778 End of Penal Laws; many Catholic registers date from this time.

1801 Ireland unites politically with Great Britain to form the United Kingdom of Great Britain and Ireland.

1837 Queen Victoria begins her reign (-1901) and civil registration begins.

1859 Charles Darwin publishes *On the Origin of Species.*

1814 Treaty of Ghent ends final war between England and its former American colonies.

1825 An overpopulated Great Britain repeals anti-emigration laws.

1843 Charles Dickens writes *A Christmas Carol.*

January, February, and March became the first three months of the year instead of the last three months.

Thus, a child born on 4 March 1605 to parents married 14 April 1605 may look like he was born out of wedlock but was, in fact, born eleven months after the marriage. Also, September, October, November, and December may be abbreviated as 7ber, 8ber, 9ber, and 10ber, respectively, even though they are now the ninth through twelfth months.

VITAL INFORMATION

From the time of the Reformation until 1837, the local clergy of the Church of England were charged with recording vital records for everyone in their community. But the number of church dissenters and the onus of forcing the clergy to work, in practice, as unpaid civil servants caused problems. So Parliament created a new civil registration system that began 1 July 1837. The country was divided into twenty-seven regions. The regions were divided into 618 districts, and these districts were divided into subdistricts with local registrars. By 1838 there were 2,193 local registrars.

English law required all births to be reported within six weeks, although many births went unrecorded. Marriages and deaths were usually registered because the person performing the marriage registered it, and deaths had to be recorded to receive a burial license.

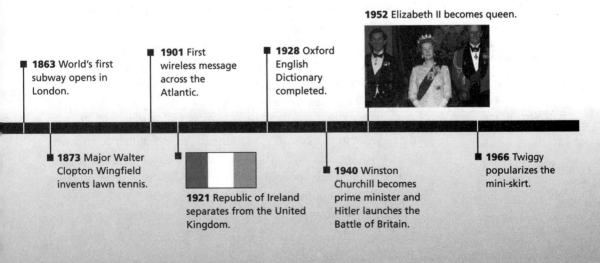

1952 Elizabeth II becomes queen.

1863 World's first subway opens in London.

1901 First wireless message across the Atlantic.

1928 Oxford English Dictionary completed.

1873 Major Walter Clopton Wingfield invents lawn tennis.

1921 Republic of Ireland separates from the United Kingdom.

1940 Winston Churchill becomes prime minister and Hitler launches the Battle of Britain.

1966 Twiggy popularizes the mini-skirt.

CHAPMAN COUNTY CODES

These three-letter abbreviations identify English counties (pre-1974):

BDF	Bedfordshire	HUN	Huntingdonshire	SFK	Suffolk
BRK	Berkshire	KEN	Kent	SRY	Surrey
BKM	Buckinghamshire	LAN	Lancashire	SSX	Sussex
CAM	Cambridgeshire	LEI	Leicestershire	WAR	Warwickshire
CHS	Cheshire	LIN	Lincolnshire	WES	Westmorland
CON	Cornwall	LND	London (city only)	WIL	Wiltshire
CUL	Cumberland	MDX	Middlesex	WOR	Worcestershire
DBY	Derbyshire	NFK	Norfolk	YKS	Yorkshire
DEV	Devon	NTH	Northamptonshire	ERY	Yorkshire—East Riding
DOR	Dorset	NBL	Northumberland		
DUR	Durham	NTT	Nottinghamshire	NRY	Yorkshire—North Riding
ESS	Essex	OXF	Oxfordshire		
GLS	Gloucestershire	RUT	Rutland	WRY	Yorkshire—West Riding
HAM	Hampshire	SAL	Shropshire (Salop)		
HEF	Herefordshire	SOM	Somerset		
HRT	Hertfordshire	STS	Staffordshire		

Opposite page:
Tower Bridge,
London

Estimates indicate that more than 90 percent of all births since 1837 have been registered, and the percentages are even higher for marriages and deaths. Since technology has made recording data more effective, very few events have gone unrecorded in England in the twentieth century, and copies of all of these records are in the General Register Office in London.

In addition to well-indexed vital records, England also has a number of other well-preserved record types that will make your family history quest easier:

Census: England took its first national census in 1801, and since then, a new census has been taken every ten years with the exception of the war year of 1941. The 1801, 1811, 1821, and 1831 censuses were nothing more than population head counts. The 1841 census, and every one since, theoretically listed everyone in the country by name. But the English census was taken on a specific night so it was actually a snapshot of society on that date: Only people who were at home that night were supposed to be enumerated.

Because of how the census was completed, families may be

Hope Village

listed incompletely. If someone isn't listed, don't jump to the conclusion that he or she had died. Men, especially sailors and soldiers, might have been working away from home that night.

The 1841 census lists genders, occupations, exact age of children, age of adults rounded down to the nearest multiple of five, and whether a person was born in the county where enumerated. From 1851 on, the census recorded exact ages (as reported), relationship to the head of the household, marital status, and exact place of birth.

English censuses remain confidential for one hundred years, so, for example, the 1901 census was opened in January 2002. While it's common practice to start with the most recent census and move backwards, for these records, the 1881 census is usually a better starting point because it's indexed by surname for the entire nation. Other censuses may not be indexed by surname, so you need to know where your ancestor was living.

As with any set of records, especially when indexed, there will be some spelling errors of surnames, people may not be listed by the same names found in civil or church records, some records have been lost or damaged, and some people have been missed.

Probate records: English probate records can be divided into post- and pre-1858. Prior to 1858, probate was the responsibility of the Church of England. Since 1858, all records have been processed in one central court system for England and Wales. Probate records include wills and administrations of the estates of those who died without making a will. Before 1540, inheritance was set so that only testaments could be written; law predetermined the division of land.

Before 1837, boys age fourteen or older and girls twelve or older could make wills, but after 1837, anyone making a will had to be at least twenty-one years old. Wills would have been probated by the court where the deceased held property. If property extended from one ecclesiastic unit to another, the will would be moved up to a higher church court. The rank (from smallest to largest) of the divisions is parish, Peculiar (Peculiar Court), Rural Deanery (Rural Deans Court), Archdeaconry (Archdeacon's Court), Diocese (Bishop's Court), and Province.

Most pre-1858 probate records that survived are now in the Public Record Office or at county or diocesan archives. A majority have been microfilmed. To get started in searching these records, you need to have a date of death and a location of property to determine what court would have jurisdiction.

For post-1858 records, a nationwide Probate Calendar recorded every will since probate jurisdiction was given to the state. To use the Probate Calendar, you will only need to know your ancestor's name and enough information to pick him out from others with the same name. The calendar will tell you when and in what court the will was executed and may also give details not found in the will.

Harrod's department store, London

English research isn't painless, and it still takes plenty of time to find the results you want. But most researchers can eventually find what they are looking for and put together a relatively complete family history—something that's not always possible with other European record systems.

Remember that your English ancestors have beautiful and often heart-wrenching stories to tell. It is up to you to tell them. You, your family members, and researchers for generations to come will be glad you did.

CENSUS

The English government has taken a census every ten years since 1801 (with the exception of 1941, due to World War II). Prior to 1841, the censuses are merely a head count of the people in a certain area, with no real genealogical use; however, some parishes collected the names of their parishioners and a few of these lists still survive.

The 1841 census was conducted on June 7. All censuses between 1851 and 1931 were taken between March 31 and April 8. Only the people who spent the night in each household were enumerated; those travelling, away at school, or working nights were listed where they spent the night.

The following information is included in these censuses:

1841: This document lists the members of every household, including name, sex, address, occupation, and if they were born in England. Note that census-takers rounded the ages of those over fifteen down to a multiple of five, so 48 became 45.

1851 and later: Here you will find the names, ages, occupations, relationship to the head of the household, and parish and county of birth (except foreign births, which may only give a country).

The censuses are organized by civil registration districts and then subdivided into enumeration districts. The 1841 census is an exception, arranged by "hundreds" (administrative subdivisions of land). On census films, you will find a title page with the district number and a description of the area covered by each enumeration district.

The original census records for 1841 to 1901 are held in the

National Archives' Public Records Office (PRO). (The National Archives was formed in 2003 with the merger of the Public Records Office and the Historical Manuscripts Commission.) Another good resource is England's Family Records Centre (FRC). Regardless of which resource you use, keep in mind that records less than a century old are confidential.

You can contact the National Archives' Public Records division at:

The National Archives (PRO)
Ruskin Ave.
Kew, Richmond
Surrey
TW9 4DU
United Kingdom
Tel: 020 8876 3444
enquiry@nationalarchives.gov.uk
<www.nationalarchives.gov.uk>
You can contact The Family Records Centre at:

The Family Records Centre
1 Myddelton St.
London
EC1R 1UW
Tel: 087 0243 7788
Fax: 017 0455 0013
<www.familyrecords.gov.uk/frc/research/censusmain.htm>

You must provide the name and address (at the time of the census) of the individual you are seeking, as well as the written consent of the person on the record or a direct descendant.

WALES

LISE HULL

On the Wales side of the Severn Bridge, a red dragon signals "Croeso i Cymru: Welcome to Wales." You have entered a tiny nation with its own Celtic language, rich heritage, and distinctive landscape.

Boasting the cities of Cardiff, Swansea, and Newport, South Wales is the most heavily populated part of Wales. It is dominated by English-speakers and industrialization, thanks to King Coal, which has been mined and exported from the Valleys since the onset of the Industrial Revolution. Highlighted by rich, undulating farmland, West Wales features Pembrokeshire, long known as "Little England Beyond Wales," and Carmarthenshire, with its vocal pocket of Welsh-speaking residents whose voting strength helped create the National Assembly. Scenic Mid Wales, with its small villages, seaside vistas, and Welsh-speaking communities, is often unwittingly bypassed by travellers anxious to reach Snowdonia National Park, where hulking grey crags are scattered not just with sheep but also with hikers. In the late thirteenth century, the mountainous terrain offered refuge to Welsh rebels fighting Edward I's army. Though the English king's mighty fortresses still dominate North Wales and slate mining has reshaped the land, the region is renowned for its beauty.

EMIGRATION TO AMERICA

You probably don't know that the Welsh actually discovered America well before Columbus sailed the Atlantic. In about 1169, Prince Madog ab Owain, a son of Owain Gwynedd, King of North Wales, voyaged from Wales to seek his fortune. Upon his return, he bragged of visiting a new land where the people lived peacefully. Many believe the land was America, and plaques commemorating the discovery have been laid at Rhos-on-Sea in North Wales, Madog's departure point, and also at Mobile Bay, Alabama, the prince's landing site across the ocean.

Despite Madog's momentous discovery, it took another five hundred years before the Welsh began emigrating to America. According to David Peate, who details the pathway of Welsh emigration in *Welsh Family History*, "Despite the Toleration Act of 1688, religious dissenters were still excluded from many aspects of the political and social life of the nation. The American colonies offered the golden opportunity of relief; there was land available and the real prospect of religious and political liberty. It was against this background that the first sizeable

BEGIN RESEARCHING YOUR WELSH HERITAGE

What do you need to know to begin researching your Welsh heritage? Annie Lloyd, *Ninnau's* (The North American Welsh newspaper) genealogy writer, offers the following guidelines:

1. You must know the name of the ancestor.

2. You need a date of baptism, marriage, death or burial, residence, or immigration. Did your ancestor emigrate? What town did he live in? Where was he buried?

3. Do you know where in Wales your ancestor came from? Has a name of a parish or town or county come down through traditional stories in your family?

4. If your ancestor immigrated to the U.S. after 1905, there will be lots more information than if he immigrated before. Before will only give you the name of the country, not where (such as all those nice things like parish or town and county). If your ancestor immigrated to the U.S. in colonial times (during the seventeenth and eighteenth centuries), then look for county or town histories and family histories. Look at pedigree charts. If they came into New England, you probably have a better chance of finding them because they kept records very early.

5. Your ancestor might have been in the military so check those records.

Lloyd notes, "For all Welsh ancestors, you should check the following information: census records, tax records (you can use these as census records as well), land and property records, probates and wills (they will list relationships), county and family histories (as mentioned above), emigration records, church records, and school records (this is late nineteenth century). Lastly, look at any record of an area where your ancestor lived."

emigrations from Wales occur." By the end of the seventeenth century, some 3,000 Welsh people had sailed to America, clustering together to continue practising their individual religions.

In the 1790s, Wales suffered a severe economic and agricultural depression, which led to another wave of emigration. Sailing from Liverpool, Bristol, Milford Haven, Caernarfon, and other ports, thousands of Welsh farmers, weavers, artisans, and gentry sought relief in America, where land was abundant and inexpensive and the economy was stable. Others emigrated to Australia, Canada, New Zealand, and South Africa.

Between 1815 and 1850, Welsh emigration to America soared, the new residents settling in New York, Pennsylvania, Vermont, Ohio, Wisconsin, and Illinois. Some journeyed west to California to take advantage of the 1849 gold rush, while later in the century, opportunities in the higher paying industrial areas of Pennsylvania attracted Welsh miners and ironworkers. By 1900, Welsh settlers had also moved into Iowa, Kansas, and Missouri, and a large number headed to Utah to join the Church of Jesus Christ of Latter-day Saints (LDS). Ultimately, Peate says, "On a rough and ready basis, it is considered that, during the years from 1820 to 1950, a conservative estimate of emigrants from Wales to the United States exceeds 250,000."

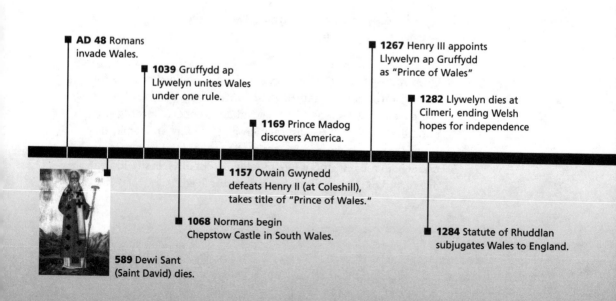

AD 48 Romans invade Wales.

1039 Gruffydd ap Llywelyn unites Wales under one rule.

1169 Prince Madog discovers America.

1267 Henry III appoints Llywelyn ap Gruffydd as "Prince of Wales"

1282 Llywelyn dies at Cilmeri, ending Welsh hopes for independence

1157 Owain Gwynedd defeats Henry II (at Coleshill), takes title of "Prince of Wales."

1068 Normans begin Chepstow Castle in South Wales.

1284 Statute of Rhuddlan subjugates Wales to England.

589 Dewi Sant (Saint David) dies.

WHERE TO START

Tracing your Welsh roots can take several pathways, each of which should connect you to your ancestors. Start at home by recording whatever family members know about your heritage. Also, talk to distant relatives. Look for names, dates, and places in letters, family records, the family Bible, photo albums, newspaper entries, and any other documents that may offer clues. Then, check out the research guidance on FamilySearch, the LDS website. Go to <www.familysearch.org> and select the "Search" tab. Under "Search," choose "Research Helps," and then select "W" for Wales. The comprehensive guide offers tips on deciding which ancestor to research, how to approach the mammoth task, and where to go to find all sorts of information. You may want to visit the Family History Library (FHL) Web site, <www.familysearch.org>, or one of their Family History Centers scattered around the world to review microfilm or microfiche and purchase copies of records. (The FHL is located at 35 North West Temple Street, Salt Lake City, Utah 84150-3400.) Your local library is another fine starting point.

Consider joining your local St. David's Society or attending a *gymanfa ganu* to learn more about Wales and network with others digging up their Welsh roots. Gather as much informa-

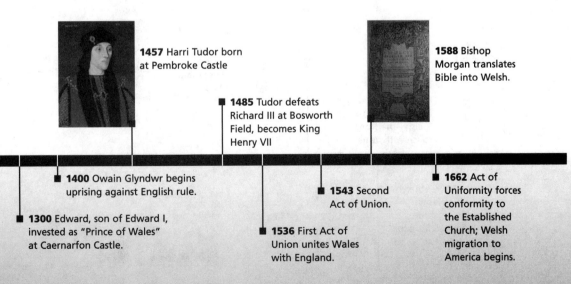

1457 Harri Tudor born at Pembroke Castle

1588 Bishop Morgan translates Bible into Welsh.

1485 Tudor defeats Richard III at Bosworth Field, becomes King Henry VII

1400 Owain Glyndwr begins uprising against English rule.

1543 Second Act of Union.

1662 Act of Uniformity forces conformity to the Established Church; Welsh migration to America begins.

1300 Edward, son of Edward I, invested as "Prince of Wales" at Caernarfon Castle.

1536 First Act of Union unites Wales with England.

tion as possible, not only about your particular Welsh ancestor but also about the nation and its history.

WHAT'S IN A NAME?

Before delving too deeply into your roots, you will need to educate yourself about Welsh surnames. Even though their Anglo-Norman conquerors had fixed surnames, the Welsh continued to use the patronymic system of naming, at least in some parts of the country, until well into the nineteenth century. While most people use fixed surnames, some modern-day Welsh are reasserting their national identity by returning to patronymics, whereby children are identified in relation to their father.

Derived from "mab," which is similar to the Scottish "mac," the use of "ap" (before a name beginning with a consonant) or "ab" (prior to a name beginning with a vowel) indicates "son of." So, Madog ab Owain indicates that Prince Madog was Owain Gwynedd's son. Likewise, Llywelyn ap Gruffydd, the first and last native Prince of Wales, was the son of Gruffydd ap Llywelyn. Indeed, like most medieval Welshmen, Llywelyn claimed a lengthy pedigree:

■ **1839** Rebecca Riots, Chartist Riots, Newport Rising.

■ **1851** *Y Drych* (*The Mirror*) founded in New York City to keep Welsh-Americans in touch with Wales.

■ **1885** Welsh Language Society (Cymdeithas yr Iaith Gymraeg)established.

1916 David Lloyd George becomes first Welsh Prime Minister.

■ **1847** "Treachery of Blue Books" blames Welsh language for poor state of education.

■ **1872** Wales' first university established in Aberystwyth.

1913 Senghenydd colliery explosion kills 439 men.

■ **1797** Last invasion of Britain (by France) occurs near Fishguard.

■ **1865** Patagonia founded by Michael Jones of Bala.

**Llywelyn ap Gruffydd ap Llywelyn ab Iorwerth
ab Owain ap Gruffydd ap Cynan . . . and so on**

Common Welsh names like Bowen and Powell reflect patronymic origins. Bowen derives from ab Owain or ab Owen and Powell from ap Hywel. Price comes from ap Rhys, while Pritchard originated as ap Richard.

Besides using "ap" or "ab," the Welsh also added an "s" at the end of a father's forename to reflect kinship ties. So, John's son adopted the surname Johns, Jones, or Jenkins. The same rule applies to Roberts, Williams, and Richards. You need to be aware of these variations and cross-verify records to be certain you have identified the correct ancestor.

Sheila Rowlands (1998) adds, "Daughters were known by their father's name: Gwenllian 'verch' ('ferch' in modern orthography) (daughter of) Rhys; the relationship was shortened to 'vch' or 'vz' in documents and appears also as 'ach.' Traditionally, this led to women retaining their maiden names (that is, their father's name rather than their husband's)."

The idiosyncrasies of the Welsh language also affect the research process. For example, over time, Llywelyn ap

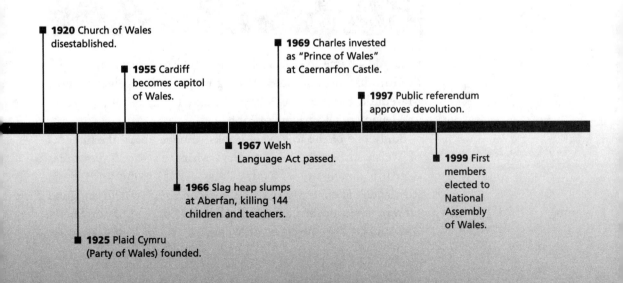

1920 Church of Wales disestablished.

1955 Cardiff becomes capitol of Wales.

1969 Charles invested as "Prince of Wales" at Caernarfon Castle.

1997 Public referendum approves devolution.

1967 Welsh Language Act passed.

1999 First members elected to National Assembly of Wales.

1966 Slag heap slumps at Aberfan, killing 144 children and teachers.

1925 Plaid Cymru (Party of Wales) founded.

Tower Bridge over Thames, London

Gruffydd's name may have been mutated to Gruffudd, Griffith or Griffiths, or even Guto. Madog may also be spelled Madoc; Maredudd has become Meredith; and Evan, Bevan, Jeavons, and Ieuan are all variants of John.

Study one of the following books to bone up on the nuances of Welsh surnames: T.J. and Prys Morgan's *Welsh Surnames* (Cardiff: University of Wales Press, 1985), John and Sheila Rowlands' *The Surnames of Wales: For Family Historians and Others* (Baltimore: Genealogical Pub. Co., 1996), or Sheila Rowlands' "The Surnames of Wales," in *Welsh Family History:*

A Guide To Research (Birmingham, England: Federation of Family History Societies, 1998).

HOME, SWEET HOME

Once you have determined your ancestor's name and any spelling variations that you might want to double check, you need to locate the parish where the person lived. Again, it's not as easy as it sounds. As Bedwyr Lewis Jones (Rowlands, 1998) states, "The main concern of family historians is to be able to identify and locate parishes. In doing this, there is one thing which has to be remembered—namely, that until fairly recently the spelling of place-names, even in official documents, could vary considerably. It is especially true in Wales where Welsh place-names have often been recorded by persons unfamiliar with the Welsh language. Cricieth in Caernarfonshire can appear as Crickaeth, Crikeith, Krickieth, Criccieth, etc."

To add to the confusion, Lewis Jones says, "In Wales, as in other countries, the same name may be borne by more than one parish." Trefdraeth is the Welsh name for Newport in Pembrokeshire and the name of a parish near Aberffraw on the Isle of Anglesey, yet the newest city in Wales is Newport, Monmouthshire. So, when you note which parish your ancestor was associated with, be sure to also write down what county or diocese they belonged to as well. Then, you can use that information as a good starting point for searching parish records or bishop's transcripts.

And, just when you thought you had the parish and county figured out . . . be aware that in 1974—and again in 1996—Wales underwent major structural reorganization. Counties came and went. Local authorities were carved out of historic counties; historic counties were reborn. Whereas Newport is now in Monmouthshire, it has also been part of Gwent. The Pembrokeshire Newport has also been in Dyfed. Most records refer to the pre-1974 counties, so it's vital that you identify the correct historic county for your search. Take a look at the LDS guide to Wales or the Data Wales Web site (www.data-wales.co.uk/walesmap.htm) for help verifying a place or parish name.

WALES AT LAST!

Once you have exhausted all research avenues at home, it's time to visit the land of your fathers or mothers. When you arrive, head to the National Library of Wales (NLW) in Aberystwyth or to the county archives office where your ancestor's records may be stored.

According to Eirionedd Baskerville, assistant archivist, the best place to start at the NLW is the Department of Manuscripts and Records.

"In its catalog room, you will find reference books listing the parish registers and the Nonconformist registers of Wales; volumes of indexes to wills proved in the dioceses of Wales before 1858 and lists of the available copy wills, 1858–c. 1940; lists of parochial records held by the department and diocesan records; personal name indexes and subject indexes; an index to wills, letters of administration, etc., other than those in the official probate records; marriage settlements; and inquisitions post mortem—all relating to documents whose descriptions are to be found in the typescript schedules (catalogs) arranged along one side of the catalog room. Many of the estate records and personal papers held by the library are cataloged in some detail in the typescript schedules." Use of the library's records is free of charge, but you will have to obtain a "reader's ticket" upon proof of identity to view the documents.

Generally speaking, each county archives office holds copies of parish registers and/or bishop's transcripts (in some cases dating to the sixteenth century); civil registrations of births, marriages, and deaths after 1837; other ecclesiastical records; school, hospital, and council records; census records; wills and other probate records; maritime records; trade directories; tax records; and quarter sessions records. They also hold copies of regional publications and newspapers, maps, poor-law union records, police records, and even medieval manuscripts and town charters.

Contact the NLW or archives office prior to your arrival to set up an appointment, to be certain they have the information you seek, and to prepare the staff for your visit. Staff are more than willing to work with you and to advise you on what documents they may have related to the names you are interested in. In many cases, they will even photocopy information if you cannot go there in person. However, some county archives will charge you to undertake postal research, and others don't have enough staff to do private searches. Our resource listings provide contact details.

Last, but certainly not least, remember to explore the "old mountainous Cambria, the Eden of bards." When you return home, don't be surprised if you, like so many before you, suffer from the malady called "hiraeth," a gut-level yearning to return to the land of your forebears. You may just find yourself returning time and again.

RESOURCES

ENGLAND

ORGANIZATIONS AND ARCHIVES

British Isles Family History Society–USA
2531 Sawtelle Blvd.
PMB 134
Los Angeles, CA 90064 USA
<www.rootsweb.com/~bifhsusa>

The British Library at St. Pancras
96 Euston Rd.
London NW1 2DB
England

British Library Newspaper Library
Colindale Ave.
London NW9 5HE
England

The Guildhall Library (Occupational and business records)
Aldermanbury
London EC2P 2EJ
England

Historical Manuscripts Commission
Quality House
Quality Court
Chancery Ln.
London WC2A 1HF
England
<www.hmc.gov.uk>

The Office for National Statistics
(formerly known as the General Register Office)
Census Legislation,
Room 4303
Segensworth Rd.
Titchfield Fareham
Hampshire PO15 5RR
England

Public Record Office
Ruskin Ave., Kew
Richmond, Surrey TW9 4DU
England
<www.pro.gov.uk>

Indexes by County

Cambridgeshire County Free Look-Up Index
<www.genealogy-links.co.uk/html/cam.lookup.html>

Derbyshire County Free Look-Up Index
<www.genealogy-links.co.uk/html/dby.lookup.html>

Lincolnshire County Free Look-Up Index
<www.genealogy-links.co.uk/html/lin.lookup.html>

Nottinghamshire County Free Look-Up Index
<www.genealogy.links.co.uk/html/ntt.lookup.html>

Suffolk County Free Look-Up Index
<www.genealogy-links.co.uk/html/sfk.lookup.html>

BOOKS

Ancestral Trails: The Complete Guide to British Genealogy and Family History
By Mark D. Herber
(Baltimore: Genealogical Publishing Co., 2000)

Basic Facts About Using the Family Records Centre
By Audrey Collins (Bury, England: Federation of Family History Societies, 1998)

The Family Tree Detective: Tracing Your Ancestors in England and Wales
By Colin D. Rogers (Manchester, England: Manchester University Press, 1997)

A Genealogical Gazetteer of England
By Frank Smith (Baltimore: Genealogical Publishing Co., 1968)

An Introduction to the Census Returns of England and Wales
By Susan Lumas (Bury, England: Federation of Family History Societies, 1992)

Never Been Here Before? A Genealogist's Guide to the Family Records Centre
By Jane Cox and Stella Colwell (Kew, Surrey: PRO Publication, 1997)

The Phillimore Atlas and Index of Parish Registers
By Cecil Humphrey-Smith

(Baltimore: Genealogical Publishing Co., 1995)

GUIDES

British Archives: A Guide to Archive Resources in the United Kingdom
By Janet Foster and Julia Sheppard, 3rd ed. (New York: Stockton Press Ltd., 1995)

Directory of British Associations & Associations in Ireland
S.P.A. Henderson and A.J.W. Henderson, eds. 13th ed. (Beckenham, Kent: CBD Research Ltd., 1996)

Enjoying Archives: What They Are, Where to Find Them, How to Use Them
By David Iredale (Chichester, Sussex: Phillimore & Co. Ltd., 1985)

A Genealogist's Guide to Discovering Your English Ancestors
By Paul Milner and Linda Jonas (Cincinnati: Betterway Books, 2000)

Genealogical Resources in English Repositories
By Joy Wade Moulton (Columbus, Ohio: Hampton House, 1988. Supplement published 1992)

Guides to Sources for British History Based on the National Register of Archives. Guide to the Location of Collections Described in the Reports and

Calendars Series 1870–1980
(London: Her Majesty's Stationery Office, 1982)

Historical, Archaeological and Kindred Societies in the United Kingdom: A List
By Malcolm Pinhorn (Isle of Wight: Pinhorns, 1986)

In and Around Record Repositories in Great Britain and Ireland
By Rosemary Church and Jean Cole, 3rd ed. (Birmingham: Federation of Family History Societies, 1992)

An Introduction to . . . Census Returns in England & Wales
By Susan Lumas (Birmingham: Federation of Family History Societies, 1992)

Libraries in the United Kingdom and the Republic of Ireland 1991
Ann Harold, ed. 18th ed. (London: The Library Association Publishing Limited, 1991)

Making Sense of the Census
By Edward Higgs (London: HMSO, 1989)

Making Use of the Census
By Susan Lumas, 2nd ed. (London: PRO Publications, 1993)

Marriage and Census Indexes for Family Historians
Jeremy Gibson and Elizabeth

Hampson, eds. 7th ed. (Birmingham: Federation of Family History Societies Publications, Ltd., 1998)

Pre-1841 Censuses & Population Listings in the British Isles
By Colin R. Chapman, 4th ed. (Dursley, England: Lochin Publishing, 1994)

Record Repositories in Great Britain: A Geographical Guide
10th ed. (London: Her Majesty's Stationery Office, 1997)

PERIODICALS

British Heritage
<www.thehistorynet.com/BritishHeritage/>

Family History
1962–. Published by the Institute of Heraldic and Genealogical Studies, Northgate, Canterbury, Kent CT1 1BA.

Family History News and Digest
1975–. Published by the Federation of Family History Societies, c/o Benson Room, Birmingham & Midland Institute, Margaret Street, B3 3BS Birmingham.

Family Tree Magazine
1984–. Published by Michael Armstrong, 15/16 Highlode Industrial Este, Stocking Fen Road, Ramsey, Huntingdon, Cambridgeshire PE17 1RB. <www.family-tree.co.uk>

The Genealogists' Magazine
1925–. Published by the Society of Genealogists, 14 Charterhouse Buildings, London EC1M 7BA.

WEB SITES

Absent Voters of Grimsby & Cleethorpes 1919 (England)
<www.angelfire.com/de/delighted/voters.html>

Ancestry Search, West Cumbria, United Kingdom

Ashover Parish, Derbyshire

Birmingham and Midland Society for Genealogy and Heraldry (Staffordshire, Warwickshire, and Worcestershire)

The Black Country Pages
<www.geocities.com/Heartland/Prairie/6697/ >

Cornwall GenWeb
<www.rootsweb.com/~engcornw/>

Cyndi's List: England
<www.cyndislist.com/england.htm>

Derbyshire Family History & Genealogy

Devon Genealogy Supplement Page
<www.geocities.com/PicketFence/1704/Devon.html>

EnglandGenWeb
<www.rootsweb.com/~engwgw>

England Marriages posted by GeneaLinks' visitors
<http://genealinks.com/cgi-bin/marriages.cgi?England>

England Sites on A Surname Site
<www.surnamesite.com/names/Europe/England>

England's Lost Female Ancestors
<http://geneasearch.com/females/females.cgi?england>

England—Yorkshire
<www.geocities.com/yshireuk/>

English Origins
<www.englishorigins.com>

Family History Archive: Bristol, Gloucestershire and Somerset, England from 1086 to present
<www.hometown.aol.com/k2m3/index.html>

Family History Unit— Kingston up Hull City Libraries
<www.hullcc.gov.uk/genealogy/>

Federation of Family History Societies
<www.ffhs.org.uk>

Genealogical Sources of Darwen & Blackburn, Lancashire
<http://ourworld.com

puserve.com/homepages/GA FOSTER/>

The Genealogical Storage and Retrieval Center
<http://jrose.dynip.com/gsrc/>

Genealogy 4U, North East Lincolnshire
<http://genealogy4u.co.uk/>

Hampshire Genealogical Society
<www.hgs-online.org.uk/>

Herefordshire-Gen UK
<www.herefordshire-gen.co.uk/>

Lincolnshire and North East Lincolnshire Lines
<www.linc2u.com>

Local History and Genealogy Reading Room: Sources for Research in English Genealogy
<www.loc.gov/rr/genealogy/bib_guid/england.html>

Notes on medieval English genealogy
<www.medievalgenealogy.org.uk/>

Old Yorkshire; Yorkshire's local and family history magazine
<www.oldyorkshire.co.uk/>

Salisbury Genealogy Site
<http://members.aol.com/dalesman/>

UK Mailing Lists
<www.rootsweb.com/~jfuller/gen_mail_country-unk.html>

Yahoo!
<uk.dir.yahoo.com/Arts/Humanities/History/Genealogy/>

Maps
Alan Godfrey Maps
<www.alangodfreymaps.co.uk/>: Catalog of detailed maps from the late 19th and early 20th century.

Ordnance Survey
<www.ordnancesurvey.co.uk>: Britain's national mapping agency.

UK Street Maps
<www.streetmap.co.uk/>: Online street maps for greater London and road maps for the rest of the country.

Research Help
FamilySearch
<www.familysearch.org/sg/ht_list.html>: Under "England," you'll find the LDS Research Outline for England, maps, census worksheet, and guide to the 1881 British census.

GENUKI
<www.genuki.org.uk>: Virtual reference library on English genealogy, with a wealth of information on history, places, and records.

Records Resources
County Record Offices
<www.oz.net/~markhow/englishros.htm>: Links to sites for individual English counties.

Public Record Office
<catalogue.pro.gov.uk>: Online catalog of the largest repository of original English documents.

Family Fact Sheets
<familyrecords.gov.uk>

Office for National Statistics
<www.ons.gov.uk>: You can download a form for ordering birth certificates by mail (order only the full certificate, not the "short" certificate). The address for correspondence is:
General Register Office
P.O. Box 2
Southport, Merseyside
PR8 2JD, England

WALES

ORGANIZATIONS AND ARCHIVES

Anglesey County Record Office
Shire Hall, Llangefni, Anglesey, Wales LL77 7TW
Tel: 012 4875 2080 (Research room code: 221)
<www.ynysmon.gov.uk/english/library/archives/archives.htm>

Association of Family History Societies of Wales
Geoff Riggs
Peacehaven, Badgers Meadow, Pwllmeyric, Chepstow Wales NP16 6UE
E-mail: secretary@fhswales.info
<www.rootsweb.com/~wlsafhs/English.htm>

Carmarthenshire Archive Service
Parc Myrddin, Richmond Terrace, Carmarthen Wales SA31 1DS
Tel: 01267 228232
Fax: 01267 228237
E-mail: archives@ carmarthenshire.gov.uk
<www.carmarthenshire.gov. uk/locserv_eng/culture/ archive.html>

Ceredigion Archives
County Offices, Marine Terrace, Aberystwyth, Ceredigion Wales SY23 2DE
Tel: 01970 633697/633698
E-mail: archives@ ceredigion.gov.uk
<www.llgc.org.uk/cac/ cac0009.htm>

Conwy Archive Service
The Old Board School
Lloyd St., Llandudno
Wales LL30 2YG
Tel/fax: 01492 860882
E-mail: archifau.archives@ conwy.gov.uk
<www.conwy.gov.uk/English/ 2council/library_ information_archives/ archservices/Ec1.html>

Denbighshire County Council Record Office
46 Clwyd St., Ruthin, Denbighshire, Wales LL15 1HP
Tel: 00 44 (0)1824 708250
Fax: 00 44 (0)1824 708258
E-mail: dcc_archives@ denbighshire.gov.uk
<www.llgc.org.uk/cac/ cac0011.htm>

Flintshire Record Office
The Old Rectory
Hawarden, Flintshire
Wales CH5 3NR
Tel: 01244 532414 (County Archivist)
Fax: 01244 538344
<www.flintshire.gov.uk/ webcont/realweb.nsf/ vwa_pagesareatitle/ Homearchives>

Glamorgan Record Office
The Glamorgan Building
King Edward VII Ave.
Cathays Park, Cardiff
Wales CF10 3NE
Tel: 029 2078 0282
Fax: 029 2078 0284
E-mail: glamRO@ cardiff.ac.uk

Gwent Record Office
County Hall, Cwmbrân
Gwent Wales NP44 2XH
Tel: 01633 644886/644888
Fax: 01633 648382
E-mail: gwent.records@ torfaen.gov.uk
<www.llgc.org.uk/cac/ cac0004.htm>

Gwynedd County Archives
Caernarfon Branch:
County Offices, Caernarfon
Gwynedd Wales LL55 1SH
Tel: 01286 679095
Fax: 01286 679637
E-mail: archives. caernarfon@gwynedd. gov.uk
Meirionnydd Branch:
Cae Penarlâg, Dolgellau
Gwynedd Wales LL40 2YB
Tel: 01341 424443
Fax: 01341 424505
E-mail: archives.dolgellau@ gwynedd.gov.uk

<www.gwynedd.gov.uk/adra nnau/addysg/archifau/index. english.htm>

Haverfordwest Library
Dew St., Haverfordwest, Pembrokeshire, Wales SA61 1SU
Tel: 01437 762070
Fax: 01437 769218

Llyfrgell Genedlaethol Cymru/The National Library of Wales
Aberystwyth, Ceredigion, Wales SY23 3BU
Tel: +44 (0)1970 632800
Fax: +44 (0)1970 615709
E-mail: holi@llgc.org.uk
<www.llgc.org.uk/cac>

Madog Center for Welsh Studies
Wood Hall
University of Rio Grande
Rio Grande, OH 45631 USA
Tel: (740) 245-7186
E-mail: welsh@rio.edu
<www.urgrcc.edu/Madog/ English/default.htm>

NAASWCH—North American Association for the Study of Welsh Culture and History
c/o John S. Ellis
Green Mountain College
One College Circle
Poultney, VT 05764 USA
E-mail: jellis@greenmtn.edu
<spruce.flint.umich.edu/ ^ellisjs/naaswch.html>

Ninnau—The North American Welsh Newspaper
NINNAU Publications
11 Post Terrace
Basking Ridge, NJ
07920-2498 USA

Tel: (908) 766-4151
Fax: (908) 221-0744
E-mail: ninnau@
poboxes.com

The National Welsh American Foundation
Post Office Box 1827,
Shavertown, PA 18708 USA
Tel: (570) 696-NWAF
E-mail: nwaf@epix.net

Pembrokeshire Record Office
The Castle, Haverfordwest,
Pembrokeshire, Wales
SA61 2EF
Tel: 01437 763707
Fax: 01437 768539
<www.llgc.org.uk/cac/
cac0002.htm>

Powys County Archives Office
County Hall, Llandrindod
Wells, Powys, LD1 5LG
Tel: 01597 826088
Fax: 01597 826087
E-mail: archives@
powys.gov.uk

Wales International (Undeb Cymru a'r Byd)
E-mail: secretary@
wales-international.org
<www.wales-
international.org>

Welsh-American Genealogical Society
60 Norton Avenue
Poultney, VT 05764 USA
E-mail: wagsjan@sover.net
<www.rootsweb.com/
~vtwags/>

The Welsh National Gymanfa Ganu Association
Dr. Ellis J. Jones, Executive
Director
Gustavus Adolphus College
800 West College Ave.
St. Peter, MN 56082 USA
Tel: (507) 933-7540
E-mail: ellis@gustavus.edu

West Glamorgan Archive Service
County Hall, Oystermouth
Road, Swansea,
Wales SA1 3SN
Tel: (01792) 636589
Fax (01792) 637130
E-mail: westglam.archives@
swansea.gov.uk
<www.swansea.gov.uk/
archives/Default.asp>

Wrexham Archives Service
Wrexham County Borough
Museum
County Buildings, Regent
Street, Wrexham Wales
LL11 1RB
Tel: 01978 317970
E-mail: archives@
wrexham.gov.uk
<www.wrexham.gov.uk/
english/heritage/archives/
index.htm>

BOOKS

Beginning Welsh Research
By Annie Lloyd (Culver City,
CA: Annie Lloyd, 1998)

Researching Family History in Wales
By Jean Istance and E.E.
Cann (Birmingham: The
Federation of Family History
Societies, 1996)

Second Stages in Researching Welsh Ancestry
By John and Shelia Rowlands
(Aberystwyth: The
Federation of Family History
Societies and the
Department of Continuing
Education, University of
Wales, 1999)

The Surnames of Wales: For Family Historians and Others
By John and Shelia Rowlands
(Birmingham: Federation of
Family History Societies,
1996)

Welsh Family History: A Guide to Research
By John and Shelia Rowlands
(Birmingham: The
Federation of Family History
Societies, 1998)

Welsh Surnames
By T.J. Morgan and Prys
Morgan (Cardiff: University
of Wales Press, 1985)

WEB SITES

Cyndi's List: Wales/Cymru
<www.cyndislist.com/
wales.htm>

Flintshire
<www.rootsweb.com/
~wlsflnsh/>

Genealogy Wales, Wales/Cymru, the culture, language and history of Wales
<http://members.tripod.com/
%7ECaryl_Williams/
index-2.html>

Gwent Family History Society
<www.rootsweb.com/~wlsgfhs.index.htm>

Kidwelly History

North Wales & Cheshire Genealogy
<www.marl.com/lds/genealogy.html>

Rhayader & District History Archives

Sources for Research in Welsh Genealogy
<www.loc.gov/rr/genealogy/bib_guid/wales.html>

SouthWales UK Genealogy Sites
<www.south-wales.org.uk/southwales/welsh_genealogy.shtml>

South & West Wales Genealogy Index
<http://members.aol.com/swalesidx/>

V Wales Audio Dictionaries
<www.red4.co.uk/welsh/dictionary/dictionaries.htm>

Wales & Associated Norfolk Families Genealogy
<www.geocities.com/heartland/fields/9939>

Wales/Cymru
<http://britannia.com/celtic/wales/index.html>

Wales Genealogy Links
<www.genealogylinks.net/uk/wales/index.html>

The WalesGenWeb Project

Welsh Genealogy Photography Requests
<http://genealogyphotographs.com/>

Scotland

REGIONAL GUIDE
PAUL MILNER AND LINDA JONAS

As well as kilts and bagpipes, people of Scottish descent may have inherited the fierce nationalism and unmatched determination that mark the history of this strong-willed country. The first occurrence of Scotland in recorded history is from the first century A.D., written by the Roman historian Tacitus, who described the natives as "savages" and "fierce enemies," as any country who has ever tried to invade Scotland has discovered.

Holyrood Palace, Edinburgh

The name "Scotland" can be attributed to Kenneth MacAlpin, King of the Scots of Dalriada, who around 843 changed the name of his kingdom from "Alban" to "Scotia." The rest of mainland Scotland was added to the kingdom by Duncan I, who made an appearance in Shakespeare's *Macbeth*.

The bad blood between Scotland and England began with Edward I of England, who eventually earned the nickname "Hammer of the Scots." After fighting off a Scottish invasion, Edward rampaged through Scotland, setting off what would become many years of Scottish rebellion against English tyranny.

In 1306, Robert the Bruce (*Braveheart*, anyone?) had himself crowned king of Scotland. Though his uprising was defeated, he became an infamous outlaw, known for uniting Scottish nobleman and harassing the English armies with guerilla tactics. Robert drove the English out of every city in Scotland, except Stirling, by 1314.

In 1502, James IV of the Scottish royal house of Stuart signed a treaty of enduring peace with England and married the daugh-

ter of King Henry VII of England, looking towards the eventual union of the house of Stuart to the English Tudors.

The house of Stuart came to an end with Mary, Queen of Scots. Mary, a Catholic, was forced to abdicate from the throne of her Protestant country in favor of her one-year-old son, James VI. She fled to her cousin, Queen Elizabeth I, and was beheaded in 1587 due to her claims to the English throne.

However, Mary's short life was not to be in vain; her son, James VI, went on to become James I of England and James VI of Scotland. He is credited with the translation of the Bible known as the King James Bible, a version still favored by many Protestants.

In 1642, civil war broke out in England, as King Charles I battled for power with Oliver Cromwell. When Cromwell won and had Charles I executed, the Scottish declared Charles' son their king. An incensed Cromwell invaded Scotland and united the two countries under a central English government, and when Cromwell died, the English monarchy was restored to the throne. This restoration of English power over Scotland led many Scots to feel they had lost their independence, which gave rise to the Jacobite rebellions of the 1700s.

The English responded to these uprisings with malice and savagery, slaughtering clansmen and burning their villages to the ground. In an effort to further decimate the clan system, the English passed the Disarming Act of 1746, which declared clan tartans, bagpipes, and the bearing of arms illegal.

Gradually, these restrictions were dropped, and Scotland now lives in peace as part of Great Britain. Thankfully, many Scottish traditions survived their oppression and act as a reminder of the strength and determination of the Scottish people, your ancestors.

GETTING STARTED

As with many other ethnicities and nationalities, it often is easier to trace your ancestors from outside Scotland than from within it. Scottish record repositories are scattered. Thanks to microfilmed records and indexes available on CD-ROM, online, and through the Family History Library <www.familysearch.org>, it's easier than ever before to research your Scottish ancestors from home.

In the excitement of discovering their possible Scottish ancestry, many family historians have made the mistake of finding someone by the same name in Scotland and assuming they've found their ancestors. Even worse, they may assume that because their ancestors had a surname associated with a particular clan, they were members of that clan. Don't make the same mistake. Find out as much as you can about your ancestors in the records of the area in which they settled. Were they Scots-Irish? Highland Scots?

It's helpful to know your ancestor's full name; precise place of origin; dates of birth, marriage, and death; parents', spouse's, and children's names; date of immigration; occupation; religion; and names of cousins, friends, and associates. Of course, you don't have to know all of this before tracing your Scottish heritage, but the more information you have, the easier it will be to identify your ancestor in Scottish records.

Start by looking for information you or other family members may have in your homes. Ask your aunts, uncles, cousins, and even family friends. Some of your ancestors may have left diaries or told their stories to their children. Search for diaries, letters, photos, and family Bibles, as well as personal items such as tools, clothing, and sewing implements. The more you can find, the more you'll know about your ancestors' lives.

Once you've examined home sources, look for documents from the area where your ancestor settled. Always begin by researching the end of a relative's life. Look for family histories and local histories published after death that may contain details about your relative and the community. You may be able to find additional information online. Some people have entire Web sites devoted to a particular family. Others post queries about families they are researching. Be sure to verify the accuracy of any information you find online by getting documentation from the provider. Always be wary of online sources until you can verify them in original records.

SETTING THE RECORDS STRAIGHT

After contacting relatives, searching online, and looking through books, you're ready for the most exciting part of family history: finding the original records. Often, the most revealing records are those written after your ancestor's death. Start first with probate records (wills, inventories of estates, etc.), then look for obituaries. Different types of newspapers will publish separate obituaries—your relative may be mentioned in church, ethnic, society, or town newspapers. When looking for documents about your ancestor, look for the same documents for your relative's spouse and each child, brother, and sister. Search for passenger lists, court records, baptism and marriage records, military records, and death records. Each will tell you more about your ancestor and your ancestor's hometown.

A crucial piece of the puzzle in immigrant research is determining when your ancestor left Scotland. The best source for this is William Filby and Mary K. Meyer's *Passenger and Immigration Lists Index: A Guide to Published Arrival Records of About 500,000 Passengers Who Came to the United States and Canada in the Seventeenth, Eighteenth and Nineteenth Centuries* (Detroit: Gale Research Co, 1981). This series of books, which you can find in libraries with genealogy sections, indexes all records that allude to immigrant status—census records, land records, and naturalization records, to name a few.

Scotland's yard
Scotland is a country of its own, but it is also part of Great Britain, the United Kingdom, and the British Isles. Great Britain was formed in 1707 from the Kingdom of England and Wales and the Kingdom of Scotland. In 1801, Ireland united politically with Great Britain to form the United Kingdom of Great Britain and Ireland. When most of Ireland separated from the United Kingdom in 1921, the full name became the United Kingdom of Great Britain and Northern Ireland.

The term Great Britain thus refers only to England, Wales, and Scotland, whereas the United Kingdom includes England, Wales, Scotland, and Northern Ireland. Traditionally, British Isles describes the two major islands of Great Britain and Ireland (both Northern Ireland and the Republic of Ireland), plus the Channel Islands, the Isle of Man, and the other islands surrounding the coast.

Until recently, all countries of the United Kingdom were

controlled by a single parliament based in London. In July 1999, Queen Elizabeth II opened a new Scottish parliament, which now has legislative power over domestic issues. The government in London retains control over defense, foreign affairs, and macro-economic policy. The Isle of Man and the Channel Islands are dependencies of the British Crown but have their own parliaments.

Scouting sources

For family historians interested in the Scottish part of Great Britain, the good news is that Scottish indexes are among the best in the world. Many background materials are easily available over the Internet or by loan through a public library. Your three main sources will be the Internet; local public, private, and university libraries; and Family History Centers.

Birth, marriage, and death records: Most early Scottish records were created by either the national government or the Church of Scotland's parishes. The government created census records and probate records and since 1855 has kept birth, marriage, and death records in a system called "civil registration." These records can be timesavers, especially when you don't know where your ancestor lived. The civil registration records are indexed for all of Scotland and stored at the General Register Office in Edinburgh. More than 90 percent of all births since 1855 have been registered, and that percentage is even higher for marriages and deaths.

Post-1854 birth, marriage, and death indexes for Scotland are available in more than one format. The most easily accessible indexes are on the Scots Origins Web site <www.scots origins.com>, but this option is also the most expensive. Most births and marriages from 1855 to 1875 are indexed in the International Genealogical Index, accessible for free at Scots Origins or at <www.familysearch.org>. For deaths after 1855 or births and marriages after 1875, the indexes you will probably use most are available on microfilm.

Civil registration indexes: You need to know the name of your ancestor and the approximate year of the event. If your ancestor's name was common, you'll also need to know the parish or district where the event occurred. Be sure to have a gazetteer or list of parishes and counties before using the indexes on microfilm or at the Scots Origins Web site.

Census records: Scotland conducted its first census in 1801 to determine the number of men available for the Napoleonic Wars. It has taken a census every ten years since then, except for 1941. The 1801 through 1831 censuses rarely gathered information about individuals. The first genealogically significant census came in 1841. This and subsequent censuses theoretically contain the names of everyone in the country. If you had ancestors born in Scotland in 1770 or later, search for them or their relatives in the census returns from 1841 on. The 1851 and later censuses include the exact age and place of birth for each household member as reported to the enumerator.

Because census schedules list only those people actually present on census night, it's common to find incomplete families in the records. If household members were working on census night but would return in the morning, they weren't included in that household's tally. Don't assume that a family member was deceased by a given year because he isn't enumerated with his family. The person may have been enumerated elsewhere. Those whose work required travel, such as soldiers or sailors, are likely listed in a place other than family residence.

Church records: A tumultuous past

Church records are the most important resource for tracing your Scottish family tree. In Scotland, government and religion were intimately intertwined. The Church of Scotland became Protestant in 1560, and for the next 130 years, church leadership alternated between Episcopalians, whose bishops appointed their ministers, and the more egalitarian Presbyterians.

In 1690, the Presbyterian Church became the Established Church of Scotland, prompting a flurry of breakaways and mergers that blur the easy classification of church records. Your ancestor may have been Presbyterian, but because of this history, you may not find him in the major Scottish church record indexes. Or he may have belonged to one of Scotland's smaller religious groups.

One major effect of this turbulent history is that many Scottish families at some time or another had connections with "nonconformist" groups. This means that not all family baptisms may appear within one church register. A register may show gaps, as some children were baptized elsewhere. Marriage records may not be where you expect to find them, either. Nonconformist burials may not have been recorded at all.

To use church records, a knowledge of local history is essential. A parish history, for example, might tell you how your ancestor lived, what he did for a living, what the predominant religions were, and when diseases were rampant. You can waste a lot of time searching in surrounding areas when a parish history may provide the answers you need. You can find a short history of your ancestor's parish in the Statistical Accounts of Scotland <edina.ac.uk/stat-acc-scot/>, but a more extensive history of the parish or county may also exist in print sources.

Before the Scottish government began civil registration in 1855, baptism, marriage, and burial records were recorded by Scottish churches. The Scottish Church Records index on CD includes all pre-1855 baptisms and marriages from parish registers of the Church of Scotland. It also includes some nonconformist baptisms and marriages. You can search the Scottish Church Records CD for free at your local Family History Center. (Find the center nearest you at <www.familysearch.org/Eng/Library/FHC/frameset_ fhc.asp>.) You can search the same information for a fee on the Scots Origins Web site. Most of the names are also in the International Genealogical Index, which you can access for free through the FamilySearch Web site and Scots Origins.

Ancient Celtic cross, Isle of Mull

GLOTTAL STOP

Depending on the location and era you're researching, you may run into language barriers. There are four major languages to consider: English, Gaelic, Scots, and Latin. English is the most common, but in the Scottish Highlands, people would have spoken Gaelic. Outside of the Highlands, you might encounter the Scots language in one or more of its dialects.

One of the most common problems in researching Gaelic-speaking ancestors is recognizing names and places. For example, if your immigrant ancestor said his name to an English-speaking person, did he give his Gaelic name (Hamish) or its English equivalent (James)? If he had a Gaelic accent, an English-speaking listener probably had difficulty understanding his name or birthplace. An English-speaking clerk or census taker would record what he heard and spell it phonetically. The result might be unrecognizable to the subject of the record. The pronunciation of even well-known Scottish place names can blow your mind. The county Kirkcudbright, for example, is pronounced "Kirk-coo-bree."

You also will find Latin in Scottish documents. The Scottish Services of Heirs up to 1847 are in Latin (except for 1652 to 1659), and even the indexes are in Latin until 1700. Latin terms sometimes appear in documents normally written in English, especially if the writer wanted to highlight a part of the document. You may also find Latin on tombstones.

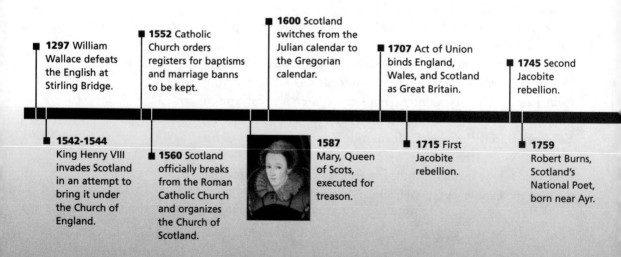

1297 William Wallace defeats the English at Stirling Bridge.

1552 Catholic Church orders registers for baptisms and marriage banns to be kept.

1600 Scotland switches from the Julian calendar to the Gregorian calendar.

1707 Act of Union binds England, Wales, and Scotland as Great Britain.

1745 Second Jacobite rebellion.

1542-1544 King Henry VIII invades Scotland in an attempt to bring it under the Church of England.

1560 Scotland officially breaks from the Roman Catholic Church and organizes the Church of Scotland.

1587 Mary, Queen of Scots, executed for treason.

1715 First Jacobite rebellion.

1759 Robert Burns, Scotland's National Poet, born near Ayr.

Even English names can be a major stumbling block in Scottish research. Names seemingly bearing no resemblance to each other can actually refer to the same person, such as Alexander and Sandy; Peter and Patrick; Elizabeth and Isobel;

Aerial view of downtown Edinburgh

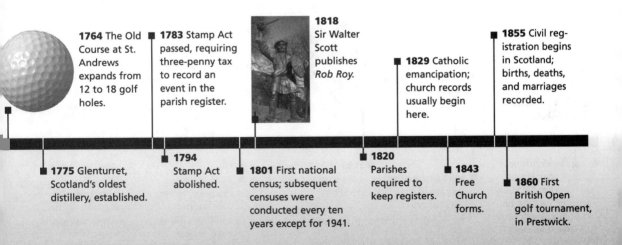

1764 The Old Course at St. Andrews expands from 12 to 18 golf holes.

1783 Stamp Act passed, requiring three-penny tax to record an event in the parish register.

1818 Sir Walter Scott publishes *Rob Roy*.

1829 Catholic emancipation; church records usually begin here.

1855 Civil registration begins in Scotland; births, deaths, and marriages recorded.

1775 Glenturret, Scotland's oldest distillery, established.

1794 Stamp Act abolished.

1801 First national census; subsequent censuses were conducted every ten years except for 1941.

1820 Parishes required to keep registers.

1843 Free Church forms.

1860 First British Open golf tournament, in Prestwick.

and Agnes, Ann, and Nancy. To compound the problem, your ancestor's name may be written in English, Gaelic (especially in the Highlands), or Latin (often in land and probate records).

BE THERE NOW

The information you gather leads to a wonderful benefit for you. Having found the town or village of your ancestors, you're ready to walk in your ancestors' footsteps. Visiting their Scottish homeland will give you a glimpse into their lives. Scotland is a wonderful place to visit. It is one of the easiest countries to access.

One reason is the Book a Bed Ahead program from the Scottish Tourist Board <www.visitscotland.com>. Simply book your first two nights and last two nights from your home. Once in Scotland, you can use the Book a Bed Ahead program through the local Tourist Information Center (TIC) to schedule your next night's lodging for wherever you wish to go. This allows you great flexibility and costs just three pounds per booking. Purchase a BritRail Pass <www.britrail.com> before you leave for Scotland. (You cannot buy one there.) The pass allows you unlimited train access not only to Scotland but also to England and Wales. Even if you take a train, you may often take a bus to your ancestors' village.

Schedule a trip to your ancestors' village at the beginning of

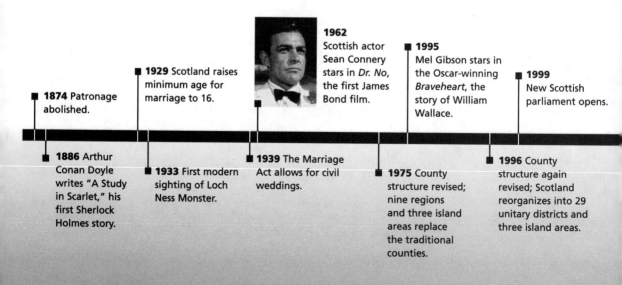

1874 Patronage abolished.

1886 Arthur Conan Doyle writes "A Study in Scarlet," his first Sherlock Holmes story.

1929 Scotland raises minimum age for marriage to 16.

1933 First modern sighting of Loch Ness Monster.

1939 The Marriage Act allows for civil weddings.

1962 Scottish actor Sean Connery stars in *Dr. No*, the first James Bond film.

1975 County structure revised; nine regions and three island areas replace the traditional counties.

1995 Mel Gibson stars in the Oscar-winning *Braveheart*, the story of William Wallace.

1996 County structure again revised; Scotland reorganizes into 29 unitary districts and three island areas.

1999 New Scottish parliament opens.

WHAT'S IN A NAME?

Scottish first names typically follow a traditional pattern, which may offer clues to your ancestral puzzles. This naming pattern is a potential guide but not a hard-and-fast rule:

Child		Given the name of
1st son	=	father's father
2nd son	=	mother's father
3rd son	=	father
4th son	=	father's brother
1st daughter	=	mother's mother
2nd daughter	=	father's mother
3rd daughter	=	mother
4th daughter	=	mother's sister

your vacation, not at the end. That way if you find a wealth of information, you can plan an extra day or two there and skip some other sightseeing.

Tracing your Scottish ancestry can be exciting, challenging, and fun. Share this joy with your family, and preserve the stories of your ancestors so that their lives—and your heritage—won't be forgotten. You, your family, and researchers for many generations to come will be glad you did.

SCOTS ORIGINS

The Scots Origins service <www.scotsorigins.com> offers a wealth of records to aid your research. You can access Scottish births/baptisms and marriages/banns from 1553 to 1900, deaths from 1855 on, and the 1891 census. Every year an additional year of indexes is added.

You can search by surname, forename, sex, event, year (or year range) of registration, age (deaths and census only), parish, or registration district and county (1553 to 1854). Before you decide to use the service, try the free demo so you have an idea how the site works. Searching the indexes costs six pounds (about $8) for thirty "page credits" in a 24-hour period. Each page credit is good for at least one entry and at most fifteen entries. If you feel confident you've found the right person, you can order an extract through the site for ten pounds (about $14.50).

Be aware that you can access some of the information in Scots Origins from other sources for free. To compare the resources available, see <www.scotlandgenweb.org>.

CENSUS

A Scottish national census has been taken every ten years since 1801, with the exception of 1941. The censuses from 1841 to 1891 are available for public use.

Enumerators were instructed to list only those present in the household the night the census was taken. People who were traveling, at boarding schools, or working away from home were listed where they spent the night. Here's a breakdown of the information in the Scottish censuses:

1801 to 1831. These records contain only statistical information. However, some parishes compiled lists of names while gathering the census information.

1841. This census was taken on 7 June 1841. It lists each member of every household's name, sex, address, occupation, and whether or not they were born in the county. Note that the census takers usually rounded the ages of those over fifteen down to a multiple of five years.

1851 and later. From 1851 to 1931, censuses were taken between 31 March and 9 April. These records list the names, ages, occupations, relationships to the head of the household, and parish and county of birth (except foreign births, which give country only) of each person.

For more information, contact:

>Registrar General
>Search Unit
>New Register House
>Edinburgh, EH1 3YT
>Scotland

RESOURCES

ORGANIZATIONS AND ARCHIVES

Aberdeen University Library
Manuscripts and
Archive Section
King's College
Aberdeen AB9 2UB
Scotland

British Isles Family History Society—USA
2531 Sawtelle Blvd.
PMB 134
Los Angeles, CA 90064 USA
<www.rootsweb.com/~bifhsusa>

Court of the Lord Lyon
New Register House
Edinburgh EH1 3YT
Scotland

National Library of Scotland
Department of Manuscripts
George IV Bridge
Edinburgh EH1 1EW
Scotland

The Public Record Office
Ruskin Ave., Kew
Richmond, Surrey TW9 4DU
England
Guide to this tool:
Tracing Your Ancestors in the Public Record Office, by Amanda Bevan and Andrea Duncan, 4th ed. (London: Her Majesty's Stationery Office, 1990)

The Registrar
General Search Unit
New Register House
Edinburgh EH1 3YT
Scotland

Scottish Record Office
HM General Register House
Princes Street
Edinburgh EH1 3YY
Scotland
Guide to this tool:
Tracing Your Scottish Ancestors: A Guide to Ancestry Research in the Scottish Record Office, by Cecil Sinclair (Edinburgh: Her Majesty's Stationery Office, 1990)

Tracing Scottish Local History: A Guide to Local History Research in the Scottish Record Office, by Cecil Sincair (Edinburgh: Her Majesty's Stationery Office, 1994)

University of Edinburgh Library
George Square
Edinburgh EH8 9LJ
Scotland

University of Glasgow Archives
The University
Glasgow G12 8QQ
Scotland

BOOKS

1993 National Genealogical Directory
Iris Louise Caley, ed. (Stoke St. Michael, Somerset: National Genealogical Directory, 1993)

British Archives: A Guide to Archive Resources in the United Kingdom
By Janet Foster and Julia Sheppard, 3rd ed. (New York: Stockton Press Ltd., 1995)

The British Isles Genealogical Register (BIG R)
(Federation of Family History Societies, 2000 edition microfiche)

The Clans, Septs, and Regiments of the Scottish Highlands
By Frank Adam and Sir Thomas Innes (Baltimore: Genealogical Publishing Co., 1970)

Collins Scottish Clan & Family Encyclopedia
By George Way and Romilly Squire (Glasgow: HarperCollins, 1998)

Concise Scots Dictionary
By Mairi Robinson (Edinburgh: Polygon, 1999)

A Dictionary of the Older Scottish Tongue, From the Twelfth Century to the End of the Seventeenth
By Sir William Alexander Craigie (London: Oxford University Press, 1937)

Genealogical Research Directory
By Keith A. Johnson and Malcolm R. Sainty (Sydney: Genealogical Research Directory Editors, 1996)

A Genealogist's Guide to Discovering Your Scottish Ancestors
By Paul Milner and Linda Jonas (Cincinnati: Betterway Books, 2002)

The Highland Clans
By Sir Iain Moncrieffe of
that Ilk (London: Barrie &
Jenkins, 1982)

Highland Clans and Tartans
By R.W. Munro (London:
Octopus Books, 1977)

*Libraries in the United
Kingdom and the Republic
of Ireland*
18th ed. (London: The
Library Association
Publishing Limited, 1992)

*Scottish Christian Names: An
A-Z of First Names*
By Leslie Alan Dunkling
(London: Johnston & Bacon,
1978)

Scottish Family Histories
By Joan P.S. Ferguson
(Edinburgh: National Library
of Scotland, 1986)

*Scottish Library and
Information Resources*
Gordon Dunsire and Brian
Osborne, eds. (Motherwell:
Scottish Library Association,
1991)

*The Scottish Nation, or
The Surnames, Families,
Literature, Honours, and
Biographical History of the
People of Scotland*
By William Anderson (Bowie,
Md.: Heritage Books, 1995)

*The Surnames of Scotland:
Their Origin, Meaning
and History*
By George Black (Edinburgh:
Birlinn Limited, 1996)

PERIODICALS

*Current Periodicals in the
National Library of Scotland*
(Edinburgh: National Library
of Scotland, 1987–.)

*The Scottish Association of
Family History Societies
Bulletin*
Published bi-annually by The
Scottish Association of
Family History Societies.

*The Scottish Genealogist:
The Quarterly Journal of the
Scottish Genealogy Society*
1954-. Published by the
Scottish Genealogy Society.

Scottish Local History
1960-. Published three times
a year by Scottish Local
History Forum.

WEB SITES

Alan Godfrey Maps
<www.alangodfreymaps
.co.uk>

AncestralScotland
<www.ancestralscotland
.com/>

**Ar Turas: Independent
Research on Scotland & the
Scots**
<www.ar-turas.co.uk/>

**BIFHS-USA National
Inventory of Documentary
Sources**
<www.rootsweb.com/~
bifhsusa/nids/nids.html>

**CensusDiggins: Scottish
Genealogy**
<www.censusdiggins.com/
scottish_genealogy.html>

Cyndi's List: Scotland
<www.cyndislist.com/
scotland.htm>

**Edinburgh City Libraries:
Family History Links**
<www.edinburgh.gov.uk/
CEC/Recreation/Libraries/
Historysphere/Genealogylinks/
famhistlinks.html>

**Electric Scotland: Scottish
Genealogy Research &
Advice**
<www.electricscotland.com/
webclans/scotroot.htm>

Gathering of the Clans
<www.tartans.com>

GENUKI
<www.genuki.org.uk>

GENUKI: Scotland
<www.genuki.org.uk/
big/sct/>

**The Highland Clearances:
Stories of Scottish Ancestry**
<www.theclearances.org/>

**The Internet Guide
to Scotland**
<www.scotland-info.co
.uk/bk-gene.htm>

**National Archives
of Scotland**
<www.nas.gov.uk>

**New Scottish
Council Regions**
<www.trp.dundee.ac.uk/
data/councils/newregions
.html>

Ordnance Survey Gazetteer
<www.ordnancesurvey.co
.uk>

Public Record Office
<www.pro.gov.uk>

Rampant Scotland Directory of Scottish Web Sites
<www.rampantscotland.com>

Roots in Scotland
<www.rootsinscotland.com/>

ScotFind.com
<www.scotfind.com/links/ Community/Genealogy/>

ScotGenes
<www.scotgenes.com/>

Scotland Royal Genealogy
<www.scotlandroyalty.org/>

Scotland's People
<www.scotlandspeople .gov.uk/>

ScotRoots
<www.scotroots.com/>

Scotsmart
<www.scotsmart.com/c/ genealogy.html>

Scots Origins
<www.scotsorigins.com>

Scottish Association of Family History Societies
<www.safhs.org.uk>

Scottish Census Transcriptions
<www.scotlandsclans.com/ census.htm>

Scottish Clans
<www.scotlandsclans.com/>

Scottish Genealogy Help
<www.dbaptie.freeserve. co.uk/>

The Scottish Genealogy Society
<www.scotsgenealogy.com/>

Scottish Roots
<www.scottish-roots.co.uk/>

Scottishweb
<www.scottishweb.net>

Sources for Research in Scottish Genealogy
<www.loc.gov/rr/genealogy/ bib_guid/scotland.html>

Statistical Accounts of Scotland
<edina.ac.uk/statacc/>

The Tartan Pages: Scotland's Internet
<www.scotlands.com/tp/clan/>

Tracing your Scottish Ancestry
<www.geo.ed.ac.uk/home/ scotland/genealogy.html>

Undiscovered Scotland
<www.undiscovered scotland.co.uk/uslinks/ genealogy.html>

Your Scottish Kin
<www.scottish- genealogy.co.uk/>

Scandinavia

Denmark
Finland
Iceland
Norway
Sweden

REGIONAL GUIDE
DAVID A. FRYXELL

Although Scandinavia sometimes seems remote from the rest of Europe, throughout history, the peoples of present-day Norway, Sweden, Finland, Iceland, and Denmark have made their mark on the continent. Indeed, you may have Scandinavian ancestors far back in the mists of history and never know it: The Normans of France, after all, originally came from the frozen and ferocious north, and Dublin, Ireland, was founded by the Vikings. Scandinavians frequently traveled far from home while doing the exploring, conquering, and colonizing for which they've been romanticized, and they both fought against and allied with each other over the centuries to define and redefine the Scandinavian region.

No matter which country in this group your ancestors hailed from, Scandinavians through the years were (and still are) known for their adventure, exploration, and achievement.

For example, during the ninth century, Aud the "Deep Minded" lived her own Viking Age odyssey. The daughter of a Norwegian chieftain in the Hebrides, she married a Viking living in Dublin and, when both her husband and son had died, took charge of the family fortune, chartering a ship to take her and her granddaughters to Orkney, Faroe, and Iceland. Once she dropped anchor in Iceland, she began distributing land to her followers. Aud was remembered as one of Iceland's four most important settlers and as a notable early Christian.

Eric the Red, born Erik Thorvaldsson in Norway in the mid-

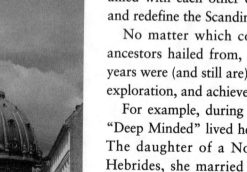

Frederick's Church, Copenhagen

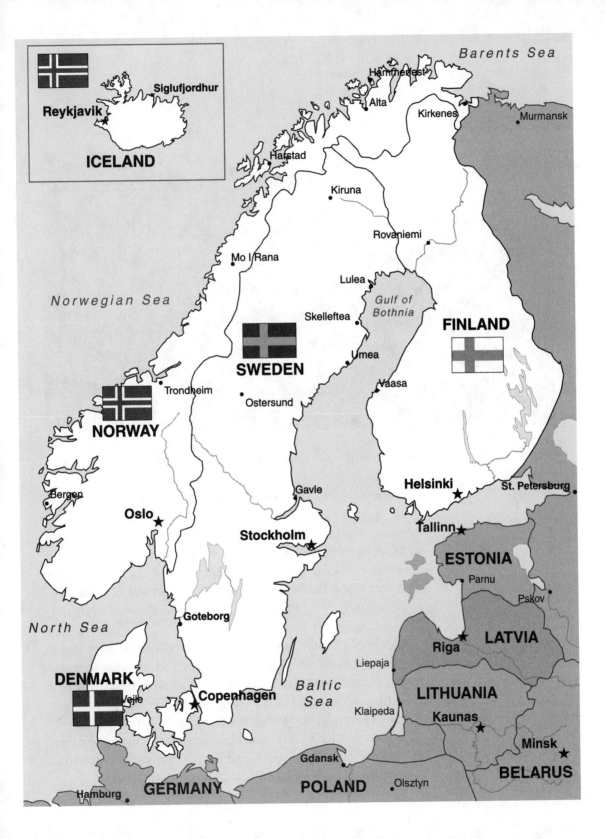

Wharf,
Trondheim,
Norway

tenth century and a descendent of Viking chieftains, discovered Greenland.

Norse explorer Leif Eriksson, son of Erik the Red, was born in the latter part of the tenth century and reached North America about the year 1000. He grew up in Greenland but visited Norway just before the turn of the millennium, where he converted to Christianity. According to one account, he was then commissioned by King Olaf I to convert the Greenlanders to Christianity, but he was blown off course, missed Greenland, and reached North America.

Thorfinn Karlsefni, an Icelandic explorer, attempted to found a settlement in North America soon after Leif Eriksson's voyage there. According to two Icelandic stories, Karlsefni was a wealthy trader who led a Viking expedition to the territory called Vinland, in North America, and wintered there. Archaeologists have since found proof of the Vikings' settlement of Vinland at L'Anse aux Meadows, Newfoundland, putting them in the New World a half-century before Columbus.

The Scandinavian spirit of adventure carried over into the twentieth century. Sven Hedin (1865–1952), explorer of Asia, acclaimed writer, and geographer, was the last person to receive a Swedish knighthood in 1902 for the accounts of his travels. In 1930, Hedin received the first Hedin medal, which was founded the same year for significant geographic, especially cartographic, research of lesser-known areas. It is also said that Hedin's excellent panoramic drawings have been instrumental in interpreting satellite photographs.

Thor Heyerdahl, born in Larvik, Norway, in 1914, made history in 1947 when he crossed the Pacific Ocean from Peru to Polynesia on a balsa wood raft. Heyerdahl led several other expeditions, including The Galapagos Expedition (1952) and the Easter Island Expedition (1955–56).

With such passion for discovery in their blood, it's no wonder that so many of Scandinavian descent embark on the quest to uncover their lineage.

Latterday "Vikings" hoping to explore their heritage will find some advantages not enjoyed by many other ethnic groups. The conscientious Scandinavians have kept excellent records, which have been mostly spared the ravages of Europe's wars. Almost everyone for centuries belonged to the state Lutheran church, which maintained voluminous parish registers. And many Scandinavians today speak and write English. On the other hand, in some ways these were relatively backward, largely agricultural countries, on the cold and remote northern edge of Western civilization. For example, Christianity didn't make it to Sweden until almost nine hundred years after Rome. The slow northward march of progress affects the historical records: Don't expect to trace your family back beyond the mid-seventeenth century in much of Scandinavia.

(Truly isolated Iceland is a special case. A genetic-research company, Decode Genetics, is developing a database of all known Icelanders for the past 1,100 years, which eventually will include more than 700,000 individuals—half of all the people born in Iceland since its settlement in 874. To learn more, see <www.decode.is>.)

Wooden woman sail-
boat mast, Stockholm

Here are six steps to get started discovering your Scandinavian roots:

Step 1: Start at home

As in all genealogy, success begins at home. "Do your home-work," advises Christopher Rumbaugh, who coordinates the Finland page for the WorldGenWeb genealogy project <www.open.org/rumcd/genweb/finn.html>. "Get as much information about your ancestors as you can from living relations and family papers. Then and only then should you attempt to tackle the microfilm."

"Resist the urge to jump headfirst into the sources," adds John Follesdall, creator of the Ancestors from Norway site <homepages.rootsweb.com/~norway/>. "Take the time to read background information. It will save you a lot of headaches."

Once you've interviewed your relatives, combed your family archives, and grounded yourself in your heritage, tap the vast resources of your local Family History Center. These centers—more than 3,400 around the globe—let you access the records on more than two billion people at the Church of Jesus Christ of Latter-day Saints' Family History Library in Salt Lake City, Utah. (See <www.familytreemagazine.com/articles/apr00/fhc.html> for tips on finding and using your nearest Family History Center. You can also search many of these records via the LDS church's FamilySearch Web site <www. family-search.org>.) The Family History Library has more than 82,000 microfilm and microfiche Swedish records, for example, and 14,000 Norwegian records. You can search the catalog <www.familysearch.org/Search/searchcatalog.asp> for microfilms and other holdings, then borrow the actual resources via your Family History Center.

Step 2: Retrace immigrants' roots

Before the American Civil War, only a small number of Scandinavian settlers were living on the East coast and in the midwest of the North American continent. After 1865, however, many Scandinavians left home, fleeing either the poor agricultural areas of northern Europe's forests or the population explosion caused by (as a Swedish poet put it)

Rural woman, Geiranger

"peace, vaccination, and potatoes"—unchecked by war, smallpox, and malnutrition—for the boundless frontiers of America.

Governments encouraged emigration, and the United States was depicted as a land of milk and honey—as the Danish writer Hans Christian Anderson described it in 1836: "Ducks and chickens raining down, geese land on the table." The Gold Rush of 1849 and the American Homestead Act of 1862 also helped to transform the trickle of Scandinavians to America into a flood. Jobs laying railroads across the growing nation also beckoned. U.S. railroad tycoon James J. Hill once boasted, "Give me snuff, whiskey, and Swedes, and I'll build you a railroad to hell." By 1890, there were almost one million Scandinavian immigrants living in North America, mainly in the upper Midwest.

In the last decade of the nineteenth century, land was most

available in the Canadian Prairies and North Dakota, and many Scandinavians settled in these areas. Some historians have characterized this nineteenth-century immigration era as the dividing of the Scandinavian people into two branches—one in Europe and one in America. (Today, for example, the number of Americans of Norwegian descent almost equals the population of Norway.) If your family was among the many that settled in North America, you need to try to find the link between your Scandinavian-American ancestors and your roots across the Atlantic.

Scandinavian emigration records were typically kept by the police. In Denmark, these archives from 1869–1904 have been computerized; you can use an English-language search menu online at <www.emiarch.dk/search.php3?l=en>. Norwegian police emigration records date from 1867, and these are being computerized by the Norwegian Emigration Center in Stavanger and the Digital Archive of Norway <digitalarkivet.uib.no>.

Records of passports and passenger lists from Finland are being computerized by the Institute of Migration <www.utu.fi/erill/instmigr/eng/e_rekist.htm>. In Sweden, parish ministers were required to report annually on emigrants. These records, along with passenger lists, can be accessed on microfilm through your Family History Center.

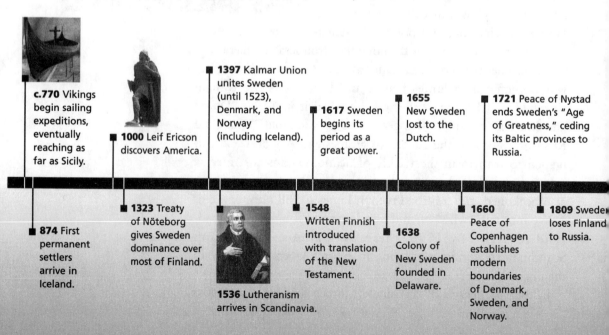

c.770 Vikings begin sailing expeditions, eventually reaching as far as Sicily.

1000 Leif Ericson discovers America.

1397 Kalmar Union unites Sweden (until 1523), Denmark, and Norway (including Iceland).

1617 Sweden begins its period as a great power.

1655 New Sweden lost to the Dutch.

1721 Peace of Nystad ends Sweden's "Age of Greatness," ceding its Baltic provinces to Russia.

874 First permanent settlers arrive in Iceland.

1323 Treaty of Nöteborg gives Sweden dominance over most of Finland.

1536 Lutheranism arrives in Scandinavia.

1548 Written Finnish introduced with translation of the New Testament.

1638 Colony of New Sweden founded in Delaware.

1660 Peace of Copenhagen establishes modern boundaries of Denmark, Sweden, and Norway.

1809 Sweden loses Finland to Russia.

Step 3: Get the name right

To trace your roots back in Scandinavia, it's crucial to know your ancestor's correct name in the old country. That's not quite as simple as it sounds.

"One of the hardest things for people to realize is that the name of their ancestor in the U.S. is not necessarily the name they used in Norway," says Linda Schwartz, who coordinates the WorldGenWeb site for Norway <www.rootsweb.com/~wgnorway>. "Thus they spend a lot of time searching for someone who didn't exist in Norway."

For centuries throughout Scandinavia, it was common to take your last name from your father's first name ("patronymic" naming): If your father's first name was Magnus, in Sweden your last name would be Magnusson (or Magnusdotter, for Magnus' daughter). Families in Norway and Denmark also took the father's name for the surname, adding -sen or -datter. The permanent surname, passed on from one generation to the next, didn't become official until 1901 in Sweden and 1923 in Norway, and patronymics persist in Iceland.

Other names came from the land. Norwegians often used a second last name, which might change depending on the farm they were working: Your ancestor might be Olav Petersen Dal

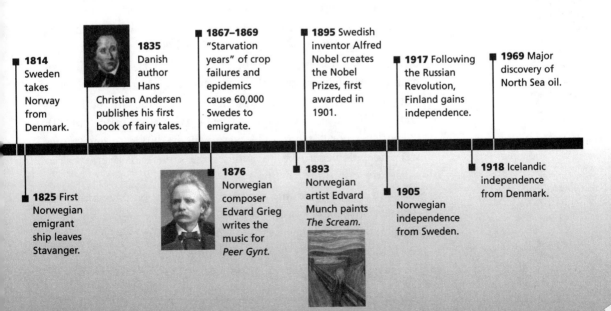

1814 Sweden takes Norway from Denmark.

1835 Danish author Hans Christian Andersen publishes his first book of fairy tales.

1867–1869 "Starvation years" of crop failures and epidemics cause 60,000 Swedes to emigrate.

1895 Swedish inventor Alfred Nobel creates the Nobel Prizes, first awarded in 1901.

1917 Following the Russian Revolution, Finland gains independence.

1969 Major discovery of North Sea oil.

1825 First Norwegian emigrant ship leaves Stavanger.

1876 Norwegian composer Edvard Grieg writes the music for *Peer Gynt*.

1893 Norwegian artist Edvard Munch paints *The Scream.*

1905 Norwegian independence from Sweden.

1918 Icelandic independence from Denmark.

while he was on the Dal farm, but Olav Petersen Li after he moved to Li.

Still other names were changed in the military and may or may not have been changed back. So my Swedish relative John Magnusson, for example, chose the last name Fryxell to differentiate himself from all the other Magnussons in his barracks. When he and his brother came to America, the immigration officials told them it was a bad idea for brothers to have different last names, so we all became Fryxells.

Changing your name in America was common. The Danish Johansen, Jorgensen, and Jensen families might all have become Johnsons. Schwartz says, "My great-grandfather's Norwegian name was Mens Arntsen from the Skaarvold farm, but he became Mike Score in the U.S. His cousin Ole Johnson from Gunhildsøien farm also took the surname Score in the U.S."

Step 4: Identify your ancestor's parish

Not only is Scandinavia overwhelmingly Lutheran, the Lutheran church is actually to varying degrees the official state church. That means many of the vital records you might expect to be handled by the government have historically been kept by the church. So the key to tracing your ancestors back in Scandinavia is knowing the name of their church parish.

Identifying the parish can unlock a wealth of scrupulously maintained records dating back centuries. In Finland, for example, "church books" began keeping vital records in 1686, though most surviving records begin about 1735. You'll also find valuable information in communion books (*rippikirjat*), where Finnish pastors recorded not only their parishioners' mastery of the faith but also family relationships and events. Parish records in Denmark began in 1573, though few survive from prior to 1660; all parish records from 1814 were kept in duplicate and copies were not allowed to be kept under the same roof overnight, so these are complete. From 1815–1874 Danish churches also recorded who arrived and who left the parish. Norwegian parish registers (*kirkebøker*) may go as far back as the 1600s, but most begin in the 1700s; they were standardized about 1800.

Sweden, where the government didn't start keeping its own

Amalienborg Guard,
Copenhagen

vital records until 1950, is perhaps the most extreme example of
the importance of parish records (*kyrkoböcker*). There the
church laid down regulations for records in 1686, though many
parishes had already begun keeping records. Printed forms were
introduced in the 1780s, when the parish lists began doubling as
official population registers. Conveniently for genealogists,
churches kept special records of anyone moving in or out of a
parish. You may also be able to learn more about your Swedish
ancestors from the records of the annual "questioning" (*husförhörslängd*) that tested parishioners' knowledge of the church
and the Bible: These listed all the farms in the parish, with
names and vital statistics about everyone living there, and even
included personal notes (*fräjd*) from the pastor about these
members of his flock.

Many Scandinavian church records have been microfilmed
and can be accessed through your local Family History Center.
These records are also increasingly available in computerized
databases, through the Web, or on CD-ROM.

Step 5: Explore other records

Besides parish records, Scandinavian countries have census, property, probate, military, and other records that can help fill in the gaps in your family tree. Census lists can be particularly useful for finding Danish ancestors. The earliest Danish censuses date from 1787, 1801, 1834, and 1840; from 1845 on, censuses were taken every five or ten years and included each person's place of birth. You can search some Danish census lists online at the Danish Demographic Database site <ddd.sa.dk/kiplink_en.htm>.

Norway also has excellent archives of its censuses (1664–1666, 1701, mid-1700s, 1801, 1815, and every ten years thereafter through 1875). Many of these censuses can be searched online via the Digital Archive (see Step 2).

Swedish census records, which date to 1652, can be a useful supplement to church records. Many of these have been microfilmed and can be accessed through your Family History Center.

Other types of records that can help in your research include probate and estate records, military and conscription records (especially in Denmark), land records (Norway), and city directories (Sweden). Many of these resources, particularly those from Sweden, are available from your Family History Center.

Step 6: Decipher your discoveries

All the Scandinavian languages are related except for Finnish, which is related to Estonian and distantly to Hungarian. And there are linguistic overlaps: Swedish is also an official language in Finland and records there were kept in Swedish until the early 1800s. Prior to 1915, most Norwegian records were written in a language that's actually closer to written Danish. All written Scandinavian languages employ extra letters beyond the twenty-six of the Roman alphabet, such as Å, Ä, and Ö (Swedish), or Æ and Ø (Danish and Norwegian, plus Å in recent usage). These are usually alphabetized at the end, following Z. Icelandic is the only one with extra consonants, which stand for the two pronunciations of "th" (as in "thing" and as in "them").

You can find dictionaries of each Scandinavian language on the Web. The Family History Library publishes guides to commonly used words in genealogy in Danish, Swedish, Finnish, and Norwegian (order from 801-240-2331; order online at <www.ldscatalog.com>).

Foreign handwriting can also be a challenge. Until about 1900, the Danish used a style known as the "German hand." Pre-1800 Norwegian records are likely to be in Gothic script.

But the rewards of discovering your Scandinavian roots are well worth overcoming such challenges. As Norwegian-American author Ole Rølvaag wrote, "When a people becomes interested in its past life, seeks to acquire knowledge in order better to understand itself, it always experiences an awakening of new life."

Sweden's Census

There are some things that researchers should keep in mind with regard to the Swedish census records. First, between 1652 and 1840, only people between the ages of fifteen and sixty-three were listed. The earliest records often contain only the given name of the head of the household, while other family members are listed as numbers in columns. After 1841, people between the ages of seventeen and sixty-three were recorded. After 1887, the ages were eighteen to sixty-three. Also, if your ancestor was in the military, you may not find his name because soldiers did not have to pay taxes, so only their wives and children are listed. Until 1810, noble families and their servants were also exempt from paying taxes and are usually not recorded. It's also important to remember that spellings of names and places in census records may differ from those in other records.

Once you find your family listed in a census, you should search that same location in the earlier and later census records for other family members. If you are in need of a good guide to the early census records, try *Mantalsskrivningen i Sverige före 1860 (Census Records in Sweden before 1860)* by Gösta Lext. (Göteborg: Göteborgs Universitet, 1968).

Denmark's Census

In the late eighteenth and early nineteenth centuries, censuses were taken sporadically. The first Danish census of value to

Wooden dragon figurehead in an Oslo, Norway marina

genealogists was taken in 1787. Beginning in 1840, information was collected every five years until 1860 and then every ten years until the end of the century. The five-year system began again in 1901.

The types of useful information you will find vary from year to year, but there are some general guidelines to help you know what to expect from your searches. The 1787, 1801, 1834, and 1840 censuses list the name, age, sex, marital status, and occupation of each member of the household, in addition to their relationships to the head of the household. Beginning with 1845, the censuses record the name, age, occupation, religious affiliation, and birthplace (county and parish) of each member of the household, in addition to their relationships to the head of the household. For more information, refer to the Danish Demographic Database <ddd.sa.dk/DDD_EN.htm>.

Finland's Census

Finnish population registration records, similar to census records, have been kept since 1634 and are called *henkikirjat/mantalslängder*. In addition, various taxation lists have been preserved from the 1530s until the present, though they are not as thorough. The *henkikirjat/mantalslängder* even precede the earliest church records, so you can use them when the time comes to look further into the past or supplement incomplete church-record information.

The age group recorded in the early *henkikirjat/mantalslängder* varies; here's a breakdown so you'll know what to expect while navigating these documents.

Between 1634 and 1651, only persons over the age of twelve were enumerated. Records from 1652 on included those between the ages of fifteen and sixty-three. (After 1655, heads of households over sixty-three were also listed.)

Also note that before 1765 (when the government started using these records to gather national statistics), those who did not have to pay taxes, such as nobility and their servants, large-estate owners, soldiers, and the destitute, are often not registered in *henkikirjat/mantalslängder.*

A good index for these records is *Luettelo henkikirjamikrofilmien käyttökopioista 1634–1808/Förteckning över brukskopior av mikrofilmer av mantalslängder 1634–1808 (Inventory of Microfilms of the 1634–1808 Censuses)* Matti Walta, ed., 2nd rev. ed. (Helsinki: Valtionarkisto, 1989).

A composite research resource unique to Finland with which you should become familiar is *Suomen asutuksen yleisluettelo/ Generalregistret över bosättningen i Finland (The General Register of Settlement in Finland)*, or SAY. Keep in mind that it doesn't cover the entire country, but you are likely to find some valuable information about southwestern Finland, in particular.

SAY is important to genealogists because it has amassed the information in its tables from various sources from the country's Old and New Collections of Accounts (1539–1809). For each residence, you will find the name of farm owners and members of the household mentioned in original record sources, such as land records, tithing records, and tax and military rolls.

A Finnish/Swedish guide to SAY is available: *Suomen asutuksen yleisluettelon opas: Generalregistret över bosättningen i Finland, en handledningen (The General Register of the Settlement in Finland: A Guide)* (Helsinki: Valtion painatuskeskus, 1975).

Norway's Census
This Digital Archive site <digitalarkivet.uib.no> is in both Norwegian and English and includes several of the censuses for Norway. Unfortunately, only the 1801 and 1900 censuses are complete for the whole country.

RESOURCES

SCANDINAVIA

ORGANIZATIONS AND ARCHIVES

Nordic Heritage Museum
3014 NW 67th St.
Seattle, WA 98117 USA
Tel: (206) 789-5707
<www.nordicmuseum.com>

Scandinavian-American Genealogical Society
P.O. Box 16069
St. Paul, MN 55116 USA
Publishes *Scandinavian Saga*

BOOKS

The Scandinavian American Family Album
By Dorothy and Thomas Hoobler (New York: Oxford University Press, 1997)

A Student's Guide to Scandinavian American Genealogy
By Lisa Olson Paddock and Carl Sokolnicki Rollyson (Phoenix, Ariz.: Oryx Press, 1996)

WEB SITES

L'Anse aux Meadows National Historic Site
<whc.unesco.org/sites/4.htm>

Nordic genealogy newsgroup/mailing list
<www.rootsweb.com/~jfuller/gen_mail_country-den.html>

Nordic Notes
<www.nordicnotes.com>

Nordic Pages
<www.markovits.com/nordic/>

Societas Heraldica Scandinavia
<www.heraldik.org/shshome2.html>

Society for the Advancement of Scandinavian Study
<www.montana.edu/sass/resource.htm>

TravelGenie
<showcase.netins.net/web/travelgenie>

Viking Heritage Server and Database

Viking Network

SWEDEN

ORGANIZATIONS AND ARCHIVES

American Swedish Historical Museum
1900 Pattison Ave.
Philadelphia, PA 19145 USA
Tel: (215) 389-1776
<www.libertynet.org/ashm/>

American Swedish Institute
2600 Park Ave.
Minneapolis, MN 55407 USA
Tel: (612) 871-4907
<www.americanswedishinst.org>

Federation of Swedish Genealogical Societies
Box 30222
SE-104 25 Stockholm, Sweden
<www.genealogi.se/roots>

Landsarkivet i Göteborg
(Göteborg och Bohus, Älvsborg, Skaraborg, and Värmland counties)
Box 3009
S-400 10 Göteborg, Sweden
Tel: 011-46-31-778 68 00
Fax: 011-46-31-778 68 25
<www.ra.se/gla/>

Landsarkivet i Härnösand
(Gävleborg, Västernorrland, Västerbotten, and Norrbotten counties)
Box 161
S-871 24 Härnösand, Sweden
Tel: 011-46-611-835 00
Fax: 011-46-611-835 28
<www.ra.se/hla/>

Landsarkivet i Lund
(Malmöhus, Kristianstad, Halland, and Blekinge counties)
Box 2016
S-220 02 Lund, Sweden
Tel: 011-46-19 70 00
Fax: 011-46-19 70 70
<www.ra.se/lla/>

Landsarkivet i Östersund
(Jämtland County)
Arkivvägen 1
S-831 31 Östersund, Sweden
Tel: 011-46-63-10 84 85
Fax: 011-46-63-12 18 24
<www.ra.se/ola/>

Landsarkivet i Uppsala
(Stockholm, Uppsala, Södermanland, Örebro,

Västmanland, and
Kopparberg counties)
Box 135
S-751 04 Uppsala, Sweden
Tel: 011-46-18-65 21 00
Fax: 011-46-18-65 21 03
<www.ra.se/ula/>

Landsarkivet i Vadstena
(Östergötland, Kalmar,
Jönköping, and Kronoberg
counties)
Box 126
S-592 00 Vadstena, Sweden
Tel: 011-46-143-130 30
Fax: 011-46-143-102 54
<www.ra.se/vala/>

Landsarkivet i Visby
(Gotland County)
Box 2142
S-621 57 Visby, Sweden
Tel: 011-46-498-21 05 14
Fax: 011-46-498-21 29 55
<www.ra.se/vila/>

**Riksarkivet
(National Archive)**
Box 12541
S-102 29 Stockholm, Sweden
Tel: 011-46-8-737 63 50
Fax: 011-46-8-737 64 74
<www.ra.se/en/>

Royal Swedish Embassy
Watergate 600
600 New Hampshire Ave. NW
Washington, DC 20037 USA

**Swedish Ancestry
Research Association**
PO Box 70603
Worcester, MA 01607 USA
<sarassociation.tripod.com>

**SVAR (Swedish
Archive Information)**
Box 160
S-880 40 Ramsele, Sweden

Tel: 011-46-623-725 00
Fax: 011-46-623-725 55

**Swenson Swedish
Immigration Research
Center**
Augustana College
639 38th St.
Rock Island, IL 61201 USA
Tel: (309) 794-7204
<www.augustana.edu/
administration/swenson>

BOOKS

Cradled in Sweden
By Carl-Erik Johansson
(Logan, Utah: Everton
Publishers, Inc., 1995)

The Emigrants
By Vilhelm Moberg,
translated by Gustaf
Lannestock (New York:
Simon & Schuster, 1951)

*Hembygdsforska!
Steg för steg
(Guide to Local History)*
By Per Clemensson and
Kjell Andersson (Stockholm:
LTs förlag, 1990)

*Riksarkivet 1618-1968
(National Archives 1618-
1968)*
By Olof Jägerskiöld
(Stockholm: P.A. Norstedt &
Söner, 1968)

*Släktforska!, Steg för steg
(Guidebook to Swedish
Genealogy)*
By Per Clemensson and Kjell
Andersson (Stockholm: LTs
förlag, 1983)

*Släktforskning–väg en
till din egen historia
(Genealogy, The Road
to Your Own History)*
By Elisabeth Thorsell and Ulf
Schenkmanis (Västerås:
ICA-Förlaget, 1993)

*Svensk slägt-kalender
(Genealogies of
Swedish Families)*
Lars Magnus Viktor Örnberg,
ed. (Stockholm: [s.n.],
1885–1888)

*Svenska ättartal
(Genealogies of
Swedish City Dwellers)*
Lars Magnus Viktor Örnberg,
ed. (Stockholm: [s.n.],
1889–1908)

*Svenska sälktkalendern
(Genealogies of Well-Known
Swedish Families)*
Gustaf Elgenstierna and Ulla
Elgenstierna, comps.
(Stockholm: Albert Bonniers
förlag, 1912–1950)

*Svenska släktkalendern.
Ny följd (Genealogies of
Well-Known Swedish
Families. Continued)*
Gösta Berg, ed. (Stockholm:
Albert Bonniers förlag,
1962–)

*The Swedish Americans
(The Immigrant Experience)*
By Allyson McGill (New York:
Chelsea House, 1988)

PERIODICALS

*Personhistorisk tidskrift
(Journal of Personal History)*
Stockholm: P.A. Norstedt,
1900–.

Släkt och hävd: tidskrift
(Family and Tradition)
Stockholm: Genealogiska
Föreningen, 1950–.

WEB SITES

American Swedish Institute
<www.americanswedishinst
.org>

Angel's Cloud:
Swedish Genealogy
<www.geocities.com/
Heartland/Park/7147/
swedegen.html>

CityGuide Sweden
<cityguide.se>

Demographic Data Base
<www.ddb.umu.se/index_eng
.html>

ExploreNorth
<www.explorenorth.com/
gen-swe.html>

Föreningen Släktdata
<www.slakdata.org/en/start>

Genealogy Pro: Professional
Genealogists & Research
Services for Sweden
<genealogypro.com/
directories/Sweden.html>

Have You Found
a Swedish Ancestor?
<www.geocities.com/
Heartland/Meadows/7095/
swede.html>

Master Index to
Swedish Genealogical Data
Ordered by last name
<www.dcs.hull.ac.uk/
public/genealogy/swedish/>

Minnesota Genealogical
Society
<mngs.org>

Online Swedish-English
Dictionary
<www.freedict.com/onldict/
swe.html>

Rötter

The Scandinavian, Swedish,
Norwegian-American page
of Genealogy
<www.geocities.com/coast
water/nina_moller_nordby
.html>

Scandinavian/USA
Genealogy Links

Svensk släktforskning
(Swedish language only)
<www.abc.se/~m6921/
geneal.html>

Sweden Genealogy Forum
<genforum.genealogy.com/
sweden/>

Sweden Genealogy
Mailing Lists
<members.aol.com/gfsjohnf/
gen_mail_country-swe.html>

SwedGenCo Swedish
Genealogy Company
<hem.passagen.se/
jonmyren/swedgenco>

Swedish 1890 Census
<www.foark.umu.se/census/
Index.htm>

Swedish Ancestry
Research Association (SARA)
<members.tripod.com/~SAR
Association/sara/SARA_
Home_Page.htm>

Swedish Archives
<www.geocities.com/
EnchantedForest/Creek/4968/
List.html>

Swedish Church
Records Online
<www.genline.com/
databasen>

The Swedish
Colonial Society

Swedish Emigrants
on CD-ROM
<www.ssd.gu.se/cdprod.html>

Swedish Emigration
to America
<www.americanwest.com/
swedemigr/pages/emigra.htm>

Swedish Genealogy Club
<www.libertynet.org/ashm/
genealo.html>

Swedish Resources
<www.tc.umn.edu/~pmg/
swedish.html>

SweGGate: Genealogical
Research in Sweden
<www.rootsweb.com/~
swewgw/>

The Swenson Center at
Augustana College:
Swedish Immigration
Research Center
<www.augustana.edu/
administration/swenson/>

ICELAND

ORGANIZATIONS AND ARCHIVES

National Archives of Iceland
Laugavegur 162
105 Reykjavik, Iceland
<www.archives.is>

National and University Library of Iceland
Arngrímsgata 3
IS-107 Reykjavik, Iceland
<www.bok.hi.is/english/>

WEB SITES

Antique Maps of Iceland
<www.bok.hi.is/kort/english.html>

FREELANG: Icelandic-English Dictionary
<www.freelang.net/dictionary/icelandic.html>

History of Iceland
<www.iceland.org/history_people.html>

Iceland Genealogy Mailing Lists
<www.rootsweb.com/~jfuller/gen_mail_country-ice.html>

Icelandic Genealogy Society
<www.vortex.is/aett>

Samkoma
<www.samkoma.com/cgi/home.pl.cgi>

DENMARK

ORGANIZATIONS AND ARCHIVES

Archive for the counties of Åbenrå, Sønderborg, Haderslev, and Tønder: Landsarkivet for Sønderjylland
Haderslevvej 45
DK-6200 Åbenrå, Denmark
<www.sa.dk/laa/omarkiverne/default.htm>

Archive for the counties of Ålborg, Århus, Hjørring, Randers, Ribe, Ringkøbing, Skanderborg, Thisted, Viborg, and Vejle: Landsarkivet for Nørrejylland
Ll. Sct. Hansgade 5
DK-8800 Viborg, Denmark
<www.sa.dk/lav/omarkiverne/default.htm>

Archive for the counties of Bornholm, Frederiksborg, Holbæk, Maribo, København and København City, Præstø, and Sorø: Landsarkivet for Sjælland m.m.
Jagtvej 10
DK-2200 Copenhagen N
Denmark
<www.sa.dk/lak/omarkiverne/default.htm>

Archive for the counties of Odense and Svendborg: Landsarkivet for Fyn
Jernbanegade 36
DK-5000 Odense
Denmark
<www.sa.dk/lao/omarkiverne/default.htm>

Copenhagen's Archive
Københavns Stadsarkiv
Rådhuset
DK 1599 Copenhagen V
Denmark

Danish Emigration Archives
Arkivstræde 1
Box 1731, DK-9100,
Aalborg, Denmark
<www.emiarch.dk>

Danish Immigrant Museum
2212 Washington St.
Box 470
Elk Horn, IA 51531 USA
Tel: (800) 759-9192 or
(712) 764-7001
<dkmuseum.org>

Danish Parishes
Kordegns kontor
(Name of the parish) Sogn
(Name of the parish)
Denmark

Frederiksberg Kommunebibliotek (Fredriksberg Community Library)
Solbjergvej 25
DK-2000 Copenhagen
Denmark

Kongelige Bibliotek (The Royal Library)
Christians Brygge 8
DK-1219 Copenhagen K
Denmark

Military Archive
Hærens Arkiv
Slotsholmgade 4
DK-1216 Copenhagen K
Denmark

Minnesota Genealogical Society
5768 Olson Memorial Highway
Golden Valley, MN 55422 USA
<mngs.org>

National Archives
Rigsarkivet
Rigsdagsgården 9
DK-1218 Copenhagen K
Denmark
<www.sa.dk/ra/engelsk/default.htm>

University Libraries
Universitetsbibliotekets
1 Af (Div.)
Fiolstræde 1
DK-1171 Copenhagen
Denmark

Universitetsbibliotekets
2 Af (Div.)
Nørre Alle 49
DK-2200 Copenhagen
Denmark

BOOKS

Definitely Danish
By Julie McDonald (Iowa City, Iowa: Penfield Press, 1993)

Find dine rødder (Find Your Roots)
By Hans H. Worsøe (Viborg: Politikens Forlag A/S, 1987)

Genealogical Guidebook and Atlas of Denmark
By Frank Smith and Finn A. Thomsen (Salt Lake City, Utah: Thomsen's Genealogical Center, 1969)

Min slægt, Hvordan-Hvornår-Hvorfor? (My Lineage, How-When-Why)
By Suno Scharling (København: Aschehoug Dansk Forlag A/S, 1989)

Searching for Your Danish Ancestors
By the MGS Danish Interest Group. To order, write to: Park Genealogical Books, Dept. WWW, P.O. Box 130968, Roseville MN USA 55113-0968; <www.parkbooks.com>

Tante Johanne: Letters of a Danish Immigrant Family, 1887-1910
By John W. Nielsen (Blair, Neb.: Lur Publications, 1996)

PERIODICALS

Fortid og Nutid (The Past and the Present)
1914–. Published by the Dansk historisk Fællesforening, Rigsarkivet, Rigsdagsgarden 9, 1218 Copenhagen K, Denmark.

Hvem Forsker Hvad (Who's Researching What)
1969–. Published by the Samfundet for Dansk Genealogi og Personalhistorie, Christian Xs Vej 27, 8260 Viby J, Denmark.

Personalhistorisk Tidskrift (Periodical and Serial of Personal History)
1880–. Published by the Samfundet for Dansk-Norsk Genealogi og personalhisto-

rie. After 1930, published by Samfundet for Dansk Genealogi og Personal-historie.

WEB SITES

Danish Demographic Database
<ddd.sa.dk/DDD_EN.HTM>

Danish Emigration Archives
<www.emiarch.dk/home.php3?l=en>

Danish-English Online Dictionary
<www.freedict.com/onldict/dan.html>

Danish Genealogy Links
<www.rootsweb.com/~mnstloui/danlnk.htm>

Danish Immigrant Museum
<www.dkmuseum.org/DenmarkDanishGenealogyTracingFindingAncestorsArchives.html>

Denmark Genealogy Mailing Lists
<www.rootsweb.com/~jfuller/gen_mail_country-den.html>

DIS-Danmark
<www.dis-danmark.dk/forenuk.htm>

Facts About Genealogical Research in Denmark
<www.genealogi.dk/factwors.htm>

Genealogy Resource Index for Denmark (GRID)

Genealogy Today:
Danish Surnames
<www.genealogytoday.com/
names/origins/danish.html>

History of Denmark
<www.um.dk/english/
danmark/danmarksbog/
kap6/6.asp>

The Society for Danish
Genealogy and Biography
<www.genealogi.dk/index
_us.htm>

FINLAND

ORGANIZATIONS
AND ARCHIVES

Ålands landskapsarkiv
(Ahvenanmaa
[Åland] County)
PB 60
22101 Mariehamn, Finland
Tel: 011-358-18-253 44
Fax: 011-358-18-191 55

Finnish-American
Historical Archives
Suomi College
601 Quincy St.
Hancock, MI 49930 USA

Genealogical Society
of Finland
Liisankatu 16A
FIN-00170 Helsinki, Finland
<www.genealogia.fi/
indexe.htm>

Hämeenlinnan
maakunta-arkisto
(Häme and Uusimaa
counties)
13100 Hämeenlinna
Finland
Tel: 011-358-3-653 3801
Fax: 011-358-3-653 3810

<www.narc.fi/ma/hma/index
.html>

Immigration History
Research Center
University of Minnesota
826 Berry St.
St. Paul, MN 55114 USA

Institute of Migration
Emigrant Register
Piispankatu 3
20500 Turku, Finland
<www.utu.fi/erill/instmigr/
eng/e_rekist.htm>

Joensuun maakunta-arkisto
(Pohjois-Karjala County)
PL 146
80101 Joensuu, Finland
Tel: 011-358-13-251 4602
Fax: 011-358-13-251 4606
<www.narc.fi/ma/joma/
index.htm>

Jyväskylän
maakunta-arkisto
(Keski-Suomi County)
40100 Jyväskylä, Finland
Tel: 011-358-14-617 592
Fax: 011-358-14-610 651
<www.narc.fi/ma/jyma/
index.html>

Mikkelin maakunta-arkisto
(Kymi, Mikkeli, and Kuopio
counties; the former Viipuri
county; and the parishes
of Salla and Petsamo, which
were ceded to the USSR
in 1944)
PL 2
50101 Mikkeli, Finland
Tel: 011-358-15-321 310
Fax: 011-358-15-321 3157
<www.narc.fi/ma/mma/
mmapsivu.htm>

Military Archives
(before 1810)
Krigsarkivet
S-115 88 Stockholm, Sweden
Tel: 011-46-8-782 41 00
Fax: 011-46-8-782 69 76
<www.ra.se/kra>

Military Archives
(most begin in 1812)
Sota-arkisto
PL 266
00170 Helsinki, Finland
Tel: 011-358-9-161 6362
Fax: 011-358-9-161 6371

National Archives of Finland
Kansallisarkisto
PL 258
00171 Helsinki, Finland
Tel: 011-358-9-228 521
Fax: 011-358-9-176 302
<www.narc.fi> (Finnish)
<www.narc.fi/sve/index
.html> (Swedish)

Oulun maakunta-arkisto
(Lappi and Oulu counties)
PL 31
90101 Oulu, Finland
Tel: 011-358-8-311 7066
Fax: 011-358-8-311 7068
<www.narc.fi/ma/oma/
oulu1.htm>

Swedish-language
newspaper archive
Brages Urklippsverk
Kaserngatan 28
00130 Helsingfors, Finland

Turun maakunta-arkisto
(Turku-Pori County)
PL 383
20101 Turku, Finland
Tel: 011-358-2-2760 818
Fax: 011-358-2-2760 810
<www.narc.fi/ma/tma/index
.htm>

University of Helsinki Library
Helsingin yliopiston kirjasto
Unioninkatu 36
00170 Helsinki, Finland
<renki.helsinki.fi/hyk/kirjasto/kokoelma/arkistot.html>

Vaasan maakunta-arkisto
(Vaasa County [see also Jyväskylän maakunta-arkisto])
PL 240
65101 Vaasa, Finland
Tel: 011-358-6-317 3912
Fax: 011-358-6-312 0392
<www.narc.fi/ma/vma/finhtml/index.htm>

BOOKS

The Fabulous Family Holomolaiset:
A Minnesota Finnish Family's Oral Tradition
By Patricia Eilola (St. Cloud, Minn.: North Star Press, 1996)

Finnish Genealogical Research
By Timothy Laitila Vincent and Rick Tapio (New Brighton, Minn.: Finnish America, 1994)

Guide to the Military Archives of Finland
(Helsinki: The Military Archives, 1977)

Guide to the Public Archives of Finland
(Helsinki: National Archives, 1980)

Hometown Folks:
A Finnish-American Saga
By Gerald F. Carlson

(St. Cloud, Minn.: North Star Press, 1997)

Kansallisarkisto, asiakkaan opas
(The National Archives: A Guide)
(Helsinki: Kansallisarkisto, 1994)

Krigsarkivet: en handledning
(Guide to the Military Archives)
(Helsingfors: Statens tryckericentral, 1977)

Maakunta-arkistojen opas
(Guide to the Provincial Archives)
(Helsinki: Valtion painatuskeskus, 1976)

Riksarkivet, en handledning
(The National Archives: A Guide)
(Helsingfors: Riksarkivet, 1995)

Släktforskning, praktisk handbok för Finland
(Genealogical Research, Practical Handbook for Finland)
By Alf Brenner (Helsingfors: Söderström & Co., 1947)

Sota-arkiston opas
(Guide to the Military Archives)
(Helsinki: Valtion painatuskeskus, 1974)

Sukututkijan tietokirja
(Reference Book for Genealogists)
(Sirkka Karskela. Suomi: Finnroots, 1983)

Suomen arkistojen opas:
Arkiven i Finland, en handledning
(Guide to Archives Repositories in Finland)
(Helsinki: Valtion painatuskeskus, 1975)

Valtionarkiston yleisluettelo—Översiktskatalog för Riksarkivet
(Inventory for the National Archives)
4 vols. (Helsiniki: Valtioneuvoston kirjapaino, 1956–73)

PERIODICALS

Genos: Suomen Sukututkimusseuran aikakauskirja/Genos: tidskrift utgiven av Genealogiska Samfundet i Finland (Genealogy: Periodical Published by the Genealogical Society in Finland)
Helsinki: 1930–.

Sukutieto: datateknik (Computer Technique)
Helsinki: Sukutietotekniikka ry, 1982–.

Sukuviesti: sukumme eilen ja tänään, sukuyhteisöjen yhteyslehti (Genealogical News: Our Family Yesterday and Today, Newsletter for the United Genealogical Societies)
Espoo: SYT, 1978–.

WEB SITES

Beginner's Guide to Finnish Family History Research
<members.aol.com/dssaari/guide.htm>

DISBYT database: Pre-1909 people search
<frigg.abc.se/~disbyt/finland/english/index.html>

Enfin (Online Finnish-English dictionary)
<212.213.217.194/cd/enfin4.htm>

Family History Finland
<www.open.org/rumcd/genweb/finn.html>

Finfo
<virtual.finland.fi>

Finland Festivals
<www.festivals.fi/english/keskioikea.lasso>

Finland Genealogy Forum
<genforum.genealogy.com/finland/>

Finland Genealogy Mailing Lists
<www.rootsweb.com/~jfuller/gen_mail_country-fin.html>

Finngen Mailing List
<www.tbaytel.net/bmartin/finngen.htm>

Finnish-American Historical Society of the West
<www.finamhsw.com>

Finnish Genealogy Group
<feefhs.org/fi/frgfinmn.html>

Finnish Genealogy Links (Suomalaisia Sukututkimus Linkkeja)
<www.engr.uvic.ca/~syli/geneo/links.html>

Genealogical Society of Finland
<www.genealogia.fi/indexe.htm>

Helsinki City Library
<www.lib.hel.fi/english>

History of Finland
<www.pp.clinet.fi/~pkr01/historia/history.html>

Institute of Migration
<www.utu.fi/erill/instmigr/art/finngeneal.htm>

National Land Survey of Finland
<www.maanmittauslaitos.fi>

Online Finnish-English Dictionary
<www.freedict.com/onldict/fin.html>

RootsWeb's guide to tracing Finnish family trees
<www.rootsweb.com/~rwguide/lesson23.htm#Finns>

NORWAY

ORGANIZATIONS AND ARCHIVES

Bergen Offentlige Bibliotek (Public Library-Bergen)
Strømgaten 6
5015 Bergen, Norway
Tel: 47 55 56 85 60
Fax: 47 55 56 85 70

Bibliotek for Humania og samfundsvitenskap (University Library)
Postboks 1009 Blindern
0315 Oslo, Norway
Tel: 47 22 85 91 02
<www.ub.uio.no/unsl>

Deickmanske Bibliotek (Public Library-Oslo)
Henrik Ibsensgate 1
N-0179 Oslo 1, Norway
Tel: 47 22 03 29 00
Fax: 47 22 11 33 89
E-mail: deichman@deich.folkebibl.no
<www.deich.folkebibl.no>

Norwegian Emigrant Museum
Åkershagan
2312 Ottestad, Norway
<www.museumsnett.no/emigrantmuseum>

Norwegian Emigration Center
Strandkaien 31
N-4005, Stavanger, Norway
<www.utvandrersenteret.no>

Norwegian Historical Data Centre
University of Tromsø
N-9037 Tromsø, Norway
<www.rhd.uit.no/indexeng.html>

Riksarkivet (National Archive)
Folke Bernadottes vei 21
Postboks 4013,
Ullevål stadion
N-0806, Oslo, Norway
Tel: 47 22 02 26 00
Fax: 47 22 23 74 89
E-mail: ra@riksarkivet.dep.telemax.no

Sons of Norway
1455 W. Lake St.
Minneapolis, MN 55408 USA
Tel: (800) 945-8851 or
(612) 827-3611
<www.sofn.com>
Largest Norwegian organization outside of Norway; publishes *Viking* magazine

Statsarkivet i Bergen
(Hordaland, Bergen, and Sogn og Fjordane Counties)
Arstadveien 22
N-5009 Bergen, Norway
Tel: 47 55 31 50 70
Fax: 47 55 32 12 65

Statsarkivet i Hamar
(Oppland and Hedemark Counties)
Lille Strandgate 3
N-2304 Hamar, Norway
Tel: 47 62 52 36 42
Fax: 47 62 52 94 48

Statsarkivet i Kongsberg
(Buskerud, Vestfold, and Telemark Counties)
Frogsvei 44
N-3611 Kongsberg, Norway
Tel: 47 32 86 99 00
Fax: 47 32 86 99 10

Statsarkivet i Kristiansand
(Aust-Agder and Vest-Agder Counties)
Märthas vei 1
Serviceboks 402, 4604
Kristiansand
N-4613 Kristiansand, Norway
Tel: 47 38 14 55 00
Fax: 47 38 14 55 01

Statsarkivet i Oslo
(Østfold, Akershus, and Oslo counties)
Folke Benradottes vei 21

Postboks 4015 Ullevål stadion
N-0806 Oslo, Norway
Tel: 47 22 02 26 00
Fax: 47 22 23 74 89

Statsarkivet i Stavanger
(Rogaland County)
Bergjelandsgate.30
N-4012 Stavanger, Norway
Tel: 47 51 50 12 60
Fax: 47 51 50 12 90

Statsarkivet i Tromsø
(Troms and Finnmark counties)
N-9293 Tromsø, Norway
Tel: 47 77 67 66 11
Fax: 47 77 67 65 20

Statsarkivet i Trondheim
(Møre og Romsdal, Sør-Trøndelag, Nord-Trøndelag, and Nordland counties)
Høgskoleveien 12
Postboks 2825 Elgeseter
N-7432 Trondheim, Norway
Tel: 47 73 88 45 00
Fax: 47 73 88 45 40

Vesterheim Genealogical Center and Naeseth Library
415 West Main St.
Madison, WI 53703
<www.vesterheim.org/genealogy.html>

BOOKS

Aslak Bolts jordebok (Aslak Bolt's Land Book)
By Jon Gunnar Jørgensen
(Oslo: Riksarkivet, 1997)

Giants in the Earth: A Saga of the Prairie
By Ole Rølvaag (New York: Harper & Row, 1964)

Norway to America: A History of the Migration
By Ingrid Semmingsen
(Minneapolis: University of Minnesota Press, 1978)

The Promise of America: A History of the Norwegian-American People
By Odd Sverre Lovoll
(Minneapolis: University of Minnesota Press, 1999)

PERIODICALS

Norsk Slektshistorisk Tidsskrift (Periodical of Norwegian Family History)
Oslo: Norsk Slektshistorisk Forening, 1928–.

WEB SITES

Ancestors from Norway
<homepages.rootsweb.com/~norway>

Culture Net Norway
<www.culturenet.no/links.php?kat=2021>

Cyndi's List: Norway
<www.cyndislist.com/norway.htm>

Emigration Ship Index
<www.norwayheritage.com/ships>

Genealogy/Slekt in Troms Norway
<www.troms-slekt.com>

Genealogy Society of Norway-DIS
<www.disnorge.no>

genealogyPro
<genealogypro.com/
directories/Norway.html>

GenealogySpot: Norway
<www.genealogyspot.com/
country/norway.htm>

History of Norway
<odin.dep.no/odin/engelsk/
norway/history>

**How to Trace Your
Ancestors in Norway**
<odin.dep.no/odinarkiv/
norsk/dep/ud/1996/eng/0320
05-990804/index-dok000-b-
n-a.html>

**National Archives of
Norway Digital Archive**
<digitalarkivet.uib.no>

Norge.no
<english.norge.no/
andrelenker>

Norway Family
<www.norwayfamily.com>

Norway Genealogy
<home.online.no/~oekaas/
Ny%20web/indexeng.htm>

Norway Genealogy Forum
<genforum.genealogy.com/
norway>

**Norway Genealogy
Mailing Lists**
<www.rootsweb.com/
~jfuller/gen_mail_
country-nor.html>

**Norway Genealogy:
WorldGenWeb**
<www.rootsweb.com/
~wgnorway>

Norway Online Information
<www.norway.org>

The Norway Post (English)
<www.norwaypost.no>

**The Norway Post:
Genealogy/Roots**
<www.norwaypost.no/
default.asp?folder_id=72>

Norway Roots
<www.geocities.com/
Heartland/3856>

**Norwegian American
Homepage: Genealogy**
<www.lawzone.com/
half-nor/ROOTS.HTM>

**Norwegian Genealogy
Resources on the Internet**
<www.hfaa.org/bygdelag/
links.shtml>

**Online Norwegian-English
Dictionary**
<www.freedict.com/onldict/
nor.html>

**Uffda: Genealogical Links to
Norway**
<www.fromnorway.net/
uffda_norwegian_
directory/geneol.htm>

US Embassy Norway
<www.usa.no/norway/
genealogy.html>

France

Gargoyle
overlooking Paris

REGIONAL GUIDE
MAUREEN A. TAYLOR

Those with French ancestry should be very proud. From the impressive list of French authors and philosophers—such as Victor Hugo, Gustave Flaubert, and Marcel Proust—to the innovative achievements of French artists like Paul Gaugain, Claude Monet, Pierre Auguste Renoir, and Edgar Degas, the French have been an important part of the advancement of the arts for centuries. The essential need for the arts in France has probably been influenced by their lavish and tumultuous history.

The Romans dubbed the Celtic people of western France "the Gauls" around 120 B.C., but the name that stuck came around 486 A.D. from invaders from the north, the Franks. The France we know today came about when Charlemagne, crowned Holy Roman Emperor in 800, united all of present-day France and revived the Latin culture of refinement and education.

Relative peace reigned until 1337, when war with England erupted over the validity of the current French dynasty and English control over a few provinces. A French peasant you may have heard of, the young and divinely-inspired Joan of Arc, rallied the French troops and led them to victory over the English in 1429. A year after her victory, she was captured and exported to England, where she was burned as a witch, but her nationalist goal was completed—she brought about the end of England's political control of France.

Louis XIV's infamous love of the arts, and his buying of lands

Doorway in Eze

to expand the borders of France, resulted in an almost-depleted French treasury. He died in 1715, leaving a disgruntled constituency and a financial disaster for his successor, Louis XV, who was also an ineffectual ruler. The stage was set for a revolution.

Louis XVI and his wife, Marie Antoinette, were the next to ascend the throne, and the sins of the past kings came to rest on their heads—literally. On 14 July 1789, French peasants attacked and took the Bastille, a great medieval prison at the eastern end of Paris that was long regarded as a symbol of political oppression. Eventually this lead to the end of the monarchy and the beheading of Louis XVI on 21 January 1793 and Marie Antoinette on 16 October 1793.

In 1799, Napoleon Bonaparte seized control of France, crowned himself king in 1804, and started on a quest to conquer Europe. He was exiled after his defeat on the Russian front but returned in 1815 and went to war with England in Waterloo. He again lost and lived out his life exiled on St. Helena Island, where he died on 6 May 1821, from stomach cancer.

The 1800s saw a rise of the working and middle class, due to the ongoing industrial revolution. In 1870, the region of Alsace-Lorraine was captured by Germany, but the area was reclaimed by France after their victory over Germany in World War I. France lost 10 percent of its men and nearly half of its industry during the war.

In 1940, after a short-lived, unsuccessful defense, France surrendered to Germany. General Charles de Gaulle became head of the resistance and, after World War II, eventually became President of France.

So where do you fit in? How can you find out more about your own French heritage? Fortunately, the French kept excellent records. To get started, it takes only an understanding of some basic sources, a list of words that frequently appear in French documents, and these six steps:

Step 1: Start with sources close to home

As with all genealogical research, it's best to start with yourself and work backwards. Don't forget oral history and home sources such as letters, diaries, and family Bibles. Clues to your ancestry may be part of your daily life, hidden in family traditions or community celebrations.

To be successful with your research in France, you'll need to know the town your immigrant ancestor came from—unfortunately, nationwide indexes to vital records in France do not exist. Since you're trying to uncover your family's specific point of origin in France, it's important to be methodical about your research in areas your ancestors settled after leaving France. Obviously the type of documents you use depends on the time period during which your ancestor emigrated. For tips on finding your immigrant ancestors, see Sharon DeBartolo Carmack's *A Genealogist's Guide to Discovering Your Immigrant and Ethnic Ancestors* (Cincinnati, Ohio: Betterway Books: 2000).

Always gather facts on your immigrant ancestor at home before attempting research in French records. Don't assume that the port of embarkation is also the town of origin—emigrants from the French countryside left through various port cities. And many groups left France with an interim stop in another country. If tracing Cajun ancestors, follow them back to their initial settlement in Atlantic Canada before making the leap to France.

Step 2: Follow French immigration patterns

Unlike some immigrant groups, who came largely in one or two big waves, the French left home in many smaller ripples over a period of centuries. Try to determine which category of French immigration brought your ancestors to their new homes:

Acadians—Defined as French immigrants to Atlantic Canada (Nova Scotia, Cape Breton, New Brunswick, Prince Edward Island), these were the people immortalized by Longfellow in *Evangeline*. In 1755, the British forced the Acadians to leave

Canada. Some Acadians went to French-controlled areas, such as Louisiana, while others moved to the American colonies. The Acadian Cultural Society maintains a list of surnames for Acadian immigrants at <www.acadianculture.org>.

French—Some merchants and scholars traveled abroad for business purposes and education, so it's important to differentiate between immigrants and temporary residents. Other individuals fled at the conclusion of the French Revolution.

French Canadians—French citizens and soldiers who originally settled in the Quebec region of Canada often immigrated to industrial areas of the United States seeking work. These groups formed distinctive communities within cities in the Northeast, retaining their ethnic identity, culture, and language by founding schools and community organizations.

Cajun—Acadians who fled Canada to Louisiana became known as Cajuns. This includes seven shiploads of Acadians who escaped to Spain and were subsequently sent to Louisiana in 1785.

Creole—Settlers in Louisiana with a mixture of French and Spanish descent or mixed European and African roots are called Creoles. They have a self-contained culture with their own patois—archaic French mixed with other languages.

Alsatian-Lorraine—In the nineteenth century, immigrants from this region, historically tossed back and forth between France and Germany, settled in Louisiana and Texas, U.S.

Huguenots—Protestant French citizens sought refuge in other countries after the revocation of the Edict of Nantes in 1685 made their religion illegal in Catholic France. Even as early as 1562, some Huguenots settled in South Carolina and Florida, U.S., until Spanish troops destroyed their colonies.

Opposite page:
Notre Dame
over the Seine, Paris

Step 3: Understand naming practices

Some confusing French naming practices can complicate your research. *Prénoms* or Christian names can be multiple and nicknames can be used instead of given names. Check both the birth certificates and baptismal records for name verification. Be prepared for surprises. In one Bessette family, for example, all the sisters have the same first name with different middle names; all their lives, however, they've been known by still other, unrecorded

Eiffel Tower, Paris

names—Loretta, Rita, and Alice. So remember: With given names, be sure to keep good notes and never make assumptions.

French surnames follow the same rules as in other cultures, but with some additions. For example, French Canadian settlers often added an additional surname or *dit* name to further distinguish themselves. This means you may have to identify and search for information under several different surnames. Confused? The American French Genealogical Society offers a list of common French Canadian surnames and variations, including *dit* names, at <homepages.roots web.com/~afgs/index1.html>. There are also cases of double surnames in families from the mountainous areas of France.

Step 4: Tackle the challenges of reading and writing

Before you jump to conclusions about having French ancestry because your family speaks the language, remember that's not necessarily an indication of ancestry from France. French is spoken in some Caribbean islands, a few provinces of Belgium, the French cantons of Switzerland, and in countries that were French colonies, such as Algeria. The opposite is also true: Some individuals have French ancestry but are from the non-French speaking areas of Alsace and the Basque regions.

But assuming you do have French ancestors, you're probably thinking you only need to be familiar with French to understand records in France—well, *au contraire*. Records may be in Latin, German, or Italian in addition to French, depending on when and where the event took place. Don't forget that names also change when they're translated into another language—so Jean becomes John, for instance.

Unless you're fluent in French, you'll need a list of words commonly found in the records to help you decipher the data and request information. The Family History Library has an excellent list of terminology and a letter-writing guide on its site <www.familysearch.org> to help you formulate a letter.

Eze, village cat

Online translation tools can help you bridge the language gap. Babelfish <babelfish.altavista.com> automatically translates up to forty sentences at a time from English to French or vice versa. Or try a free online French-English dictionary to translate documents yourself, such as <www.freedict.com/onldict/fre.html>. If you prefer to have translations done by an experienced human, try contacting a local college or university's French department.

Step 5: Explore French records—four basic types

Once you get to the point of actually tapping French records, you'll find four basic types that will help you trace your ancestry in France: vital records (church and civil), notarial documents, military papers, and emigration records. The wealth of information in some of these documents will amaze you, especially if you're unfamiliar with church documents. Others present special challenges.

Vital records. To find French vital records—birth, marriage, death, and so on—you'll want to check not only government documents but also those of your ancestor's church. Until 1792, only churches kept vital records. Once civil records began, church documents became less complete, but it's still worth investigating both types of records.

Because of the importance of church records, you'll want to try to learn not only your ancestors' town of origin but also their religious affiliation. If you have Catholic ancestors, bone up on the various religious feast days, which is often the only way to date a baptism, marriage, or death. Baptismal documents record the child's name, parents' names, baptism date, godparents' names, sometimes birth date, and father's occupation. Marriages took place in the bride's home parish, except for 1798 to 1800, when weddings took place in the canton rather than the hometown. Marriage records include the bride's maiden name and sometimes her mother's maiden name, too.

1534 Jacques Cartier begins French exploration of North America.

1541 Protestantism attracts converts in France.

1579 Death and marriage records are filed for the first time.

1685 Revocation of the Edict of Nantes makes Protestantism illegal, causing Huguenots to flee France.

1698 Dom Pérignon creates champagne.

1539 Date and hour of birth first appear in French baptismal registers. French replaces Latin as official language.

1559 Protestant pastors start keeping baptisms and marriage registers for their congregation. Many of these are later destroyed during Protestant persecutions.

1632 French settle Quebec and Acadia (Canada).

1722 First wave of settlers begins moving from Alsace-Lorraine to colonies in the Banat (Austria-Hungary, in southeastern Europe).

The Family History Library has microfilms of the records of about 60 percent of all French parishes, which you can borrow through your local Family History Center. To see if your ancestor's parish is covered, go to <www.familysearch.org>, click on "Library," "Family History Library Catalog," and "Place Search."

For civil records, you'll find two sets—one in the town hall, the other in the archives of the *département*. (France today is divided into twenty-two *régions*, similar to the provinces of French history; the *régions* are subdivided into a total of ninety-six *départements*, which date to the French Revolution. *Départements* are further subdivided into *arrondissements*, then *cantons*, and finally *communes*.) The record books are arranged chronologically and usually have annual indexes.

You can request civil birth, marriage, and death records from the town registrar. Only direct descendants can have access to records that are less than a century old, however. Civil authorities collected the same types of information as churches, with the exception of godparents' names.

Notarial records. Notarial records are some of the best sources of French genealogical information, but they're also difficult to locate unless you know the name of the notary and where he

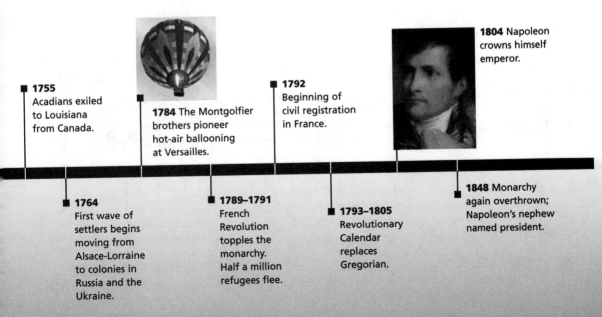

1755 Acadians exiled to Louisiana from Canada.

1784 The Montgolfier brothers pioneer hot-air ballooning at Versailles.

1792 Beginning of civil registration in France.

1804 Napoleon crowns himself emperor.

1764 First wave of settlers begins moving from Alsace-Lorraine to colonies in Russia and the Ukraine.

1789–1791 French Revolution topples the monarchy. Half a million refugees flee.

1793–1805 Revolutionary Calendar replaces Gregorian.

1848 Monarchy again overthrown; Napoleon's nephew named president.

lived. These officials recorded legal events, such as marriage contracts, wills, property divisions, guardianships, and household inventories. Theirs are the oldest type of record kept in France.

Archived chronologically under the name of each notary, notarial documents older than 125 years are usually—but not always—located in the departmental archives. Try to determine the name of the notary in the area your ancestor lived from the departmental archives so that you can check those documents first. Families typically used the same notary for several generations, but not necessarily the one closest to them geographically.

Notarial records are mostly unindexed, though you may find lists of indexed records in local genealogical society publications. French notarial papers are only in France, so you may need to hire a professional genealogist there to assist you. However, similar materials for French Canada are on microfilm, available through the Family History Library.

Military records. When researching French male ancestry, place the gentleman in historical context in terms of military service. French armies participated in many long-term conflicts in Europe, as well as against the British in America. The government began keeping lists of soldiers organized by regiment and date of origin of the group in 1716. Unindexed military censuses

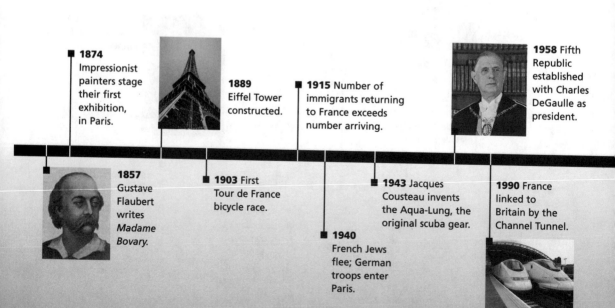

1874 Impressionist painters stage their first exhibition, in Paris.

1889 Eiffel Tower constructed.

1915 Number of immigrants returning to France exceeds number arriving.

1958 Fifth Republic established with Charles DeGaulle as president.

1857 Gustave Flaubert writes *Madame Bovary.*

1903 First Tour de France bicycle race.

1943 Jacques Cousteau invents the Aqua-Lung, the original scuba gear.

1990 France linked to Britain by the Channel Tunnel.

1940 French Jews flee; German troops enter Paris.

Abbey of Senanque, Gordes, Provence

were compiled yearly and list alphabetically the names of men nineteen and twenty years old. In order to access these records, you need to hire someone to search the documents; you'll have to provide the man's birth year and the department that recorded his birth.

Emigration documents. Published indexes to different types of emigration materials exist, but they depend on where in France your ancestors lived, the specific group with which they left, and the time period. For instance, very few nineteenth-century passenger lists from the major port of Le Havre still exist. Whatever passenger lists still exist for France are unindexed, but usually contain the name, age, occupation, place of origin, and sometimes birthplace of the emigrant.

Step 6: Embrace your cultural heritage

If you're finding that the pursuit of your French roots may take you a little while, don't worry about it. As you do your research, take time to explore French culture at every opportunity. If you live in a major city, participate in a Bastille Day (July 14) celebration. Let the charm of an imitation French bistro in your country encourage you on a frustrating day. Visit Montreal for a taste of life in a French-speaking city, or plan a trip to France itself.

It may be that your French roots are indisputable even if you never discover the original town in France your ancestors were from. My mother's family settled in the province of Quebec, but didn't immigrate to the United States until the twentieth century. Our French heritage is a combination of cultural traditions from France as transformed by centuries living in Canada. So far, the original town has eluded our efforts to uncover it, but ultimately it doesn't matter—we have the French sense of *joi de vivre*.

CENSUS

French national censuses have not been transferred to microfilm, are not indexed, and are, therefore, rarely used for genealogical research. Unlike the U.S., Canadian, or British censuses, they cannot be easily searched to locate families. Church and civil records are better sources.

RESOURCES

ORGANIZATIONS AND ARCHIVES

Acadian Cultural Society
Box 2304
Fitchburg, MA 01420 USA
<www.acadiancultural.org>

American-Canadian Genealogical Society
Box 6478
Manchester, NH 03108 USA
<www.acgs.org>

American French Genealogical Society
Box 2113
Pawtucket, RI 02861 USA
Tel: (401) 765-6141
<www.afgs.org>

Archives des Affaires étrangères (Foreign Affairs Archives)
5 et 6 boulevard Louis-Barthou
B.P. 1056
44035 Nantes Cedex
France

Archives Militaires (Military Archives)
Château de Vincennes
94304 Vincennes Cedex
France

Archives Nationales (National Archives)
11 rue des Quatre-Fils
75141 Paris 3e
France

Bibliothèque Généalogique et d'Histoire Social
3 rue de Turbigo
75001 Paris, France
Tel: +33 (01) 42 33 58 21
<www.geocities.com/Eureka/1568>

Bibliothèque Nationale (National Library)
58 rue de Richelieu
75084 Paris Cedex 02
France

Bibliothèque publique d'information (Library of Public Information)
Centre Georges Pompidou
rue Saint-Martin
Paris, France

Les Archives d'Outre-Mer
(Overseas Archives)
29 Chemin du Moulin
de Testas
13090 Aix en Provence,
France

Minitel Services Company
888 7th Ave. 28th Floor
New York, NY
10106-1301 USA
Tel: (212) 399-0080
Fax: (212) 399-0129

National Huguenot Society
9033 Lyndale Ave. S. #108
Bloomington, MN
55437 USA
Tel: (952) 885-9776

U.C.G.L. (Genealogical
Society of Lorraine)
Madame la Secrétaire
B.P. 8
54131 Saint Max Cedex
France

BOOKS

*Ancestral Research in
France: The Simple Guide to
Tracing Your Family History
Through French Records*
By Patrick Pontet (self-
published, send twenty-
three British pounds to 31
Collingwood Walk, Andover
Hampshire SP10 1PU)

*Beginning Franco-American
Genealogy*
By Rev. Dennis M. Boudreau
(Pawtucket, R.I.: American-
French Genealogical Society,
1993)

*État des inventaires des
archives départementales,
communales et hospitalières
au 1er janvier 1983
(Report on archive inventories of departments, com-
munities, and hospitals)*
France. Direction des
Archives. 2 vols. (Paris:
Archives nationales, 1984)

*Fiches op de registers,
collectie La Rochelle,
1602–1685
(Card index of Huguenots of
La Rochelle, Charente-
Maritime, France,
1602–1685)*
Bibliothèque Wallonne,
Leiden. (Salt Lake City:
Genealogical Society of
Utah, 1950)

*Fiches op de registers,
collectie Montauban,
1647–1682
(Card index of Huguenots of
Montauban, Tarn-et-
Garonne, France, 1647–1682)*
Bibliothèque Wallonne,
Leiden. (Salt Lake City:
Genealogical Society of
Utah, 1950)

*Fiches op de Waalse register,
1500–1828
(Card index of Huguenots,
1500–1828)*
Bibliothèque Wallonne,
Leiden. (Salt Lake City:
Genealogical Society of
Utah, 1950)

*A Genealogist's Guide to
Discovering Your Immigrant
& Ethnic Ancestors*
By Sharon DeBartolo
Carmack (Cincinnati, Ohio:
Betterway Books, 2000)

*Genealogy: an introduction
to continental concepts*
By Pierre Durye
(New Orleans: Polyanthos,
1977)

*Guide des recherches
sur l'histoire des familles
(Family history research
guide)*
By Gildas Bernard (Paris:
Archives Nationales, 1981)

*Guide to Quebec Catholic
Parishes and Published
Parish Marriage Records*
By Jeanne Sauve White
(Baltimore: Clearfield Co.,
1998)

*Huguenot Genealogies:
A Selected Preliminary List*
By Arthur Louis Finnell, 16
volumes (Baltimore:
Clearfield Co., 1999)

*Immigrants to America
from France and Western
Switzerland, 1859–1866*
By Clifford Neal Smith
(McNeal, Ariz.: Westland
Publications, 1983)

*In Search of Your
Canadian Roots: Tracing
Your Family Tree in Canada*
By Angus Baxter, 3rd ed.
(Toronto: McClelland &
Stewart, 1999)

*Annuaire
international des archives
(International Directory
of Archives)*
International Council on
Archives. (München;
London; New York; Paris:
Saur, 1992)
Archivum; vol. 38. Text in
French.

*La généalogie: histoire
et pratique
(Genealogy: History and
Practice)*
By Joseph Valynseele (Paris:
Larousse, 1992)

*Les familles Protestantes
en France (XVIe siècle-1792)
(French Protestant families
from the 16th century to
1792)*
France. Archives nationales.
(Paris: Archives Nationales,
1987)

*The New Orleans French,
1720–1733: A Collection of
Marriage Records Relating
to the First Colonists of the
Louisiana Province*
By Winston De Ville
(Baltimore: Genealogical
Publishing Co., 1973)

*Nouveau guide
de généalogie
(New guide to genealogy)*
By Robert Aublet
(Evreux: Ouest-France, 1986)

*Recensement des
dépouillements
systématiques réalisés
en France pour faciliter les
recherches généalogiques
(Inventory of the systematic
extraction made in France
to help genealogical
researchers)*
(Paris: Bibliothèque
généalogique, 1988)

*Répertoire de généalogies
françaises imprimées
(French genealogical bibliography)*
By Étienne Arnaud, 3 vols.

(Paris: Berger-Levrault, 1978-
1982)

PERIODICALS

*Acadian
Genealogy Exchange*
1972–. Published by Janet
Jehn, Acadian Genealogy
Exchange, 863 Wayman
Branch Road, Covington, Ky.
41015 USA.
English text. It includes
Acadian/Cajun families
throughout the world.

*Bulletin de la Société de
l'Histoire du Protestantisme
Français
(Bulletin of the Society for
the History of French
Protestantism)*
1852–. Published by the
Society for the History
of French Protestantism
[Société de l'histoire du
Protestantisme Français]
54 rue des Saints-Pères,
75007 Paris, France.

*Cahiers du Centre de
Généalogie Protestante
(Notices of the Center
for Protestant Genealogy)*
1978–. Published by the
Society for the History of
French Protestantism
[Société de l'histoire du
Protestantisme Français]
54 rue des Saints-Pères,
75007 Paris, France.

*Cercle de Généalogie Juive
(Jewish Genealogical
Society)*
1985–. Published by the
Cercle de Généalogie Juive,
Centre Edmond Fleg, 8bis

rue de l'Eperon, 75006
Paris, France.

*Gé[néalogie] Magazine
(Genealogy Magazine)*
1982–. Published by Editions
Christian, 5 rue Alphonse
Baudin, 75011 Paris, France.

*Geschichtsblätter
des Deutschen
Hugenotten-Vereins*
Sickte: Verlag des Deutschen
Hugenotten-Vereins, 1892–.
Place of publication varies.
This is the German Huguenot
Society's historical series
on international Huguenot
leaders, churches, and
settlements. The text is in
German. Volumes 1-14 are
indexed in Cordier, Leopold.

*Héraldique et généalogie
(Heraldry and genealogy)*
1969–. Published by
Héraldique et Généalogie,
B.P. 526, 78005 Versailles
Cedex, France.

*Je me souviens
(I remember)*
1978–. Published by
American French
Genealogical Society,
P.O. Box 2113, Pawtucket, RI
02861 USA. English text.
Indexes available through
Summer 1985.

*La revue française
de généalogie
(French Genealogical
Review)*
1979–. Published by
La Revue, 12 rue
Raymond-Poincaré,
55800 Revigny, France.

Les Voyageurs
(The Voyagers)
1980–. German-Acadian
Coast Historical and
Genealogical Society,
P.O. Box 517, Destrahan, LA
70047 USA. English text.

Lifelines
1984–. Published by
Northern New York
American Canadian
Genealogical Society,
P.O. Box 1256,
Plattsburgh, NY 12901 USA.
English text.

WEB SITES

**1755: The French and
Indian War**
<web.syr.edu/~laroux>

**Acadian Genealogy
Exchange**
<www.acadiangenexch
.com>

**American-French
Genealogical Society**
<www.afgs.org>

**Beginner's Guide to
Researching Your French
Ancestry**
<genealogy.about.com/
hobbies/genealogy/library/
weekly/aa070700a.htm>

**Bibliothèque Nationale
de France**
<www.bnf.fr/site_bnf_eng/
index.html>

Cyndi's List: France
<www.cyndislist.com/france
.htm>

France.com
<www.france.com>

France Genealogy Forum
<genforum.genealogy.com/

France Genealogy Links
<www.genealogylinks.net/
europe/fra.htm>

France GenWeb
<www.francegenweb.org>

France Mailing Lists
<www.rootsweb.com/~
jfuller/gen_mail_country-
fra.html>

Franco-Gene
<www.francogene.com>

**French Government Tourist
Office**
<www.francetourism.com>

French Heraldry
<www.heraldica.org/topics/

**French Migration Resource
Center**
<www.frenchmigration.com/
default.asp>

Geneactes
<www.geneactes.org>

GeneaGuide
<www.geneaguide.com>

**Genealogie & Histoire
en France**
<www.gefrance.com>

**Genealogy: Acadian
and French Canadian Style**
<ourworld.compuserve.com/
homepages/lwjones>

**GeneaLor: Genealogy in
Lorraine**
<genealor.net>

**Guide Practique de
Genealogie en France
(A Practical Guide to French
Genealogy [in French])**
<www.genealogy.tm.fr>

**The Habitant: Acadian and
French Canadian Genealogy**
<habitant.org>

**Le Centre de Genealogie
Francophone d'Amerique
(The Center of Genealogy
for French-speaking
Americans [in French])**
<www.genealogie.org/
accueil.htm>

**Les Pages Jaunes
(French Yellow Pages)**
<www.pagesjaunes.fr/pj
.cgi?lang=en>

National Archives of Canada
<www.archives.ca>

**RootsWeb's Guide to Tracing
Family Trees, Lesson 24**
<www.rootsweb.com/~
rwguide/lesson24.htm>

Theriault Acadian Family
<www.terriau.org>

YourDictionary.com
<www.yourdictionary.com/
languages/romance.html#
french>

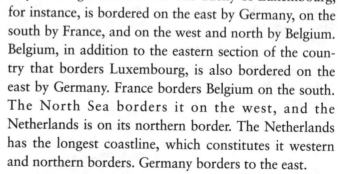

Benelux

Belgium
Luxembourg
The Netherlands

REGIONAL GUIDE
RHONDA R. McCLURE

Millions of people can trace their ancestry to the Benelux region, most of whom find their connection to the Netherlands. Now known as the Benelux, an economic union between the countries of Belgium, the Netherlands, and the Duchy of Luxembourg, it gets this name from the customs union of these countries that took place in 1948. However, more people may recognize these countries as the north part of the former Low Countries. They are situated along the coast of northwest Europe.

Since some family historians are geographically confused when it comes to this region, it's a good idea to get out an atlas or map so you can get a feel for it. The duchy of Luxembourg, for instance, is bordered on the east by Germany, on the south by France, and on the west and north by Belgium. Belgium, in addition to the eastern section of the country that borders Luxembourg, is also bordered on the east by Germany. France borders Belgium on the south. The North Sea borders it on the west, and the Netherlands is on its northern border. The Netherlands has the longest coastline, which constitutes it western and northern borders. Germany borders to the east.

THE NETHERLANDS
Of the countries that make up the Benelux region, the Netherlands has the highest number of emigrants, particularly to the United States; though with the exception of the period after World War II, there was no actual forced migration as a result of crop failures or other problems, as was

Manneken Pis
fountain, Brussels,
Belgium

experienced by so many other countries. Once you discover where in the Netherlands your ancestors came from, however, you may find that they were encouraged to migrate because of some economic, colonial, or religious influence within that specific region.

Those with ancestors from the Netherlands have their genealogical work cut out for them. The country is marked by several other nations who've taken control of the area throughout history, including England, France, Spain, and Austria. The Dutch began setting up colonies in the East Indies in 1595, and over the next few centuries, they had occupied or settled in such places as Curacao, the Virgin Islands, Martinique, Java, the Moluccas, New Zealand and Tasmania, St. Helena, western Australia, South Africa, and Manhattan Island. Although families in the early part of the seventeenth century were not eager to brave the dangers of ocean crossing or to carve out new beginnings in uncharted wilderness, political power struggles, the colonial drive, and long-standing religious tensions between Protestants and Catholics (resulting in alternating periods of persecution) caused many to consider relocation.

It's also important to note that the Belgian revolution started in 1830 as a result of language, religion, and differences in trade interests. (Belgians at the time were predominantly Catholic, spoke French, and were industrial, while Dutch were Protestant, spoke Dutch, and were traders.) This means that your Belgian relatives may have been considered "Dutch" before this uprising and Belgium's declared independence in 1839. Also, in 1831, the Grand Duchy of Luxembourg—part of the Netherlands since the Congress of Vienna—was divided into two parts, the larger of which went to Belgium.

If your Dutch ancestors emigrated in the 1800s, you will likely find that they came from the rural villages of the Netherlands. Of those coming from the Friesland area, known as Frisians, you will find that there was a large migration from this area in the latter part of the nineteenth century as a result of a depression of the local economy. Those who emigrated after World War II did so as a result of natural disasters, such as flooded farmlands, and the devastation in the country after the Nazi occupation.

Remember when you are researching your Dutch lineage that in addition to being referred to as Dutch, you may also hear them called Hollanders or Netherlanders. Be aware that if you find your ancestor referred to as a Frisian, you actually have four possible provinces from which your ancestor could have come, two of which—West Friesland and Friesland—are in the Netherlands, while the other two—East and North Friesland—are in Germany.

Ghent, Belgium canal

BELGIUM

As a kingdom, Belgium has no history before 1830. As individual territories, the ten counties and duchies from which Belgium derived its present land, the accounts are long and varied. From 57 B.C. until it became its own country in 1830, Belgium has been under the rule of the Romans, the Franks, France, the Hapsburg Empire, Spain, Austria, and the Netherlands. It was

Houses in Ghent,
Belgium

only after the revolt begun in 1830 that it was recognized as a
separate entity, the Kingdom of Belgium. From 1555 to 1700 it
was considered the Spanish Netherlands, and from 1700 to 1795
it was known as the Austrian Netherlands.

In addition to these different names, there are the ten individual counties and duchies which you will find yourself turning to
as your research in Belgium progresses beyond 1830. They
include the County of Flanders (lands now found in the
Netherlands, Belgium, and France); le Tournaisis (lands now
entirely in Belgium); the County of Hainaut (lands now found in
Belgium and France); the Duchy of Brabant (lands now in
Belgium and the Netherlands); the County of Namur (lands now
in Belgium and France); the Prince-Bishopric of Liège (lands now
in the Netherlands, Belgium, and France); Bouillon (lands now
entirely in Belgium); the Duchy of Luxembourg (lands now found
in Belgium, Germany, France, and the Grand Duchy of
Luxembourg); the Duchy of Limburg (lands now found in
Belgium, the Netherlands, and Germany); and the Duchy of

Juliers (lands now found in Belgium, the Netherlands, and Germany).

With such a varied history and the close proximity of so many countries, it is not surprising to find that the present-day population of Belgium is divided almost in half and is 52 percent Flemish and 32 percent Walloon. The Flemish, while not actually speaking Dutch, speak a German derivative that is almost indistinguishable from Dutch. The Walloons speak French. When working in the records of Belgium, you can expect to find these two languages, along with possibly some German along the eastern border. While the language may be divided, the religion is almost entirely Roman Catholic.

Even though Belgium is one of the smallest countries in Europe, you will find that if you do not know the town of origin of your ancestors, you may be stalemated. There are too many towns to search individually.

You will also find that most Belgians emigrated through the port of Antwerp and went to places as varied as the United States, Brazil, Guatemala, England, Algeria, and Portugal. Belgian immigrants tended to look for rural communities in which to settle. They were trying to leave industrialization behind and hoping to find fertile farmland upon which to reestablish their homes and communities.

When trying to find the town of origin, be creative in your record searching. Look for biographical sources, including obituaries and published directories for different professions. You may find that there are some native-language newspapers that were published, especially in the 1800s, that may help you. Passenger lists will not give you the place of birth until the 1900s, though naturalization records may. Death records, unfortunately, usually only indicate that the person was born in Belgium. Remember, if your ancestor referred to him or herself as Flemish or a Walloon that you have narrowed your search to a degree.

LUXEMBOURG

One of the smallest countries, today encompassing only 999 square miles of land, Luxembourg is also a relatively young country if you look only at the time it has been an independent duchy. However, the history of the country traces back to the tenth century. Throughout that history, Luxembourg has been occupied by the French, has been a member of the German Confederation, and was held in a sort of limbo in the 1830s when the small nation was to have been divided between Belgium and the Netherlands—a limbo that was settled in 1839, when a larger portion of the country became the province of Luxembourg in Belgium and the remaining area became the independent state. Of course, it wasn't long before it found itself again in the forefront, when Napoleon III saw the duchy as his way to offset Prussia's growing influence. It was not until May of 1867, when the European powers gathered in London, that Prussia was forced to withdraw and the duchy's neutrality was established.

Over a period of fifty years beginning around 1840, some 72,000 Luxembourgers immigrated to the United States and France. Those emigrants who opted for a new life in France were mostly craftsmen who toured the country in order to learn and improve their craft and then returned home. On the other hand, those who left for the United States tended not to return to Luxembourg. The Institut Grand-Ducal in Luxembourg asserts that if you consider the population of Luxembourg during that period (fluctuating somewhere between 175,000 and 213,000), you can deduce that the duchy lost one out of every five of its inhabitants to the United States.

Brussels café

Unlike the Netherlands, emigration was largely a result of devastating famines, although several other factors—including demographic pressure, the unavailability of land, high taxes, political discrimination of the lower classes (only the rich had the right to vote), and a military draft—also helped push Luxembourgers from their homeland.

The migration patterns reflect a strong family and village bond, as people emigrated and settled collectively. Be aware that certain settlements of immigrants from Luxembourg have corresponding specific villages and areas in the homeland.

Determining that your ancestor was from Luxembourg may at first have you thinking you were descended from an immigrant from one of the many other countries geographically close to the duchy. Many of those who came from what is now recognized as the Duchy of Luxembourg were sometimes identified as Belgian, Dutch, French, German, or Prussian. This is a direct result of the political changes during the 1800s, when Luxembourg was shuffled from one country to another. The problem is you may be trying to find a place of birth in a country from which your Luxembourger was mistakenly thought to have come.

ON TO THE RECORDS

Like so many aspects of genealogical research, the boundary changes or political issues of the region often directly affect the records and where you look for them. As we saw with the Frisians and the Luxembourgers, you may get mislead in your initial research if you are not aware of the history of those two groups. We have had a chance to cover these aspects of the Benelux region in just the basics, and you will probably want to spend a little more time learning about the country of your ancestors. As well as being beneficial in your search for records, the history is often fascinating, and it gives us a healthy new respect for the roots we have labored to discover.

You will find that there are many different records available for the Benelux region, most covering even the earlier years. A large percentage of them have been microfilmed by the Family History Library, which makes them available to you through

GOING BEYOND THE SEARCH AT FAMILYSEARCH

Most people stop at the FamilySearch site when they see the search form that lets them look for their ancestors. There is a lot of information hidden in the "Research Helps" section, however, including important research outlines and word lists that will aid you in your Benelux research. To find them:

1. go to the FamilySearch site

2. click on the "Search" tab

3. click on the "Research Helps" link

From here you can search for research outlines by place (using the alphabetical links) or change to *sort by document type* to find the word lists.

your local Family History Center. Before you can effectively search the Family History Library Catalog (FHLC) at the FamilySearch Web site <www.familysearch.org>, look at the different records so you can be introduced to them and, more importantly, what they will tell you about your ancestors.

Civil Registration

Perhaps the most frequently used records are the birth, marriage, and death records. In many countries, including the Netherlands, Belgium, and Luxembourg, they are known as civil registration. This is the subject term you will look for in the FHLC when looking for civil records of your ancestors.

You will find that in the Benelux civil registration records, you need to know more than just the country from which your ancestor came. In the case of both Belgium and the Netherlands there is no central repository for the civil records, so you will need to contact the town where the event took place. The same is true when looking for these records on microfilm. Luxembourg has moved its pre-1979 records to the state archives, but again, you need to know the town in which the event took place. Civil registration for the Netherlands began in 1795 in the southern

provinces and 1811 in the northern provinces. Belgium began keeping civil records in 1796, and Luxembourg's records go back to 1795. Many of the towns' records in all three countries are available on microfilm.

Façade over canal, Ghent, Belgium

Remember that you will be faced with certain language issues. The FHLC generally lets you know which languages are used, and you may find more than one language in each type of record. Luxembourg offers ten-year indexes for many of the towns. Interestingly enough, the indexes are in French, whereas many of the actual town records are in German. Don't worry if you don't read or speak the language. The FamilySearch Web site offers word lists in Dutch, French, and German. The word lists concentrate on those words unique to genealogical research, so most of the time you can decipher the records. If you are going to be spending a lot of time with a particular country's records, you might want to invest in a translation dictionary.

Church Records

When you run out of civil records, usually you will find that church records continue back another century or more. Of course, in addition to having to identify the town in which the event took place, there is also the issue of the parish. Larger towns usually have more than one parish church, and as a result, you may need to look in the records of more than one church. In some of the Benelux countries, the question of religion is not as paramount, but it is still a good idea to be familiar not only with your ancestor's religion but also with the history of religion in the country from which he or she came. For the Netherlands, you will find a great deal of information about church history in the Netherlands research outline available on the FamilySearch Web site.

The church records for Belgium have been deposited in the state archives, at least up until the start of civil registration in 1796. Likewise, while the parish registers for Luxembourg are

10th-11th cent. Belgium is made up of 17 counties, including Luxembourg.

1556 Belgium becomes part of the Spanish Netherlands, under the kings of the Spanish monarchy.

1703–1706 French occupy Belgium; the French remained in Luxembourg until 1714.

Jan. 1790 United Belgian (or Netherlands) States are formed, but Luxembourg remains under Austrian rule.

1792 - 1794 Belgium occupied again by France.

1548 Belgium under the Habsburg dynasty.

1606 Dutch Baroque-era artist and engraver Rembrandt van Rijn is born.

1713 As a consequence of the War of the Spanish Succession, the Spanish Netherlands passes to the Archdukes of Austria (Austrian Netherlands).

Dec. 1790 Austrian rule restored.

1795 Belgian territory is divided into nine departments, which quickly become annexed by France.

still housed in the individual churches, microfilmed copies can be found in the national archives. There is no centralization of the church records in the Netherlands. In researching them, you may discover some of the Catholic registers are written in Latin, while the Lutheran records are usually in German or the old German or Dutch script. You may find these old scripts difficult to read.

Census Records

In some countries, researchers turn to census records in an effort to get an overview of a family unit. Many times we have come to expect the release of census records after a certain amount of time has passed. Belgian census records begin in 1846, but unfortunately these records are not open for public research. There are a few earlier, more localized enumerations for the city of Namur and the province of Brabant that are available. In Luxembourg, censuses have been taken every ten years since 1793 and are now housed in the national archives. In the Netherlands, national censuses began in 1829 and were taken every ten years until 1929. While national in scope, they are housed at the local municipal archives and are available to the

1797 Belgium officially ceded to France by Austria.

1815 Incorporation of the Belgian lands and Liège into the Kingdom of the Netherlands.

1831 Congress proclaims Louis-Charles-Philippe-Raphaël d'Orléans, duc de Nemours, son of King Louis-Philippe of the French, to be king; his father refuses in his name. Leopold Georg Christian Friedrich, Prinz von Sachsen-Coburg und Gotha (pictured) is then chosen as king.

1898 Dutch graphic artist M.C. Escher, known for his visual puzzles, is born.

1814 Belgian territory separated from France, Government General of Belgium established.

1830 The Provional Government of Belgium proclaims independence from the Netherlands.

1878 King Leopold II of Belgium makes plans for colonization of Congo. He commissions former journalist Henry Morton Stanley to ink treaties with local chiefs.

public. A small number of the census records for each country are available on microfilm through the Family History Library, but generally researchers find the civil registration and parish registers more informative.

Notarial Records

All three countries have notarial records, court records that cover many different things from marriage contracts to wills and property rights. The Family History Library has many of these records on microfilm for the Netherlands. You will want to look in the FHLC under both the province and the town in question. The Netherlands is the best-represented country in regard to these records, though there is an alphabetical list of notaries and where the records have been deposited for all the Benelux countries. Unfortunately, none of the notarial records that are in the archives of Luxembourg have been microfilmed, so you would either need to visit the archives or hire a researcher living there.

Major Repositories

While many records are available on microfilm through the Family History Library, there are still other important reposito-

1914—1918 Germany invades and occupies first Luxembourg and then Belgium.

1940–1944 Germany occupies Belgium and rules together with the Nord and Pas de Calais departments of France.

1963-1965 First Belgian-Dutch Antarctic expedition.

2003 Justine Henin-Hardenne became the first Belgian to win a Grand Slam tennis title after a stunning 6-0 6-4 win over Belgian compatriot Kim Clijsters.

1908 Reacting to outcry over atrocities committed against Congolese, the Belgian parliament annexes Congo Free State. It is renamed Belgian Congo.

1925-42 Henri de Baillet-Latour served as the first Belgian president of the International Olympic Committee.

1944 Allied occupation.

2001 Palestinian leader Yasser Arafat and Shimon Peres, the Israeli Foreign Minister, meet for peace talks at the European Union conference in Brussels.

ries to keep in mind. Some of them offer answers by mail, while others simply do not have the staff to respond to written requests.

DON'T LET THE LANGUAGE BARRIER STOP YOU

While it is true that you may find the search for your Benelux roots frustrating, don't let the language barrier discourage you in your research. There are many helpful guides to aid you with the language differences and with record availability. One book that will introduce you to many additional records and repositories is Angus Baxter's *In Search of Your European Roots*, 3rd edition, (Baltimore: Genealogical Publishing Company, Inc., 2001).

The Belfry, Bruges

Just as you may have learned how to use various records in your country, you will learn what records exist in the homeland of your ancestors. You may be slowed by the language differences for a while, but you will soon begin to recognize the important words. By using word lists and translation dictionaries, you will be able to analyze many different records. In the end you will have a feeling of accomplishment as you look at your tree and the roots that connect you to the Benelux region. The records for these countries are plentiful and many genealogists wish for such a bounty. Enjoy the research.

BELGIUM'S CENSUS

Like in France, access to public records is restricted for the last 100 years.

THE NETHERLANDS' CENSUS

The closest thing to the first national "census" was the civil lists [*listes civiques*] or civil registers [*registres civiques*] of the French government, taken in 1811. These records are housed in the state and municipal archives; however, they contain many mistakes and little information.

The Kingdom of the Netherlands held its first national census in 1829, and from then on, censuses were taken every ten years until 1929. Censuses were again taken in 1947, 1960, and 1971. Although they were national, these census records are kept locally, usually in the municipal offices. Those records found in the municipal archives are available to the public. Locally, census records exist for the province of Friesland for 1689, 1714, 1744, and 1796. Provincial censuses are also available for Overijssel in 1748 and 1795.

RESOURCES

BELGIUM

ORGANIZATIONS AND ARCHIVES

Archives Générales de l'État
Rue de Ruysbroeck 2
1000 Bruxelles
Tel: 02 513 76 80
<http://membres.lycos.fr/
erasson/GENEA/Archives.htm>

Office Genealogique et
Heraldique de Belgique
(OGHB) (Genealogy and
Heraldry Office of Belgium)
Maison communale de
Woluwe St Pierre
Av. Charles Thielemans 2,
B-1150 Bruxelles
Tel: (02)772 50 27

Service de Centralisation des
Études Genealogiques et
Heraldiques de Belgique
(SCGD) (Centralization
Service for the Study of
Genealogy and Heraldry
of Belgium)
Maison des Arts, 147
chaussée de Haecht
B-1030 Schaerbeek

BOOKS

*Etymological Dictionary
of the Surnames in
Belgium and North France*
By Dr. Frans DeBrabandere, 2
vols. (Uitgegeven door het
Gemeentekrediet, Brussel,
1993)

PERIODICALS
Belgian Laces
Published by The Belgian
Researchers, Oregon, USA.

WEB SITES

Archives Générales de l'État
<http://membres.lycos.fr/
erasson/GENEA/Archives.htm>

Belgian cities and villages
Web index
<www.a-z.be/steden.html>

Belgium Genealogy Forum
<genforum.genealogy.com/
belgium>

The Belgium-Roots Project
<http://belgium.rootsweb.com>

Cyndi's List: Belgium
<www.cyndislist.com/
belgium.htm>

The Emigrants from
Belgium to the United States
and Canada
<www.ping.be/picavet>

The Emigration from the Waasland to the United States and Canada, 1830–1950
<www.geocities.com/ Heartland/Plains/5666/ Picavet.html>

Francetres: Genealogie en Belgique
<users.skynet.be/wallonia/ belgiq-f.htm>

Genealogy Benelux Homepage
<listserver.ufsia.ac.be/ genealogy/genealog.htm>

Genealogy Benelux Net Ring
<www.dijkgraaf.org/ benelux.htm>

Genealogy Helplist Belgium
<helplist.org/bel/index.shtml>

LUXEMBOURG

ORGANIZATIONS AND ARCHIVES

Archives Nationales du Grand-Duché de Luxembourg
Plateau du Saint Esprit
BP 6, 2010 Luxembourg
<www.etat.lu/AN/>

The Luxembourg Society of Genealogy and Heraldry
Castle of Mersch, 3rd floor
P.O. Box 118
L-7502 Mersch, Luxembourg

Luxembourg Tourist Office in London
122 Regent St.
London W1B 5SA England
Tel: 020 7434 2800

Fax: 020 7734 1205

BOOKS

Familienchronik der Gemeinden Remerschen und Bürmeringen
(All the inhabitants of Remerschen, Schengen, Wintringen/Wintrange [1668–1900], Buermeringen/Burmerange, Elvingen/Elvange and Emeringen/Emerange [1800-1900])
By Prosper Kayser and Roger Kayser (Luxembourg: Institut Grand-Ducal, Section de linguistique, d'ethnologie et d'onomastique).
Contains records for 18,000 individuals and 4,500 families.

Familienchronik der Gemeinde Wellenstein
(All the inhabitants of Wellenstein, Bech-Kleinmacher and Schwebsingen/Schwebsange 1688-1999)
By Prosper Kayser and Roger Kayser (Luxembourg: Institut Grand-Ducal, Section de linguistique, d'ethnologie et d'onomastique)
Contains records for 17,300 individuals and 4,580 families.

Familienchronik der Stadt Remich (All the inhabitants of Remich 1688–1900)
By Prosper Kayser and Roger Kayser (Luxembourg: Institut Grand-Ducal, Section de linguistique, d'ethnologie et d'onomastique)

WEB SITES

Archives Nationales du Grand-Duché de Luxembourg
<www.etat.lu/AN>

Cyndi's List: Luxembourg
<www.cyndislist.com/ luxembourg.htm>

Discussion group for genealogical research in Luxembourg
<fr.groups.yahoo.com/ group/GDLuxembourg>

Genealogie en Belgie
<users.skynet.be/sky60754/ genealbe>

Genealogylinks.net: Luxembourg
<www.genealogylinks.net/ europe/lux.htm>

GENLUX Luxembourg-American Genealogy
<www.eskimo.net/~lisanne/ index.html>

Institut Grand-Ducal
<www.igd-leo.lu>

Luxembourg Coats of Arms
<www.ngw.nl/int/lux/ luxemb.htm>

Luxembourg Genealogy and Heraldry
<www.luxembourg.co.uk/ genealog.html>

Luxembourg GenWeb
<www.rootsweb.com/~ luxwgw>

Luxembourg on My Mind
<http://members.aol.com/ StSimons1/Article5.html>

Luxembourg
Surname Navigator
<www.rat.de/kuijsten/
navigator/luxembourg/
luxembourg.html>

NETHERLANDS

ORGANIZATIONS AND ARCHIVES

Algemeen Rijksarchief (National Archives)
Prins Willem-Alexanderhof 20
Postbus 90520
2509 LM 's-Gravenhage
The Netherlands

Centraal Bureau voor Genealogie (Central Office for Genealogy)
Prins Willem-Alexanderhof 22
Postbus 11755
2502 AT Den Haag
The Netherlands
Tel: 070-3150500
<www.cbg.nl>

Centraal Register van Particuliere Archieven (Central Register of Public Archives)
Prins Willem-Alexanderhof 30
2595 BE 's-Gravenhage
The Netherlands

Commissie voor de Archieven der Nederlandse Hervormde Kerk (Commission of Church Archives)
Overgoo 11
Postbus 405

2260 AK Leidschendam
The Netherlands

General State Archives
Prins Willem-Alexanderhof 20
2595 BE The Hague
<www.nationaalarchief.nl>

Koninklijk Nederlands Genootschap voor Geslacht—en Wapenkunde (The Royal Dutch Society for Genealogy and Heraldry)
Prins Willem-Alexanderhof 24
Postbus 85630
2508 CH Den Haag
The Netherlands
<www.knggw.nl>

Nederlandse Genealogische Vereniging (Dutch Genealogical Society)
Postbus 976
1000 AZ Amsterdam
The Netherlands
E-mail: info@ngv.nl
<www.ngv.nl>

BOOKS

Church and Civil Records of Amsterdam, the Netherlands, before 1811
(Salt Lake City, Utah: Genealogical Society of The Church of Jesus Christ of Latter-day Saints, 1975)

Handleiding voor Genealogisch Onderzoek in Nederland (Handbook for Genealogical Research in the Netherlands)
By J.C. Okkema, 2nd ed. (Weesp: Fibula–Van Dishoeck, 1986)

Handleiding voor Stamboomonderzoek (Handbook for Ancestral Research)
By Roelof Vennik (Rotterdam: Donker, 1987)

PERIODICALS

De Nederlandsche Leeuw: Maandblad van het Koninklijk Nederlandsch Genootschap voor Geslacht–en Wapenkunde (The Dutch Lion: Journal of the Royal Dutch Society for Genealogy and Heraldry)
1883–. Published by the Koninklijk Nederlands Genootschap voor Geslacht–en Wapenkunde, Postbus 85630, 2508 CH Den Haag, The Netherlands.

Genealogie: Kwartaalblad van het Centraal Bureau voor Genealogie (Genealogy: Quarterly of the Central Office for Genealogy)
1995–. Published by the Centraal Bureau voor Genealogie, Postbus 11755, NL-2502 AT Den Haag The Netherlands.

Gens Nostra: Maandblad van de Nederlandsche Genealogische Vereeniging (Our Ancestry: Monthly Journal of the Netherlands Genealogical Society)
1945–. Published by the Nederlandse Genealogische Vereniging, Postbus 976, 1000 AZ Amsterdam, The Netherlands.

*Ons Voorgeslacht
(Our Ancestry)*
A journal of the South
Holland chapter of the
Dutch Genealogical Society.

*Ons Waardeel
(Our Valuable Volume)*
A journal for genealogy in
Drenthe and Groningen.

*Van Zeeuwse Stam
(Of Zeeland Origin)*
A journal of the Zeeland
chapter of the Dutch
Genealogical Society.

*Veluwse Geslachten
(Families from the Veluwe)*
A regional journal
for Gelderland.

WEB SITES

**The Central Bureau
for Genealogy**
<www.cbg.nl>

Cyndi's List: Netherlands
<www.cyndislist.com/
nether.htm>

Dutch Genealogy
<www.geocities.com/Athens/
Delphi/3453/Dutch.html>

Dutch Genealogy Links
<www.euronet.nl/users/
mnykerk/genealog.htm>

DutchGenWeb
<www.rootsweb.com/~
nldwgw>

General State Archives
<www.nationaalarchief.nl>

Holland Page
<www.users.bigpond.com/
paulvanv/homepage.htm>

Germanic Region

Austria
Germany
Lichtenstein
Switzerland

REGIONAL GUIDE
S. CHRIS ANDERSON AND ERNEST THODE

If you think you're going to end up in some Germanic castle on the Rhine or Danube after researching your Germanic family tree, you're in for a twofold shock. First, most of us came from the hearty peasant stock that made up about 99 percent of the masses. The nobility—which was often less noble than the peasants—was roughly one percent of the population. But your ancestors are worth discovering regardless. Second, the path to uncovering your family tree can be hard work, and Germanic ancestry offers its own particular pitfalls in research.

But understanding your Germanic roots can be richly rewarding, even if you don't find any castles, and there are some wonderful resources available to assist you in discovering your Germanic ancestors.

Market Square, Lubeck

WHAT'S "GERMAN"?

You've probably noticed that we keep talking about "Germanic" ancestors, rather than "German." That's because "Germanic" is a much more inclusive term. Germanic ancestors could have come from Germany, Austria, Switzerland, Alsace (part of France), much of what is now Poland, Luxembourg, southern Denmark, the present Czech Republic, or even a bit of Russia.

The German language unifies Germanic people. Even so, German speaking is not all that unified. While England, Spain, and France spent centuries under a unified monarchy, medieval Germany never consolidated under a single ruler until becoming a nation-state under Otto von Bismarck in 1871—after many Germanic people had already left the Old World.

Instead, the various kingdoms and principalities were members of the Holy Roman Empire of the German Nation, as they called it, loosely under the Holy Roman Emperor. Germany's central position in Europe meant that many conflicts were played out in what was a patchwork of hundreds or even thousands of secular and religious kingdoms, principalities, duchies, electorates, estates, free cities, and free states, each with its own rulers, laws, and local customs.

Imperial Palace, Vienna

Because these small areas fluctuated with warfare and marriage, maps of Germany are just a thin slice of history. If you compare a map of Germany from the 1600s and one from the 1700s, boundaries may have shifted yearly in some places or not for dozens of years in others. To get a real perspective on the transformation of Germanic regions, you need to imagine the map as a series of snapshots placed year by year that flow like a movie.

Step 1: Understanding the family feudal

The feudal system in Germany meant that each independent area kept its own records, leading to regional rather than national archives. Various German lands each had their own capitals, and the empire had certain major governmental/royal cities, such as Frankfurt, Regensburg, and Vienna. Berlin didn't develop into a national capital until after 1871. Even then, the other German states did not send records on to "headquarters" in Berlin. The present German national archive houses only records from the post-World War II constitutional government.

Many regional records were destroyed in the devastation of the Thirty Years' War (1618–1648), so it's unusual to find church records before 1650. Still, that means records go back 350 years in many parts of Germany, roughly ten generations, which is not too bad as family histories go.

The legacy of feudalism has a bright side for genealogists, however. Because most peasants relied on a local feudal ruler for protection, the populace was taxed at every occasion. If some-

body died, the ruler got the best ox. If the ruler needed grain, he
took 10 percent of the harvest. If a villager wanted to marry
someone in the next village, he had to wait until the ruler could
make a swap of serfs with that village's ruler. If the ruler decided
to throw a party, he took a nice goose. If someone wanted to
emigrate, the ruler took 10 percent of the person's property.
Fortunately for genealogists, taxes of all kinds generate records.

Neuschwanstein
Castle, Schwangsu

In poorer regions and in times of poverty, Germanic lands
saw a relatively high rate of out-of-wedlock births. Being born
out of wedlock meant a person was ineligible for many things—
joining a guild, owning property of any kind, or becoming a citizen in a free city. Not surprisingly, someone born out of wedlock might want to emigrate to a place where the social stigma
was not so devestating. So you may find your ancestors among
this group.

Germanic inheritance law passed property strictly through
the male line. Inheritance law becomes particularly important if
you're seeking northern German ancestors. Maintaining an
intact farm was critical in the north, especially in Westphalia.

And farm property was indivisible, so the farm name stayed with the land and the new owner had to adopt the farm name. Sons who weren't in line to inherit the farm had incentive to get a trade or to emigrate, as they'd likely never get a chance to own a farm. In other parts of Germany, where farms have been divided and subdivided among all heirs since the early nineteenth century, parcels of land kept getting smaller every generation and farmers might own widely scattered parcels. Although there were more landowners, this lead to inefficiency—another economic factor leading to emigration from those areas.

Step 2: Reading, writing, and records

Deciphering the handwriting or print of Germanic documents may be the greatest challenge in researching your Germanic roots. Worse, early records are frequently composed in open paragraph form, rather than being nicely laid out in columns of name, birth date, and father's name. (Some later records, happily, use this standard post-Napoleonic record format.) Also, not every set of records is indexed. In the absence of an index, it may be necessary to look through dozens or even hundreds of pages to find the record you need.

You don't need to read German fluently to be able to decipher most genealogical records, but you must learn to recognize the most common genealogical scripts and prints. This is

300–500
The invasion of nomadic Asian Huns causes Eastern European tribes, such as the Goths, Saxons, Franks, and Alemans, to move.

1517 Martin Luther posts his 95 theses, sparking the Protestant Reformation.

1618–1648 Germanic lands are ravaged by the Thirty Years' War. Many records and documents are destroyed.

800 Charlemagne is crowned emperor of the Holy Roman Empire, an area that included France, Switzerland, roughly half of modern-day Germany, and parts of Austria.

1545
The Catholic Church in Germany begins to record all marriages, births, and deaths.

1670s and 1680s
The French repeatedly attack the Palatinate region of Germany.

absolutely essential since very few German records have been translated. Older German records are prepared in letters similar to the style called Kurrent. To see a sample of this lettering, see the *Family Tree Magazine* Web site <www.familytreemagazine.com/articles/alphabet.html>. Also illustrated are two other styles, called Fraktur and Sutterlin, to help you see the connection between Kurrent and modern styles.

Certain Kurrent letters appear very similar. This can make your interpretation of Germanic documents difficult and lead to confusion. The handwriting of individual priests, ministers, and clerks can vary significantly from one to another, creating further confusion. The idiosyncrasies of each individual's style of forming particular letters can be baffling.

To be effective in translating a particular person's handwriting properly, make photocopies of enough samples of one person's writing to be able to decide what the letters are. By becoming familiar with numerous common words written by that person, you'll be able to better decipher each word in that person's handwriting.

Step 3: Getting the name right

Once you have the name of an ancestor, you may be ready to start researching—but first make sure you have the correct name. The name may be wrong for several reasons. The sur-

1848 Some 8,000 political refugees, known as "Forty-Eighters," flee Germany when the Frankfurt constitution fails.

1871 Germany becomes a nation-state under Bismarck.

1948 After the Soviets blockade West Berlin, the massive Berlin Airlift supplies the city of 2 million people by air for more than a year.

1708–1709 The Rhine freezes solid during a very harsh winter in the Palatinate, causing many to emigrate.

1852 The Butcher's Guild in Frankfurt introduces the frankfurter.

1881 Anti-Catholic atmosphere and the decline of cottage industries causes German emigration to the US to peak.

1989 Fall of the Berlin Wall sets Germany on a course to reunification a year later.

name may have been changed, or even translated by clerks, as a result of your ancestors having contact with English speakers, especially in the early North American colonies. Nicknames may have been used instead of the standard given name. A sloppy census enumerator may even have altered the family name.

You may think you have an early ancestor named John Snyder, for example—except that's not exactly the way he spelled it when he wrote it himself. He wrote Johann Peter Schneider. John is Johann, a common German name. And Snyder is Schneider. That sounds like Snyder, which is an anglicized version of Schneider. Dropping the middle name can also lead to trouble. In pre-nineteenth-century Germany, the middle name was usually the most frequently used name. Your ancestor may have gone by Peter Schneider, not Johann Schneider.

Because of the many forms and spellings that your ancestors' names might have taken on or been twisted into, don't limit your research to a single spelling or name. Keep records of the variations and examine all the possibilities at each step.

Family surnames followed different patterns depending on the region of Germany. If you have ancestors from northern Germany, around Ostfriesland, you may have a confusing pattern of changing names. Last names there were patronymics from the given name of the father: So Peter Hansen's offspring would have the last name of Petersen, as they were the children of Peter, or Peter's sons.

If your ancestors are from around Westphalia, their surnames may be based on the ownership of a farm. Watch to see if your ancestors' male surnames change when they marry; this would be because the woman was the heiress to a farm.

Patronymics and the use of farm names as surnames are both regional customs, not universal practices throughout the German-speaking lands. But they are things to be aware of in your research.

Step 4: Master the map

Germanic places of origin are hard to find, hard to identify, and hard to pinpoint geographically. To find any mention of the place of origin, you need to look in the obvious places—church records, censuses, death records, marriage records, obituaries, family Bibles, papers brought from overseas, and family histories. Don't forget that neighbors in the country to which your ancestors immigrated may have come from the same place. By finding the neighbors' places of origin, you may locate your own ancestor's origin.

Suppose you find your ancestor's birthplace listed on the 1880 U.S. census as Preisen. You might think the next logical step would be to try to locate a village named Preisen. But foreign birthplaces in censuses are listed as states, not specific villages, or simply as countries. The only state that resembles Preisen is the largest German state, Preussen, which translates into Prussia. Just as surnames are often misinterpreted, place names can be misunderstood, too; our Preisen example is a dialectal pronunciation of Preussen.

German Cathedral, Berlin

Another source of confusion arises when researchers misattribute whether a given place is a village, county, or district. In English, if someone comes from County Cork, Ireland, we know that it's an area and not a town. Because German is a less familiar language, it's natural, but wrong, to think that Amt, Regierungs-Bezirk, Kreis, or Oberamt are the names of villages rather than names for districts. Oberamt Balingen means "District of Balingen," for example.

The same thing occurs with mother churches and branch churches. *Kirchspiel* and *Kirchensprengel* both mean "church parish." If you find Kirchspiel Lienen, it refers to the church parish of Lienen, not a village named Kirchspiel.

Similarly, in the names of larger jurisdictions, *Konigreich* means kingdom, *Herzogtum* means duchy, and *Grafschaft* means county or earldom. One additional complication in this last example is that there are actually at least three villages in Germany named Grafschaft. In the vast majority of cases, however, the reference would be to a district or county rather than a particular village.

Mapping your ancestors can be like solving a mystery. You might run across a place that's changed its name (Veyl or Feil to Feilbingert), or one that uses an abbreviated form of a longer name (Bbronn for Büchenbronn). You might need to find a village that no longer exists (Ronnenberg is now in the Baumholder military firing range), or one that has had its name translated (Newton for Neustadt). Maybe the place you're looking for has a Latin version of its name (Treverorum from Trier) or an alternate spelling altogether (Gostyn and Gostingen). If you don't find a place name you think you should find, review older gazetteers and lists of Latin forms of place names.

Your next steps

When researching your Germanic roots, don't be an island. Make connections with Germanic genealogical societies and other Germanic-specific sources. Go to Germany after you know the exact location to research. But don't make too many assumptions about your trip. You may find a living relative who can add substantially to your store of knowledge about the family. You'll see first-hand a number of areas historically significant to your ancestors. And you can enjoy the flavor of the old country that your ancestors inhabited.

The history of one hundred percent of the world's people has been condensed and preserved through the stories of less than one percent of the world's people—those that make it into the history books shared in schools. Don't substitute the history in schoolbooks for the personal stories that can be a source of pride, laughter, or sympathy for your children and grandchildren. These stories were part of the mysterious fabric that bound a family together.

CENSUS

Censuses were not taken nationally in Germany. What few local records do exist are general, often inaccurate, and rarely accessible to the public. Researchers will have better luck with church and civil records.

RESOURCES

ORGANIZATIONS AND ARCHIVES

Austrian National Archives (emigration records from 1861–1919)
Abteilung I: Haus-, Hof- und Staatsarchiv, Bibliothek, Minoritenplatz 1, A-1010 Vienna, Austria

For Baden, write to:
Generallandesarchiv Karlsruhe
Nördliche Hildapromenade 2
76133 Karlsruhe Germany

Deutsche Zentralstelle für Genealogie (German Center for Genealogy)
Sächsisches Staatsarchiv Leipzig
Schongauerstr. 1
04109 Leipzig Germany
<www.genealogienetz.de/reg/DEU/dzfg-en.html>

Specializing in east Germany:
Arbeitsgemeinschaft ostdeutscher Familienforscher Detlef Kühn
Ritterfelddamm 219
14089 Berlin Germany
<www.genealogienetz.de/vereine/AGoFF/AGoFF-d.html>

For Elsaß-Lothringen (Alsace-Lorraine):
Archives départementales du Bas-Rhin
5 rue Fischart
67000 Strasbourg
France
Archives départementales du Haut-Rhin

Cité administrative
3 rue Fleischhauer
68026 Colmar Cedex 3
France

Archives départementales du Moselle
1 allée du château
57070 St. Julien-les-Metz
France

German Research Association
P.O. Box 711600
San Diego, CA 92171-1600
USA
<feefhs.org/gra/frg-gra.html>

Germanic Genealogical Society
P.O. Box 16312
St. Paul, MN 55116-0312 USA
<www.rootsweb.com/~mnggs/GGS.html>

Specializing in Hessen:
Hessische Familiengeschichtliche Vereinigung Staatsarchiv
Karolinenplatz 3
69289 Darmstadt
Germany
<www.genealogienetz.de/vereine/HFV/hfv.html>

Immigrant Genealogical Society
P.O. Box 7369
Burbank, CA 91510-7369
USA

Specializing in middle Germany:
Günther Unger
Materborner Allee 65
47533 Kleve Germany
<www.genealogienetz.de/vereine/AMF/AMF.html>

National Archives of the Federal Republic of Germany (since 1945)
Bundesarchiv
Postfach 320
D-56003 Koblenz Germany
<www.bundesarchiv.de>

For Ostpreußen, Westpreußen, Pommern, Posen, Schlesien, and other areas now under Polish jurisdiction:
Naczelna Dyrekcja Archiwów Panstwowych
Ul. Dluga 6, skr. poczt. 1005
00-950 Warszawa Poland
<www.archiwa.gov.pl>

Palatines to America
611 E. Weber Rd.
Columbus, OH 43211-1097
USA
<www.palam.org>

For the Pfalz (Palatinate):
Otto-Mayer-Str. 9
67346 Speyer Germany
E-mail: post@landesarchiv-speyer.de

Specializing in the Pfalz and Rheinland:
Arbeitsgemeinschaft Pfälzisch-Rheinische Familienkunde
Rottstr. 17 (Stadtarchiv)
67061 Ludwigshafen/Rhein
Germany

For Rheinland (Rhineland):
Landeshauptarchiv Koblenz
Karmeliterstrasse 1-3
56068 Koblenz
Germany
E-mail: info@landeshauptarchiv-ko.de

Specializing in Rheinland:
Westdeutsche Gesellschaft
für Familienkunde
Claus Geis
Unter Gottes Gnaden 34
50859 Koln-Widdersdorf
Germany
<www.genealogienetz.de/
vereine/wgff>

**For Schleswig-Holstein,
Oldenburg, Lübeck, or the
part of Hamburg that was
once part of Denmark:**
Landesarchiv
Prinzenpalais
Gottorfstr. 6
D-24837 Schleswig Germany
<www.archive.schleswig-
holstein.de>

Swiss National Archives
Archivstrasse 4
CH-3003 Bern
Switzerland

**Specializing in
Württemberg and Baden:**
Verein für Familien- und
Wappenkunde in
Württemberg u. Baden
Postfach 10 54 41
70047 Stuttgart Germany
<www.genealogienetz.de/
vereine/VFWKWB/
VFWKWB.html>

BOOKS

*Address Book for
Germanic Genealogy*
By Ernst Thode, 6th ed.
(Baltimore: Genealogical
Publishing, 1997)

*Bibliographie der
Ortssippenbücher in
Deutschland*

*(Bibliography of village line-
age books in Germany)*
By Franz Heinzman
(Düsseldorf: Heinzmann,
1991) This work lists both
monographs and village
lineages in periodicals.

*Bibliographie gedruckter
Familiengeschichten, 1946-
1960
(Bibliography of
printed family histories,
1946-1960)*
By Franz Heinzman and
Christoph Lenhartz
(Düsseldorf: Heinzmann,
1990)

*Deutsches Geschlechterbuch
(German lineage book)*
194+ vols. (Limburg/Lahn:
C.A. Starke, 1889–)

*Encyclopedia of
German-American
Genealogical Research*
By Clifford Neal Smith and
Anna Piszczan-Czaja Smith
(New York: R.R. Bowker,
1976)

*Genealogical Guide to
German Ancestors from
East Germany and
Eastern Europe*
Arbeitsgemeinschaft
ostdeutscher
Familienforscher e.V.,
Herne, Germany (Herne
Neustadt/Aisch: Degener,
1984)

*A Genealogical Handbook
of German Research*
By Larry O. Jensen. Rev. ed.
(Pleasant Grove, Utah:
Jensen, 1978–1983)

*A Genealogist's Guide to
Discovering Your Germanic
Ancestors*
By S. Chris Anderson and
Ernest Thode (Cincinnati,
Ohio: Betterway Books,
2000)

*German Church Books:
Beyond the Basics*
By Kenneth Lee Smith
(Camden, Maine: Picton
Press, 1989)

*German
Genealogical Research*
By George K. Schweitzer
(Knoxville: Schweitzer, 1992)

*Stammfolgen-Verzeichnisse
für das genealogische
Handbuch des Adels und das
deutsche Geschlechterbuch
(Index of the genealogical
handbook of nobility and
the German lineage books)*
(Limburg/ Lahn: C.A.
Starke, 1969)

*Taschenbuch für
Familiengeschichtsforschung
(Pocketbook for family
history research)*
By Wolfgang Ribbe and
Eckart Henning (Neustadt/
Aisch: Degener, 2001)

PERIODICALS

*Archiv für Sippenforschung
(Archive for ancestral
research)*
1941–.

Der Blumenbaum
Published by the Sacramento
German Genealogical

Society, P.O. Box 660061, Sacramento, CA 95866-0061 USA.

Deutsches Familienarchiv (German families archive)
1952–.

Familienkundliche Nachrichten: Mitteilungen, Rundfragen, Empfehlungen (Family history news: announcements, queries, suggestions)
1956–.

Genealogie: Deutsche Zeitschrift für Familienkunde (Genealogy: German periodical for family studies)
1952–.

German American Genealogy
1988–. Published by The Immigrant Genealogical Society, P.O. Box 7369, Burbank, CA 91510-7369, USA.

The German Connection
1976–. Published by the German Research Association, P.O. Box 711600, San Diego, CA 92171-1600, USA.

German Genealogical Digest
1985–. Published by German Genealogical Digest, P.O. Box 700, Pleasant Grove, UT 84062, USA.

Journal (American Historical Society of Germans from Russia)
1978–. Published by the AHSGR, 631 D St., Lincoln, NE 68502-1199, USA.

The Palatine Immigrant
Published by Palatines to America, 611 E. Weber Rd. Columbus, OH 43211-1097 USA.

Praktische Forschungshilfe (Practical research help)
1924–. This is an insert in *Archiv für Sippenforschung*.

WEB SITES

Ahnenforschung.net
(site in German)
<ahnenforschung.net>

Archives in Germany
<home.bawue.de/~hanacek/info/earchive.htm>

Catholic Churches in Germany
(site in German)
<www.kath.de>

Federation of East European Family History Societies' German Genealogy Cross-Index
<www.feefhs.org/indexger.html>

Free Access to German Genealogy Records
<searchgenealogy.net/Germany.html>

Genealogy.net
<www.genealogienetz.de/genealogy.html>

German Genealogy Forum
<genforum.genealogy.com/germany>

The German Genealogy Group
<www.germangenealogygroup.com>

German Names
<www.serve.com/shea/germusa/germname.htm>

Germanic Genealogy: The German Way
<www.german-way.com/german/gene.html>

GermanRoots
<home.att.net/~wee-monster>

Germany GenWeb
<www.rootsweb.com/~wggerman>

Society for German Genealogy in Eastern Europe
<www.sggee.org>

Stammbaum: Journal of Jewish-Germanic Genealogy
<www.jewishgen.org/stammbaum>

Poland

REGIONAL GUIDE
MELANIE RIGNEY

Forget the Polish jokes. Our ancestors persevered against the Swedes, the Prussians, the Austrians, the Russians, the Germans, and the Russians again, including a stretch of more than one hundred years when Poland didn't even exist on maps and when speaking Polish was a crime. Today, we take pride in a Polish-born pope, relish our pierogi and kielbasa, and enjoy seeing Poland take a place at the table with its former occupiers as a NATO member.

Poland's history is long and fraught with frustration, and family history researchers are likely to feel some of that same frustration when it comes to seeking their roots. The first king, Mieszko I, ruled in the tenth century—about the same time the country became part of the Holy Roman Empire. Poland reached its height politically in the late fourteenth and early fifteenth century, when the Jagiellonian dynasty united with Lithuania and defeated the Teutonic knights, who had been called in as protectors. The Swedes invaded in the mid-seventeenth century. Then, in 1772, Russia, Prussia (the rough equivalent of today's Germany), and Austria began the process of slicing up Poland. Despite that first partition, the Poles came up with Europe's first constitution in 1791; two years later, however, Russia and Prussia took more land and annulled the constitution. In 1795, Prussia, Russia, and Austria erased Poland from the map.

Several unsuccessful efforts for autonomy followed, often accompanied by the departure of great minds. For example, after a November 1830 uprising against the Russians failed, Frederic Chopin and the poet Adam Mickiewicz left their Polish homeland. Joseph Conrad, who eventually would write *Heart of*

©EPA Photo EPA Janek Skarżynski

Market Square, Krakow

Darkness, left after a failed uprising in January 1863. Fed up with Polish feistiness, the Russian and German monarchs implemented severe policies aimed at killing the spirit for independence. Between 1870 and 1914, more than 3.5 million people left what had been Poland, with the emigration relatively even between those leaving Russian- and German-controlled lands.

There was a brief, twenty-one-year interlude of Polish independence after World War I. Then, on 23 August 1939, Russia's Stalin and Germany's Hitler signed a nonaggression pact splitting Poland. During World War II, six million Poles were killed and 2.5 million were deported to Germany for forced labor. All but about 100,000 of the three million Jews who lived in Poland before the war died. The atrocities left Poland as one of the most homogeneous countries around; the U.S. State Department estimates 98 percent of the country's approximately thirty-nine million residents today are of Polish descent, and 90 percent are Catholic.

Following the war, Poland was back on the map as a Soviet satellite country. Then came the dramatic days of 1980–1983, when the Solidarity labor movement was born in the shipyards of Gdansk, and Poles dared hope for freedom again. The first postwar noncommunist government was elected in 1989, and labor leader Lech Walesa became the country's first popularly elected president the following year.

CRACK OPEN YOUR ATLAS

Because of Poland's troubled past, finding and reading records in the old country can be a nightmare. For example, if your ancestors lived in eastern Poland, records from 1868 to 1917 will be in Russian. Records from 1808 to 1868 generally should be in Polish. As for western Poland, controlled by Germany while Russia ruled the east, records generally will be in German or Latin (the language used by the Catholic Church), although you may find some in Polish. And what of Galicia, the part of the partition ruled by Austria? Most records will be in Latin, although some will be found in German and Polish.

The present is almost as confusing. Poland had forty-nine *wojewodztwo*, or provinces, until a January 1999 reorganization. There now are sixteen. In another complication, the old provinces frequently had a city with the same name as the province; that's no longer the case.

As in much of European research, knowing the precise city or village in which your family lived is essential, for either civil or church records. If you don't have a clue based on family legends, interviews, or documents, you may be in for a lengthy, perhaps ultimately unsuccessful, search. Without clear, concrete knowledge that a particular record for your ancestor exists, you'd be better off spending some time researching at your local Family History Center <www.familysearch.org/Search/search fhc2.asp> or consulting some Polish genealogy Web sites before booking your flight to Poland.

Some records simply no longer exist, especially if your ancestor went to the United States by ship. Hamburg and Bremen, both in Germany, were the most popular ports of exit for Poles during the major emigration period. Records are available for those who left from Hamburg; check out <www.hamburg.de/fhh/behoerden/staatsarchiv/link_to_your_roots/english/index.htm> for a database of five million people who passed through the port. The bad news is that twice as many Poles left via Bremen, and those records were destroyed by the German government due to lack of space and by Allied bombing during World War II. A few Poles left via Belgium and the Netherlands; records for those ports are sparse.

You may be in the same boat, pardon the pun, when it comes to checking passenger lists. From 1820 to 1882, only the passenger's name, age, sex, country of allegiance, destination, and occupation had to be recorded. Even after that date, the passenger's hometown or place of birth didn't have to be noted. Still, there can be clues in learning who else was on a particular ship:

©EPA Photo EPA Janek Skarzynski

Old Town, Warsaw

your ancestor's brother? mother? eventual spouse? Watch for similarly spelled names or names appearing immediately before or after your ancestor on the list.

While Poles and others streamed into the United States through Ellis Island <www.ellisisland.org> starting in 1892, a significant number also entered before then at Castle Garden in New York City <www.nps.gov/cacl/> as well as Baltimore, Boston, Philadelphia, and New Orleans.

Because the Polish migration began relatively early, finding a paper trail on your ancestor's arrival in the U.S. can also be difficult. Naturalization records became the purview of the federal government in 1906; before that, immigrants filed their intent to become U.S. citizens in a variety of courts, sometimes near the city where they arrived. Actual naturalization usually didn't come for another couple of years. In some cases, those early documents list nothing more than name, country of birth or allegiance, and date of application. When you look for U.S. records prior to 1922, you're most likely to find information about male ancestors; women automatically became citizens if their husbands were or became citizens.

KNOW YOUR FEAST DAYS

In many cultures, children are named after grandparents in a relatively easy-to-follow structure (first-born son, paternal grandfather; first-born daughter, maternal grandmother). Don't expect that to be the norm when it comes to Polish ancestors, because of the Catholic Church's influence on everyday Polish life. Children often were named after a saint whose feast day was near the child's birth or baptismal date. For example, my great-grandfather, known in America as John Organist, was baptized with the first name Katejan, for an Italian saint whose feast day, August 7, was close to his birthday. His daughter and my grandmother, Mary, was born on September 7, the day before the feast day for the Nativity of the Blessed Virgin Mary. You'll find great lists of saints' feast days at <www.polish roots.com> and in *Polish Roots* by Rosemary A. Chorzempa (Baltimore: Genealogical Publishing Co., 1993), generally acknowledged as the best book available on researching your Polish ancestry.

If the feast-day system doesn't provide clues, check the baptismal certificate: Sometimes children were named after their godparents. In any event, examine the names of the godparents carefully. Poles, like other immigrants when they left their native land, tended to settle in the same areas as their friends and neighbors from the old country. You may find that a godmother later married one of your direct ancestor's siblings, and such information can help you track down others researching your family line today.

This is also an appropriate place to note that Polish surnames change. Polish is an extremely complicated language, influenced by those centuries of subjugation. The language is Indo-European and similar to other Slavic languages, with a vocabulary influenced by everyone from the Romans to the Swedes to the Germans and Russians. Surnames change depending on how they appear as a singular subject. In *Introduction to the Polish Language*, 3rd ed., by Sigmund S. Birkenmayer (Kosciuszko Foundation, out of print), the author demonstrates how the surname Nowak is spelled nearly twenty different ways, depending on the grammar case, whether the name is being used in the singular or plural, and if the Nowak is male or female.

Further, be aware that the Polish alphabet consists of thirty-three letters (when X, seldom used, is included) and does not include Q and V from the English alphabet. Numerous diacritics (dots, slashes, and accents) can substantially change a word's pronunciation. When consulting old documents, consider the possibility that what looks like an R is in fact a K, or what looks like dz is really dz.

Often, Polish immigrants to the U.S., wanting to fit into their new country, Americanized their names. And what you think is your family name may be the name of the town from which they came or the estate on which they worked. *Polish Surnames: Origins and Meanings* by William F. Hoffman (Chicago: Polish Genealogical Society of America, 1993) provides the origins of 30,000 common Polish surnames, categorized by their roots.

Similarly, don't rule out Anglicanization of first names if you're having trouble matching up a relative with census, civil, or baptismal records. In our family, for example, Leokadia, the

966 Duke Mieszko I, Poland's first recorded leader, converted to Christianity after marrying Dabrowka of Bohemia. This is formally recognized as the birth of the Polish nation.

1320 Polish state is reunified.

1388 Jadwiga, Poland's Sovereign, marries Wladyslaw Jagiello, the Grand Duke of Lithuania. By this act she unites Poland and Lithuania under one crown. It becomes thereby one of the biggest countries in Europe, extending from the Baltic to the Black Sea.

1241 A Mongol army raids Poland.

1364 The Academy of Krakow, now called the Jagiellonian University, is founded by Casimir the Great. In time, Nicholas Copernicus will study there.

1493 The bicameral Polish Parliament is first convened; henceforth the King governs with the consent of the governed.

Polish equivalent of Laura, has instead evolved as LaCarda; a great-aunt identified in the 1910 census as Paulina was known to one and all as Pearl. In many cases, the Polish name and the English equivalent (Fryderyk and Frederick, for example) are spelled differently, and the Latin spelling may be different still. It's up to you whether you enter the name in your family tree as it appeared on an official record or as the person was known. But it's best to do one or the other consistently, with a notation of the other name.

DESPERATELY SEEKING PIEROGI

If you're looking for Poles in your area and can't find them on the Internet, mark March 19 on your calendar and watch for restaurants that advertise St. Joseph's Day specials. That's the Catholic feast day and traditional death day for the Virgin Mary's husband. It's a sure bet nearly everyone in the restaurant will be Italian or Polish. The feast day also provides a bit of a respite from the solemn introspective of the Lenten season. Whatever the reason, in areas where Italians and Poles live, you'll often find a fine St. Joseph's table at restaurants and some churches that day, groaning with pierogis, potato pancakes, and more; a statue of the saint; and a place to make offerings for the needy.

Of course, nothing can replace the experience of heading to

1543 Nicolaus Copernicus (Mikolaj Kopernik) publishes "On the Revolutions of the Celestial Spheres," proposing that the earth revolves around the sun.

1772 The first partition of Poland: Russia, Prussia, and Austria annex a significant portion of Poland, partitioning the territory between themselves.

1573 The Sejm guarantees religious equality. Roman Catholics, Jews, Protestants, Orthodox Christians, and Muslims all live together in Poland in peace.

1655–1660 Known as the Deluge, Sweden invades Poland with the help of the Tartars and Cossacks from the East. Poland is virtually destroyed as cities are burned and plundered. A population of 10 million is reduced to 6 million due to the wars, famine, and the bubonic plague.

1791 After the First Partition leads to some reforms, a constitution is passed, called the Constitution of the Third of May. It is only the second written document that outlines the responsibilities of the Government.

Poland for one of their many annual nationalist celebrations. Late spring and summer are a particularly good time to head to the old country for a taste of the past.

The Dominican Fair is one of Poland's oldest festivals, established by a Papal Bull in 1260. In April or May every year, it's a lively sixteen-day event which celebrates the ancient traditions of Poland with over 1,000 craftsmen and artists. Taste pastries during the Swieto Chleba (Bread Festival), listen to a brass orchestra, watch the many street performers and cabarets, and get a true feel for the medieval on Teutonic Knights day. Not bad for a party over 740 years old.

In late June every year, two Krakow festivals keep alive and celebrate age-old myths of the Polish tradition. On June 24, Wianki, the floating of magical wreaths on the Vistula River, traces its roots to a peaceful pagan ritual where maidens would float wreaths of herbs on the water to predict whom and when they would marry. This festive event also includes musical performances, a speech by the mayor, fairs, and fireworks.

Lajkonik, a procession through Krakow's Old Town streets, celebrates the defeat of the savage Tartars (the Mongol hordes) in the thirteenth century. Musicians, merrymakers, the young, and the old follow a man dressed in Mongol costume, with a decorated wooden hobbyhorse around his waist. Played every

1793 The second partition of Poland: The autocratic ruler of Russia, alarmed by Poland's democratic constitution, invades Poland and forces suspension of the constitution. More Polish territory is annexed by Russia and Prussia. Russian troops are stationed in Poland.

1870s Russia attempts to eradicate Polish culture, making Russian the official language of the Russian partition. Prussia does the same in their portion of Poland, attempting to Germanicize Poles. Under the Austrian partition, Galician Poles are allowed to retain some autonomy.

1939 Hitler attacks Poland from the west on September 1 and World War II starts. On September 17, the Soviet Union invades Poland from the east. A partition of Poland follows on September 28.

1795 The Third Partition divides the rest of Poland. Poland is "officially" non-existent for the next 123 years.

1918 Poland regains independence after World War I. It is recognized under the terms of Versailles Treaty. Marshal Jozef Pilsudski becomes President.

hour on the hour is the Hejnal trumpet call. The tune is rudely interrupted, and legend has it that a trumpet player was shot through the throat as he was warning the medieval town of the approaching Mongols. This seven-hundred-year-old tradition illustrates the devastating effect invaders had on the city.

August brings the world's largest and oldest Chopin festival in Duszniki Zdroj, which lasts nine days and features around twenty-five concerts and recitals. Stick around for Krakow's Court Dance Festival, which presents the unique opportunity to see the ballet of the Medieval, Renaissance, and Baroque eras and catch a glimpse of old, romantic court culture.

For a taste of the ancient world, visit the open air museum at Biskupin, a settlement by the shores of the Biskupin Lake that existed 2,500 years ago and has been reconstructed in detail. Thirty exhibits reconstruct ancient methods of handicraft, including horn-polishing, amber jewelry making, shoemaking, carpentry, and weaving. Learn how to use a bow and arrow, visit the local witch, and don't forget to try the old-style brewed beer.

And of course, there is the most important celebration for those of Polish descent—Independence Day, celebrated nation-wide on November 11.

Remember, our ancestors fought hard for centuries to keep that culture alive. Celebrating it is the least we can do to thank them.

1978 Karol Wojtyla, the Archbishop of Krakow, is elected Pope. Taking the name John Paul II, he is the first non-Italian pope in nearly 500 years.

1990 The first fully free election is won by Lech Walesa.

1999 Poland becomes a member of NATO, the North Atlantic Treaty Organization.

1943 The Warsaw Ghetto Uprising.

1980 Strikes and riots ensue as the economy crumbles. At the Lenin Shipyard in Gdansk, the government reaches an agreement with the workers. The workers are allowed to organize into an independent trade union, called *Solidarnosc*, or Solidarity. Strike leader Lech Walesa is elected as the head of Solidarity, and by November, 60 percent of the Polish workforce is organized. Solidarity gradually grows into a strong, non-violent sociopolitical movement.

1997 Poland's National Assembly adopts a new Constitution.

CENSUS

The first nationwide census of Poland's population, ordered by Sejm (the lower house of Parliament), took place in 1789, but the first general and complete census was taken in the Duchy of Warsaw between 1808 and 1810.

For links to Polish census history, resources, and information, go to the Web site for Poland's Central Statistical Office <www.stat.gov.pl/english/stale/przewodnik>.

RESOURCES

ORGANIZATIONS AND ARCHIVES

American Center of Polish Culture
2025 O St. NW
Washington, DC 20036 USA
Tel: (202) 785-2320
<www.polishcenterdc.org>

Consular Agency
Ulica Paderewskiego 8
61708 Poznan, Poland
Tel: 48-61-518-516

Consulate General
Ulica Stolarska 9
31043 Krakow, Poland
Tel: 48-12-211-400

Federation of Eastern European Family History Societies
Box 510898
Salt Lake City, UT 84151 USA
<www.feefhs.org>

Indiana University Polish Studies Center
1217 E. Atwater Ave.
Bloomington, IN 47401 USA
Tel: (813) 855-1507
<www.indiana.edu/~polishst>

Polish American Association
3834 N. Cicero Ave.
Chicago, IL 60641 USA
Tel: (773) 282-8206
<www.polish.org>

Polish Embassy
2640 16th St. NW
Washington, DC 20009 USA
Tel: (202) 234-3800
<www.polishworld.com/polemb>

Polish Genealogical Society of America
984 N. Milwaukee Ave.
Chicago, IL 60622 USA
<www.pgsa.org>

Polish National Tourist Office (Orbis)
275 Madison Ave.
Suite 1711
New York, NY 10016 USA
Tel: (212) 338-9412
<www.polandtour.org>

Pope John Paul II Polish Center
3999 Rose Drive
Yorba Linda, CA 92886 USA
Tel: (714) 966-8161
<www.polishcenter.org>

State Archives of Poland
Archiwum Główne Akt Dawnych
00-263 Warszawa
ul. Dluga 7
Tel: 48 22 831 54 91
<www.archiwa.gov.pl>

US Embassy
Aleje Ujazdowskie 29/31
00540 Warsaw, Poland
48-22-628-3041

BOOKS

Essentials in Polish Genealogical Research
By Daniel M. Schlyter
(Chicago: Polish Genealogical Society of America, 1993)

First Names of the Polish Commonwealth: Origins and Meanings
William F. Hoffman, and George W. Helon (Chicago: Polish Genealogical Society of America, 1998)

Index to the Newsletters, Journals, and Bulletins of the Polish Genealogical Society of America, 1979–1996
Rosemary A. Chorzempa, George W. Helon, and William F. Hoffman, comps.

(Chicago: Polish Genealogical Society of America, 1997)

Poland, 1799
Map. (Albany, N.Y.: Jonathan Sheppard Books, 1995) Illustrates the divisions of Poland in 1772, 1793, and 1795.

Polish and Proud: Tracing Your Polish Ancestry
By Janneyne L. Gnacinski and Leonard T. Gnacinski (West Allis, Wisc.: Janlen Enterprises, 1979)

Polish Family Research
By J. Konrad, Rev. ed. (Munroe Falls, Ohio: Summit Publications, 1992)

Polish Genealogy and Heraldry: An Introduction to Research
By Janina W. Hoskins (New York: Hippocrene Books, 1990)

Polish Parish Records of the Roman Catholic Church: Their Use and Understanding in Genealogical Research
By Gerald A. Ortell, 3rd rev. ed. (Buffalo Grove, Ill.: Genun Publishers, 1989)

Polish Roots (Korzenie Polskie).
By Rosemary A. Chorzempa (Baltimore, Md.: Genealogical Publishing Co., Inc., 1993)

Polish Surnames: Origins and Meanings
By William F. Hoffman (Chicago: Polish Genealogical Society of America, 1993)

Roman Catholic Parishes in the Polish People's Republic in 1984
By Lidia Mullerowa (Chicago: Polish Genealogical Society of America, 1995)

Tracing Your Polish Roots
By Maralyn A. Wellauer (Milwaukee, Wisc.: Maralyn A. Wellauer, 1979)

PERIODICALS

Bulletin of the Polish Genealogical Society of America
1994–.

Polish Eaglet
1981–. Detroit: Polish Genealogical Society of Michigan.

Polish Genealogical Society Newsletter
Volumes 1–15 (1979–1992). Became *Rodziny* in 1993.

WEB SITES

Chicago Public Library Polish Genealogy Pathfinder
<www.chipublib.org/001hwlc/litpolgenealogy.html>

Cyndi's List: Poland
<www.cyndislist.com/poland.htm>

NewPoland Genealogy
<www.newpoland.com/genealogy.htm>

PolandGenWeb
<www.rootsweb.com/~polwgw>

Poland.net
<www.poland.net>

Polish American Congress
<www.polamcon.org>

Polish Genealogy Bridge
<www.geocities.com/Silicon Valley/Haven/1538/Polishpg.html>

The Polish Genealogy Project
<polishproject.hypermart.net/>

Polish Genealogy Society of New York State— Polish Genealogy Links
<www.pgsnys.org/Links/polwwwlinks.html>

Polish government online
<poland.pl>

PolishRoots
<www.polishroots.com>

Polish World
<www.polishworld.com>

Rafal T. Prinke's Polish Genealogy Home Page
<hum.amu.edu.pl/~rafalp/GEN/plgenhp.htm>

Eastern Europe

REGIONAL GUIDE

ALLISON STACY

Travelers to Eastern Europe trek to Sighisoara to see the birthplace of Vlad Ţepeş, better known as Dracula. The house itself is ordinary, bearing only a small plaque in honor of its famous occupant. But when you roam the citadel's medieval battlements and archaic, cotton-candy-colored buildings, it's easy to understand why Transylvania has inspired so many spooky stories.

Romanians are quick to point out that the vampire lore is fiction—torture tactics aside, Vlad "the Impaler" is revered for his efforts to unite Romania. Yet Transylvanian tourist shops happily capitalize on foreigners' misconceptions by hawking Dracula merchandise, which I, of course, couldn't resist. Two "I Love Dracula" bumper stickers and a stack of Vlad postcards later, I trekked to the old Saxon cemetery behind Sighisoara's sixteenth-century Church on the Hill. Ambling between the overgrown plots, I recalled a conversation with a neighbor back home. She told me her husband had Romanian ancestry—her brother-in-law used to tease her kids that they were descendants of Dracula. She laughed and said the kids ought to look at the photos of my trip to see what their ancestors' country was really like.

Those photos hint at the rich heritage my neighbor's family—and others with Eastern European roots—have to discover. Though nothing compares to seeing the old country firsthand, you can explore much of your ancestry from home.

Eastern Europe remains mysterious and often misunderstood. Even the term is tough to define: Where does the region begin? Where does it end? For genealogy, it helps to consider historical connections between peoples and cultures. Historians put Slavic peoples into three categories. West Slavs include Czechs,

Municipal Hall,
Prague,
Czech Republic

Slovaks, and Poles. South Slavs include Bosnians, Croatians, Slovenes, Serbs, Montenegrins, Bulgarians, and Macedonians. They're separated from East Slavs—Russians, Belarusians, and Ukrainians—by Hungarians (or Magyars), who migrated from central Asia, and Romanians, who descend from the Dacians of the ancient Roman Empire.

During the early part of the twentieth century, Austria-Hungary and the Ottoman Empire were the region's dominant powers; East Slavs remained under Russian influence. So here we'll look at the modern countries carved out of those empires, including the Czech Republic, Slovakia, Hungary, Croatia, Slovenia, Romania, Bulgaria, and Yugoslavia.

Those expanding empires and changing borders mean tracing your roots here won't necessarily follow political boundaries. Grandma's naturalization papers may say she came from Hungary, but her village could now be in Croatia, Slovakia, or Romania. You may also discover a distinction between your ancestors' nationality and ethnicity. Scientist Nikola Tesla, for example, emigrated from Croatia, but his parents were ethnically Serbian. And Carpatho-Rusyns don't have their own nation—their homeland is in present-day Slovakia, Poland, and Ukraine.

BUILDING A NETWORK

Before you dive into the complexities of European research, though, you need to thoroughly explore your family history in your home country. Your first step, of course, is gleaning clues from family members. But don't stop with your closest relatives. "Talk to cousins in different branches of the family—your grandparents' brothers and sisters," advises Duncan Gardiner, a professional genealogist who specializes in Czech, Slovak, German, and Carpatho-Rusyn research. Great-uncle Marek's family may have clues you won't find anywhere else.

Look for distant cousins at online message boards, where you can post queries and search archived messages. Genforum <genforum.genealogy.com> and Ancestry <boards.ancestry.com> have boards for every Eastern European country. The Federation of East European Family History Societies (FEEFHS) has country-specific Research Lists at <www.feefhs.org/index/indexrl .html>. You'll find more queries and advice in mailing lists—research communities that do lookups, share expertise, and work together to beat brick walls.

Look for help offline, too. "The most useful thing a beginner can do is join a society," says Gardiner. "When you sign up, they usually send you an introductory packet," which contains materials for getting started. Other perks include newsletters, access to the society's resources, and help from experienced researchers. FEEFHS is an umbrella organization for ethnic- or country-focused groups, and member societies have Web pages on its site.

Use your country's records—in the United States, these would include censuses, passenger lists, and naturalization records—to fill in your family tree back to the immigrant generation. Through these records, home sources, and stories, your goal is to uncover two crucial clues: your immigrant ancestors' native name and place of origin.

FROM SHIP TO SHORE

Study your ethnic group's immigration patterns; looking at what others did provides context and can focus your search. For example, few Eastern Europeans came to North America before

Chain bridge over the Danube, Budapest, Hungary

the 1800s. Then a mid-nineteenth century potato blight drove nearly 100,000 Czechs to Texas, Missouri, and Wisconsin in the United States. Croatians and Serbs also crossed the Atlantic in the mid-1800s; most were Dalmatian sailors and fishermen who jumped ship (sometimes literally), settling across the south and west coast. A small surge of Hungarian immigration followed the nationalist revolt of 1848.

Your ancestors were far more likely to have been among the flood of Eastern Europeans that poured out near the turn of the century. By this time, the industrial revolution was overtaking the western world, but Eastern Europe lagged behind. Vestiges of feudalism persisted—Hapsburg lands had abolished serfdom only in 1848—and societies remained rural and poor. Desperate to escape overpopulation and poverty, people decided to try their luck elsewhere.

This huge wave of emigration began around 1880, and

included hundreds of thousands of northern and eastern Hungarians and southeastern Slovenes. Close to two decades later, Slovaks plunged into the tide. Before the turn of the century, most of the Romanians who emigrated were Jewish, but after that, the vast majority came from Transylvania, Bukovina, and the Banat. By 1914, Carpatho-Rusyns were also leaving their home in great numbers.

During the first decade of the twentieth century, emigration from Austria-Hungary peaked, and Balkan people—Croatians from the country's interior, Orthodox Christian Albanians from the south, and Macedonian Bulgarians—began leaving their native lands in significant numbers. (Prior to World War I, 60 percent of Bulgarian immigrants came from Macedonia; they considered themselves ethnically Bulgarian and geographically Macedonian.) Serb emigrants usually left areas outside Serbia proper—such as Vojvodina, a military frontier zone where families fled the Turks.

Illiterate male peasants made up the bulk of these immigrants, finding jobs in coal mines, mills, and factories. The nearly 100,000 Bohemians and Moravians who left during the 1880s and '90s, however, often arrived in their new country skilled and literate. And they tended to travel as a family instead of sending one person ahead. Slovenian immigrants, though peasants, also tended to be literate.

Still, the majority of Eastern Europeans were what the Macedonian Bulgarians called *gurbetchii* or *pechalbari*—fortune seekers who intended to return after a few years, once they'd earned enough for a better life back home. Some did return—Bulgarian returnees exceeded entrants from 1910 to 1929—and some became "birds of passage." For example, a quarter of Slovaks arriving in the United States in 1905 had been to the country before. But many never left America, settling in the industrial centers of the Northeast and Midwest.

Eastern European immigration to North America slowed at the start of World War I and then virtually halted when the U.S. government passed "quota" laws in 1921 and the National Origins Act in 1924. These laws limited newcomers based on how many of their countrymen had already arrived. Eastern

Europeans had only been immigrating en masse for a few decades, so they had low quotas. But the laws didn't deter everyone: Some went to Canada; others entered the United States illegally. After World War II, a smaller influx of intellectuals and artists fled to America to escape communism.

OVER THE BORDERLINE

The next step in your journey to the old country is a history lesson. "Look up your country in the encyclopedia and read about its history for the 1800s," suggests Gardiner. You'll learn both what was going on when your ancestors left and the events leading up to their departure.

Eastern Europe's recent political shakeups are deeply rooted in its past. For centuries, the common theme for Eastern European peoples was domination by a foreign power. Hungary traditionally held Slovakia, Croatia, and Transylvania. Austria's Hapsburgs ruled the Czech lands (Bohemia and Moravia). Serbia and Bulgaria dominated the Balkans until the arrival of the Ottomans (Turks) in the fourteenth century—an event that shaped the region's history for the next five centuries.

The Ottoman Empire swallowed up present-day Romania and the Balkans and constantly threatened the other powers, Austria and Hungary. Hungary fell to the Turks in 1526 at Mohács, its king died in battle, and the Hapsburgs snagged Hungary's crown. Ottoman rule introduced the Balkans to feudalism, which lasted well into the 1800s. (Serbia and Romania didn't shake off the Turks until 1878, followed by Bulgaria in 1908 and Albania in 1912.) The Hapsburgs already had a feudal system until the 1848 peasant revolts. Then in 1867, Hungary gained autonomy, resulting in the dual monarchy of Austria-Hungary. Austria retained Bohemia, Moravia, and Slovenia; Hungary ruled Croatia, Slovakia, and Transylvania. This was the political landscape late-nineteenth-century and early-twentieth-century immigrants left behind.

All that changed after World War I, when a series of treaties carved up defeated Austria-Hungary. As Angus Baxter explains in his book *In Search of Your European Roots* (Baltimore: Genealogical Publishing Co., 2001), this resulted in huge territory transfers: Romania gained Transylvania, Bukovina, and part of the Banat. Bohemia, Moravia, and Slovakia became Czechoslovakia. Bosnia-Herzegovina, Croatia, Dalmatia, Serbia, Slavonia, and Slovenia were united as Yugoslavia. The genealogical fallout: Your ancestors' country of origin may have changed overnight. And the new people in power may have assigned your ancestral village or province a new name.

WHERE'S WEISSKIRCHEN?

Actually, since lands changed hands so often in Eastern Europe, chances are good your ancestral town's name was different at some point in the past. Many cities have names in multiple languages; for example, Slovakia's capital, Bratislava, is known as Pozsony in Hungarian and Pressburg in German. In some cases, new rulers altered town names completely. And we know major cities by still different names in English—Praha as Prague, Beograd as Belgrade, Bucureşti as Bucharest.

Charles Bridge,
Prague,
Czech Republic

So how do you figure out just where your ancestors came from? First you need a place name. Search naturalization papers, baptismal records, obituaries, tombstone inscriptions, and cemetery records.

Once you find a name, though, don't make a beeline for the atlas. You'll have better luck if you do some additional research first, explains Gardiner: "The spelling you get in various sources may not be right. Consult a person who's familiar with spellings in those languages." Take advantage of your research network—mailing lists, societies, special interest groups (SIGs). Some overseas researchers will do town IDs for free.

The best tool to locate your ancestral town is a gazetteer, or index of geographical names. "If a town had different names, that will often be given," says Gardiner. Use the gazetteer to identify the town's location and the map you should look at to find it. You can find good gazetteers at major public libraries, the Family History Library (FHL), and its branch Family History Centers. Use a statistical lexicon, which is based on census data and usually includes the town's province, its native-language name, and index. Try a place search of the FHL catalog <www.familysearch.org> to turn up gazetteers that cover your ancestral country.

NAME THAT TONGUE

You'll have plenty of language hurdles besides place names, so start familiarizing yourself with your ancestors' native tongue. Get a good dictionary and try to find genealogy-specific resources, such as the FamilySearch Word Lists for Czech, Slovak, and Hungarian. You'll also find help online, including dictionaries and services such as e-Transcriptum <www.e-transcriptum.net/eng>, which offers free translations of short genealogy texts.

Eastern European languages present special challenges when dealing with ancestors' names. To trace your family in the old country successfully, you have to determine their original name. That's not always easy, and it's particularly hard if your ancestors emigrated to North America, where many immigrants "Americanized" their names. This usually happened three ways,

1254 Explorer Marco Polo born in what's now Croatia.

1389 Turks defeat Serbs at Kosovo.

1456 Hungary defeats Ottomans at Belgrade.

1563 Council of Trent orders churches to keep vital records.

1660 Croatian soldiers introduce the necktie, or "cravat."

1350 Prague is capital of Holy Roman Empire.

1402 Czech Protestant reformer Jan Hus begins preaching in Prague.

1526 Hungary defeated at Battle of Mohács; lands divided between Turks and Hapsburg Empire.

1584 Hapsburg Empire adopts Gregorian calendar.

1671 Hungary becomes province of Austria.

as outlined in Daniel Schlyter's *Handbook of Czechoslovak Genealogical Research* (Buffalo Grove, Ill.: Genun Publishers, 1985):

- Immigrants translated given and surnames to their American counterparts, such as František to Frank or Krejči to Taylor.
- They chose a similar-sounding name—Wenzel for Václav or Corrister for Kořista.
- They Anglicized the spelling so Americans could pronounce it. Kokoška might become Kokoshka, for example.

(Don't put stock in family stories asserting that Ellis Island immigration officials changed your ancestors' name—that's a myth. See <www.bcis.gov/graphics/aboutus/history/articles/NameEssay.html> for details.)

And be aware that Slavic-name spellings vary in grammatical context. Czech and Slovak surnames, for example, have male and female endings plus adjective and noun forms.

Unfortunately, language hurdles don't stop with your forebears' tongue. The region's barrage of border shifts means records—like town names—were often in the language of whoever was in power. In Austro-Hungarian lands, early records are frequently in Latin. In the Czech Republic, you may also find German; in Slovakia, Hungarian. Or consider the records of Croatia: They're a mix of Latin, German, Croatian, Hungarian,

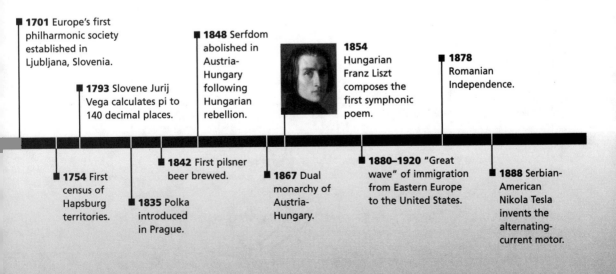

1701 Europe's first philharmonic society established in Ljubljana, Slovenia.

1793 Slovene Jurij Vega calculates pi to 140 decimal places.

1848 Serfdom abolished in Austria-Hungary following Hungarian rebellion.

1854 Hungarian Franz Liszt composes the first symphonic poem.

1878 Romanian Independence.

1754 First census of Hapsburg territories.

1835 Polka introduced in Prague.

1842 First pilsner beer brewed.

1867 Dual monarchy of Austria-Hungary.

1880–1920 "Great wave" of immigration from Eastern Europe to the United States.

1888 Serbian-American Nikola Tesla invents the alternating-current motor.

Slovene, and Italian (for coastal areas of Dalmatia and Istria), plus some use of the Serbian Cyrillic form. So your Slovak great-great grandma Alžběta may show up as Erzsébet (Hungarian) or Elisabetha (Latin); Great-grandpa Francisek from Slovenia might show up as Franz (German). Schlyter's *Handbook* has a handy table that shows Czech, Slovak, Hungarian, Latin, and English versions of given names. See <feefhs.org/slovenia/sidb1/si-names.html> for Slovenian names and English equivalents.

Learning about naming customs will help you sort through the Franciseks and the Franzes. In Eastern Europe, it was common to name children after a saint whose feast day was close to their birthday. Branka Lapajne, author of *Researching Your Slovenian Ancestors*, adds that in Slovenia, "it was almost a must for each family to have a Joseph, John, and Mary." Note that Hungarians write their surname before their given name.

Some Eastern European surnames come from patronymics—people taking their father's first name as their own surname. For example, a Romanian whose father was named Dumitru might take the surname Dumitrescu. Bulgarians used patronymics with a twist. People traditionally had three names: a given name, followed by the father's name and the family name. But when sons were named after grandfathers, you might end up with Georgi Petrov Georgiev, son of Petyr Georgiev Petrov.

You can check surname spellings by looking in the country's online telephone book.

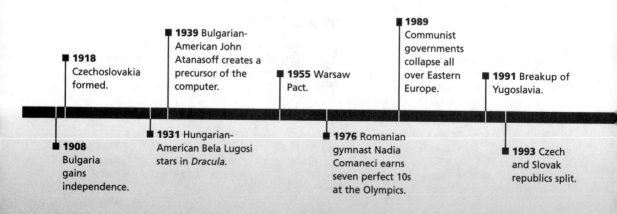

1918 Czechoslovakia formed.

1939 Bulgarian-American John Atanasoff creates a precursor of the computer.

1955 Warsaw Pact.

1989 Communist governments collapse all over Eastern Europe.

1991 Breakup of Yugoslavia.

1908 Bulgaria gains independence.

1931 Hungarian-American Bela Lugosi stars in *Dracula*.

1976 Romanian gymnast Nadia Comaneci earns seven perfect 10s at the Olympics.

1993 Czech and Slovak republics split.

GOING TO CHURCH

You have a name. You have a place. Now where do you get the records you need to trace your family in the old country?

Gardiner says a big mistake Eastern European genealogists make is assuming the records no longer exist. "In my experience, very few have been destroyed," he explains. "Always have [finding records] as a goal."

Parish registers will be the backbone of your research in these countries. The Council of Trent gave churches the responsibility of recording births, marriages, and deaths in the sixteenth century, but the dates for vital records in your country will vary. Here's a quick look at church records across the region:

- **Hungary:** Baptisms (*keresztelő*), marriages (*házasság*), and burials (*temetés*) span from the early 1700s to 1895, when civil registration began. The Church of Jesus Christ of Latter-day Saints (LDS) has filmed registers (*anyakőnyv*) up to 1895, and they're available through the FHL and FHCs. These films also cover places in Romania and Yugoslavia.

- **Slovakia:** The LDS has filmed almost all vital records (*matriky*), with roughly the same dates as Hungary's. You'll find Slovak *matriky* for both Protestant and Catholic parishes.

- **Czech Republic:** The earliest existing Catholic *matriky* are for the late 1500s, but most priests didn't comply until the 1600s. From 1620 to 1781, Austria allowed only Catholicism, so Czech Protestants' *matriky* were kept by Catholic priests. Czechoslovakia started civil registration for nonchurchgoers in 1918, but the state didn't take over vital records until 1950.

- **Croatia:** The FHL has microfilm of Catholic, Orthodox, and Greek Catholic parish registers from roughly the late 1500s to 1940s. Civil registration began in 1946.

- **Slovenia:** One parish has records as early as 1458, but that's an exception—most go back to the 1600s. Civil registration began in 1926. LDS has microfilmed some church and civil registers. Lapajne advises writing to the local archbishopric in Slovenia for records.

- **Bulgaria:** Bulgarian Orthodox parishes have registers to about 1800. Microfilmed FHL records cover the Sofia, Panagurska, and Pazardijk districts from 1893 to 1910.

- **Romania:** Government vital records began in 1865, earlier than elsewhere in Eastern Europe. For the previous three decades, Romanian Orthodox priests carried out civil registration. After one hundred years, churches transfer vital records to the district (*judet*) archive.
- **Yugoslavia:** Not surprisingly, with the recent unrest in the former Yugoslavia, the availability of records is murky. Pre-1946 parish registers are kept in local Orthodox, Catholic, and Muslim churches. For areas formerly under Ottoman control, the Turkish government may have records of your family (also true for Romania and Bulgaria).

Parliament,
Budapest, Hungary

ARCHIVING YOUR ANCESTORS

You may have luck with other types of records. For example, Hungary's 1828 tax census, which lists heads of household, is on microfilm. Austria-Hungary took a census in 1869; Zemplén County, Hungary, has been filmed, and "bits and pieces of other areas are in different archives," says Gardiner.

In some Eastern European countries, writing to archives is your best strategy for getting records. Kahlile Mehr, an FHL collection development specialist, says the Czech Republic, Romania, and Yugoslavia have been unreceptive to LDS microfilming efforts, so you won't have the bounty of microfilm your Hungarian and Slovak peers do. Gardiner says Romanian and Yugoslav archives "have not been very responsive," but the Czech Republic has a system for research requests. You fill out a form specifying your inquiry and a cost limit, and then send to the national archives. Expect to wait up to six months for a reply.

Another option is to hire someone to do research for you—either a local researcher or one in your ancestral country.

FEEFHS maintains a directory of professional genealogists at <www.feefhs.org/frg/frg-pg.html>.

Eventually, you might want to explore medieval villages and ancestral cemeteries yourself. If you plan to use a trip to the old country to further your research, exhaust all your avenues at home first. "Identify the town a year ahead of time," advises Gardiner. "Don't call the archives a week before and say, 'I'd like to look at such and such record.'"

And take Uncle Frank's stories with a grain of salt—leave the stakes and garlic at home.

RESOURCES

ORGANIZATIONS AND ARCHIVES

East European Genealogical Society
Box 2536
Winnipeg, Manitoba
R3C 4A7 Canada
Tel: (204) 989-3292
<www.eegsociety.org>

Federation of East European Family History Societies
Box 510898
Salt Lake City, UT 84151 USA
<feefhs.org>

Interlink Bookshop & Genealogial Services
4687 Falaise Dr.
Victoria, British Columbia
V8Y 1B4 Canada
Tel: (800) 747-4877
<www.genealogy unlimited.com>

BOOKS

Following the Paper Trail: A Multilingual Translation Guide
By Jonathan D. Shea and William F. Hoffman (Teaneck, N.J.: Avotaynu, 1994)

Historical Atlas of East Central Europe
By Paul Robert Magocsi with Geoffrey J. Matthews. Rev. ed. (University of Washington Press, 2002)

In Search of Your European Roots: A Complete Guide to Tracing Your Ancestors in Every Country in Europe
By Angus Baxter (Baltimore: Genealogical Publishing Co., 2001)

Our Slavic Fellow-Citizens
By Emily G. Balch (New York: Arno Press, 1969)

Overcoming Obstacles to Eastern European Research
By Serah Fleury Allen (Apollo, Pa.: Closson Press, 1990)

Where Once We Walked: A Guide to the Jewish Communities Destroyed in the Holocaust
By Gary Mokotoff and Sally Amdur Sack (Bergenfield, N.J.: Avotaynu, 2002)

Where Once We Walked Companion: A Guide to the Communities Surrounding Central and Eastern European Towns
By Gary Mokotoff (Teaneck, N.J.: Avotaynu, 1995)

WEB SITES

Cyndi's List: Eastern Europe
<www.cyndislist.com/easteuro.htm>

EastEuropeGenWeb
<www.rootsweb.com/~easeurgw>

E-Transcriptum
<www.e-transcriptum.net/eng>

Hamburg Link to Your Roots
<www.hamburg.de/fhh/behoerden/staatsarchiv/link_to_your_roots/english/index.htm>

JewishGen Shtetl Seeker
<www.jewishgen.org/ShtetlSeeker>

RecipeSource
<209.157.67.146/ethnic/
europe>

**Repositories of Primary
Sources: Europe**
<www.uidaho.edu/special-
collections/euro1.html>

Slavophilia
<www.slavophilia.com>

ALBANIA

ORGANIZATIONS
AND ARCHIVES

**Embassy of the Republic
of Albania**
2100 S St. NW
Washington, DC 20008 USA
Tel: (202) 223-4942

**National Albanian
American Council**
1700 K St. NW Suite 200
Washington, DC 20036 USA
<www.naac.org>

BOOKS

*A Dictionary of Albanian
Religion, Mythology and
Folk Culture*
By Robert Elsie (New York:
University Press, 2001)

WEB SITES

Albania Genealogy Forum
<genforum.genealogy.com/
albania>

AlbaniaGenWeb
<www.rootsweb.com/~
albwgw>

Albania Mailing Lists
<www.rootsweb.com/~
jfuller/gen_mail_country-
alb.html>

Albanian Cultural Heritage
<www.albaniancultural
heritage.com>

**Italo-Albanian
Heritage Pages**
<members.aol.com/itaalb1/
web/arb1a.htm>

Yahoo! Clubs: Albanian
<clubs.yahoo.com/clubs/
albanian>

CZECH REBULIC,
SLOVAKIA, &
CARPATHIAN RUS'

ORGANIZATIONS
AND ARCHIVES

**Archives of the Czechs
and Slovaks Abroad**
University of Chicago Library
1100 E. 57th St.
Chicago, IL 60637 USA
Tel: (773) 702-8456
<www.lib.uchicago.edu/e/
su/slavic/acasa.html>

Carpatho-Rusyn Society
125 Westland Dr.
Pittsburgh, PA 15217 USA
<www.carpathorusyn
society.org>

**Czech Republic
State Archives**
Archivní Správa
Ministerstva vnitra CR
Milady Horakove 133
166 21 Praha 6
Czech Republic
Tel: (420) (2) 321173

**Czechoslovak Genealogical
Society International**
Box 16225
St. Paul, MN 55116 USA
Tel: (763) 595-7799
<www.cgsi.org>

**Embassy of the
Czech Republic**
3900 Spring of
Freedom St. NW
Washington, DC 20008 USA
Tel: (202) 274-9100
<www.mzv.cz/washington>

**Embassy of the
Slovak Republic**
3523 International Court NW
Washington, DC 20008 USA
Tel: (202) 237-1054
<www.slovakemb.com>

**National Czech and
Slovak Museum and Library**
30 16th Ave. SW
Cedar Rapids, IA 52404 USA
Tel: (319) 362-8500
<www.ncsml.org>

Slovak National Archives
Ministerstvo vnútra SR
odbor archivníctva a spisovej
služby, Križkova 7
811 04 Bratislava
Tel: +421 (2) 52 49 60 51

BOOKS

*The Carpatho-Rusyn
Americans*
By Paul Robert Magocsi
(Philadelphia: Chelsea
House, 2000)

The Czech Americans
By Stephanie Saxon-Ford
(Philadelphia: Chelsea
House, 1999)

*Genealogical Research for
Czech and Slovak Americans*
By Olga K. Miller
(Detroit: Gale Research Co.,
1978)

*Granny: Scenes from
Country Life*
By Bozena Nemcová
(Westport, Conn:
Greenwood Press, 1976)

*Handbook of Czechoslovak
Genealogical Research*
By Daniel Schlyter
(Buffalo Grove, Ill.: Genun,
1985)

*Our People:
Carpatho-Rusyns and
Their Descendants in
North America*
By Paul Robert Magocsi
(Toronto: Multicultural
History Society of Ontario,
1984)

The Slovak Americans
By M. Mark Stolarik
(New York: Chelsea House,
1988)

WEB SITES

The Carpathian Connection
<www.tccweb.org>

**Carpatho-Rusyn
Genealogy Web Site**
<www.rusyn.com>

**Carpatho-Rusyn
Knowledge Base**
<www.carpatho-rusyn.org>

**Cyndi's List: Czech Republic
& Slovakia**
<www.cyndislist.com/czech.
htm>

Czech GenWeb
<www.rootsweb.com/
~czewgw>

Czech Republic Mailing Lists
<www.rootsweb.com/~
jfuller/gen_mail_country-
cze.html>

**Genealogical Research
in the Czech Republic**
<www.mzv.cz/washington/
cons/genealogy.htm>

It's All Relative Genealogy
<www.iarelative.com>

**Online Czech-English
Dictionary**
<www.wordbook.cz>

**RootsWeb's Guide to
Tracing Family Trees:
Czechs and Slovaks**
<www.rootsweb.com/~
rwguide/lesson27.htm#
Czechs>

Slovak GenWeb
<www.rootsweb.com/~
svkwgw>

Slovak Telephone Directory
<www.zoznamst.sk/sk>

Slovakia.org
<www.slovakia.org>

Slovakia Mailing Lists
<www.rootsweb.com/~
jfuller/gen_mail_country-
slo.html>

ORGANIZATIONS
AND ARCHIVES

**Embassy of Bosnia
and Herzegovina**
2109 E St. NW
Washington, DC 20037 USA
Tel: (202) 337-1500
<www.bhembassy.org>

WEB SITES

**Bosnia and Herzegovina
Genealogy Forum**
<genforum.genealogy.com/
bosnia>

**Bosnia-Herzegovina
GenWeb**
<www.rootsweb.com/
~bihwgw>

Bosnian Telephone Directory
<www.imenik.telecom.ba>

ORGANIZATIONS
AND ARCHIVES

**Bulgarian-Macedonian
National Educational
and Cultural Center**
223 Allenberry Circle
Pittsburgh, PA 15234 USA
<www.bmnecc.org>

Bulgarian National Archives
Centralen Da˘rz˘aven Arhiv
ul. Slavjanka
Sofia, Bulgaria

State Archives of the Republic of Macedonia
Grigor Prlichev 3
Skopje 91000
Macedonia
Tel: +389 (91) 115 783
<www.arhiv.gov.mk/Ang1.htm>

BOOKS

The Bulgarian Americans
By Claudia Carlson (New York: Chelsea House, 1990)

Macedonia: Its People and History
By Stoyan Pribichevich (University Park: Pennsylvania State University Press, 1982)

Peter Menikoff: The Story of a Bulgarian Boy in the Great American Melting Pot
By Peter Dimitrov Yankoff (Nashville, Tenn.: Cokesbury Press, 1928)

Who Are the Macedonians?
By Hugh Poulton (Bloomington: Indiana University Press, 2000)

WEB SITES

988 White Pages for Macedonia
<988.mt.com.mk>

Bulgaria Genealogy Forum
<genforum.genealogy.com/bulgaria>

Bulgaria GenWeb
<www.rootsweb.com/~bgrwgw>

Bulgaria Mailing Lists
<www.rootsweb.com/~

jfuller/gen_mail_country-bul.html>

Bulgarian Phone Directory
<db.infotel.bg:8889>

Genealogy Macedonia
<geneamac.dhs.org>

History of Bulgaria
<www.bulgaria.com/history/bulgaria>

Macedonian Republic Genealogy Forum
<genforum.genealogy.com/macedonian>

Macedonian Republic Mailing Lists
<www.rootsweb.com/~jfuller/gen_mail_country-mac.html>

Slavic Cyrillic Transliteration Table
<www.loc.gov/rr/european/lccyr.html>

HUNGARY

ORGANIZATIONS AND ARCHIVES

American Hungarian Foundation
300 Somerset St.
Box 1084
New Brunswick, NJ 08903
USA
Tel: (732) 846-5777
<www.ahfoundation.org>

Budapest City Archives
H-1052 Budapest
Városház u. 9-11, Hungary
Tel: +36 (1) 317-2033
<www.bparchiv.hu/english/english.htm>

National Archives of Hungary
Magyar Orzágos Levéltár
Postafiok 3
1250 Budapest, Hungary
Tel: +36 (1) 356-5811
<www.natarch.hu/mol_e.htm>

New York Hungarian House
215 E. 82nd St.
New York, NY 10028 USA
Tel: (212) 744-5298
<hungarianhouse.org/owners/library/library-us.htm>

BOOKS

Contents and Addresses of Hungarian Archives
By Edward Reimer Brandt, 2nd ed. (Minneapolis, Minn.: ER Brandt, 1993)

Handy Guide to Hungarian Genealogical Records
By Jared H. Suess (Logan, Utah: Everton Publishers, 1980)

The Hungarian Americans
By Steven Béla Várdy (Boston: Twayne Publishers, 1985)

WEB SITES

Austro-Hungarian Genealogy
<www.felix-game.ca>

Eötvös University Department of Cartography
<lazarus.elte.hu>

Hungarian Heraldry
<www.heraldica.org/topics/national/hungary.htm>

Hungarian Links
<www.geocities.com/
Heartland/Bluffs/9548/links.
html>

Hungarian Names 101
<www.geocities.com/Athens/
1336/magyarnames101.html>

**Hungarian Village Finder
and Gazetteer**
<www.hungarianvillage
finder.com>

Hungarotips
<www.hungarotips.com>

Hungary GenWeb
<www.rootsweb.com/~
wghungar>

Hungary Mailing Lists
<www.rootsweb.com/
~jfuller/gen_mail_country-
hun.html>

**Online Hungarian-English
Dictionary**
<www.freedict.com/
onldict/hun.html>

**Radix: Genealogy Research
in Hungary**
<www.bogardi.com/gen>

**RootsWeb's Guide to Tracing
Family Trees: Hungarians**
<www.rootsweb.com/~
rwguide/lesson27.htm#
Hungarians>

YUGOSLAVIA

ORGANIZATIONS
AND ARCHIVES

Archives of Serbia
Karnegijeva 2

11000 Beograd
Yugoslavia
<www.archives.org.yu>

Archives of Yugoslavia
Vase Pelagica 33
11000 Beograd
Yugoslavia
Tel: +381 (11) 650-755
<www.arhiv.sv.gov.yu>

**Cultural Society of
South Slavs**
3510 Xylon Ave. N.
New Hope, MN 55427 USA
Tel: (612) 544-6433
<feefhs.org/frg-csss.html>

**Montenegrin Association
of America**
805 Magnolia St.
Menlo Park, CA 94025 USA
<www.montenegro.org>

Serbian Genealogical Club
Nevesinjska 7
11000 Beograd
Yugoslavia

Serbian Unity Congress
17216 Saticoy St.
PMB 352
Van Nuys, CA 91406 USA
Tel: (818) 902-9891
<www.suc.org>

BOOKS

Americans from Yugoslavia
By Gerald G. Govorchin
(Gainesville: University of
Florida Press, 1961)

The Serbian Americans
By Jerome Kisslinger (New
York: Chelsea House, 1990)

*Yugoslav Migrations
to America*
By Branko M. Colakovic (San
Francisco: R&E Research
Association, 1973)

WEB SITES

**Montenegro Genealogy
Forum**
<genforum.genealogy.com/
montenegro>

Serbia Genealogy Forum
<genforum.genealogy.com/
serbia>

Serbia GenWeb
<www.rootsweb.com/~
serwgw>

Serbia Mailing Lists
<www.rootsweb.com/
~jfuller/gen_mail_country-
ser.html>

**Slavic Cyrillic
Transliteration Table**
<www.loc.gov/rr/european/
lccyr.html>

Yugoslavia Mailing Lists
<www.rootsweb.com/~
jfuller/gen_mail_country-
yug.html>

ROMANIA

ORGANIZATIONS
AND ARCHIVES

**Bukovina Society
of the Americas**
Box 81
Ellis, KS 67637 USA
<members.aol.com/LJensen/
bukovina.html>

Embassy of Romania
1607 23rd St. NW
Washington DC 20008 USA
Tel: (202) 332-4848
<www.roembus.org>

**National Archives
of Romania**
Bulevardul M.
Koga˘lniceanu 29
70602 Bucuresˌti
Romania

**Romanian American
Heritage Center**
2540 Grey Tower Rd.
Jackson, MI 49201 USA
Tel: (517) 522-8260
<feefhs.org/ro/frg-
rahc.html>

Romanian Culture Center
200 East 38th St.
New York, NY 10016 USA
Tel: (212) 687-0180
<roculture.net>

Romanian Cultural Centre
54-62 Regent St., 7th Floor
London W1R 5PJ
England
Tel: 020 7439 4052
<www.radur.demon.co.uk/
RCC.html>

**Romanian Ethnic Arts
Museum and Library**
St. Mary's Romanian
Orthodox Church
3256 Warren Road
Cleveland, OH 44111 USA
Tel: (216) 941-5550

Romanian Folk Art Museum
1606 Spruce St.
Philadelphia, PA 19103 USA
Tel: (215) 732-6780
<users.erols.com/romuseum>

BOOKS

The Romanian Americans
By Arthur Diamond
(New York: Chelsea House,
1988)

WEB SITES

**Emigration/Romanian
Ancestry**
<marinel.net/romania/
ancestry.html>

**Guide to Finding
Your Romanian Town**
<www.rootsweb.com/~
romwgw/romaniatown
map.html>

Links to Romania
<hometown.aol.com/
patraulius>

Romania GenWeb
<www.rootsweb.com/~
romwgw/index.html>

Romania Mailing Lists
<www.rootsweb.com/
~jfuller/gen_mail_country-
rom.html>

Romanian Cookbook
<hometown.aol.com/
simonagscu/romancook.html>

**Romanian-English
Dictionary**
<dictionar.info.uvt.ro/base/
newindex.html>

Romanian Genealogy
<members.lycos.fr/cosminc>

Romanian White Pages
<www.whitepages.ro>

**Romania (Rumania)
Homepage**
<www.feefhs.org/ro/
frg-ro.html>

SLOVENIA

ORGANIZATIONS
AND ARCHIVES

**Archives of the
Republic of Slovenia**
Zvezdarska 1, p.p. 21
1127 Ljubljana
Slovenija
Tel: +386 (01) 24 14 200
<www.gov.si/ars/1a.htm>

**Embassy of the
Republic of Slovenia**
1525 New Hampshire Ave.
NW
Washington, DC 20036 USA
Tel: (202) 667-5363
<www.embassy.org/slovenia>

**Regional Archives
of Maribor**
<www.pokarh-mb.si/
pamb.html>

**Slovenian Genealogical
Society International
Headquarters**
52 Old Farm Road
Camp Hill, PA 17011 USA
Tel: (717) 731-8804
<www.sloveniangenealogy
.org>

BOOKS

*Researching Your
Slovenian Ancestors*
By Branka Lapajne (BML
Publishing Co.; write 108
Hollywood Ave., Willowdale
Ontario, M2N 3K3, Canada)

WEB SITES

Genealogy and Heraldry in Slovenia
<genealogy.ijp.si>

Slovenia GenWeb
<www.rootsweb.com/~svnwgw>

Slovenia Mailing Lists
<www.rootsweb.com/~jfuller/gen_mail_country-slv.html>

Slovenian Genealogy Research Aids
<www.sloveniangenealogy.org/onlineresources/orgresearch-aid.htm>

CROATIA

ORGANIZATIONS AND ARCHIVES

Croatian Genealogical and Heraldic Society
2527 San Carlos Ave.
San Carlos, CA 94070 USA
Tel: (415) 592-1190
<feefhs.org/cro/frg-cghs.html>

Croatian State Archives
Marulic'ev trg 21
10000 Zagreb, Croatia
<zagreb.arhiv.hr>

Embassy of the Republic of Croatia
2343 Massachusetts Ave. NW
Washington, DC 20008 USA
Tel: (202) 588-5899
<www.croatiaemb.org>

BOOKS

Croatia: Land, People, Culture
Frances H. Eterovich, ed.
(Toronto: University of Toronto Press, 1964–)

Croatian Pioneers in America, 1685–1900
By Adam S. Eterovich (Palo Alto, Calif.: Ragusan Press, 1980)

A Guide to Croatian Genealogy
By Adam S. Eterovich (Palo Alto, Calif.: Ragusan Press, 1995)

WEB SITES

Croatia Genealogy Homepage
<www.feefhs.org/cro/frg-hr.html>

Croatia GenWeb
<www.rootsweb.com/~hrvwgw>

Croatia Mailing Lists
<www.rootsweb.com/~jfuller/gen_mail_country-cro.html>

Croatian Genealogy Links
<www3.sympatico.ca/icurkovic/links.html>

Croatian Heritage
<www.croatians.com>

Croatian Roots
<www.croatianroots.com>

How To Do Croatian Genealogy
<www.durham.net/facts/crogen>

RootsWeb's Guide to Tracing Family Trees: Croatian and Slovenian
<www.rootsweb.com/~rwguide/lesson27.htm#Croatians>

Russia and Baltic Region

Russia
Ukraine
Belarus
Latvia
Lithuania
Estonia
Moldova

REGIONAL GUIDE
ALLISON STACY

Even though the Soviet Union disappeared from the map more than a decade ago, the specter of communism remains hard for its successor countries to shake. Western perceptions of Russia still gravitate toward recollections of the Cold War.

The USSR's frosty relationship with the West certainly hasn't faded from genealogists' memories. Millions of people have emigrated from what's now Russia, Ukraine, Belarus, Moldova, Estonia, Latvia, and Lithuania—including writers, artists, scholars, scientists, and engineers whose cultural contributions have enriched the societies they settled in. And those emigrants have millions of descendants, many of whom want to learn more about their families' pasts in the old country. But for decades, family history seekers faced the ultimate brick wall: the iron curtain.

After the Soviet Union dissolved, it became easier for researchers to visit their Eastern European ancestral homelands. Opportunities for actual genealogical research have been slower to develop, though. New governments meant new jurisdictions for archives. Amidst the reshuffling, genealogists have overwhelmed archives in the former USSR with research requests. But archivists haven't leapt to keep pace with the new demand for their services. Miriam Weiner, president of Routes to Roots <www.routestoroots.com>, a travel and research firm operating in the former Soviet Union and Poland, says these countries have only recently begun to understand genealogists' interest and recognize the potential income from family history research.

© Jim Steinhart of www.planetware.com

Nineteenth century buildings of 25 October St., Moscow

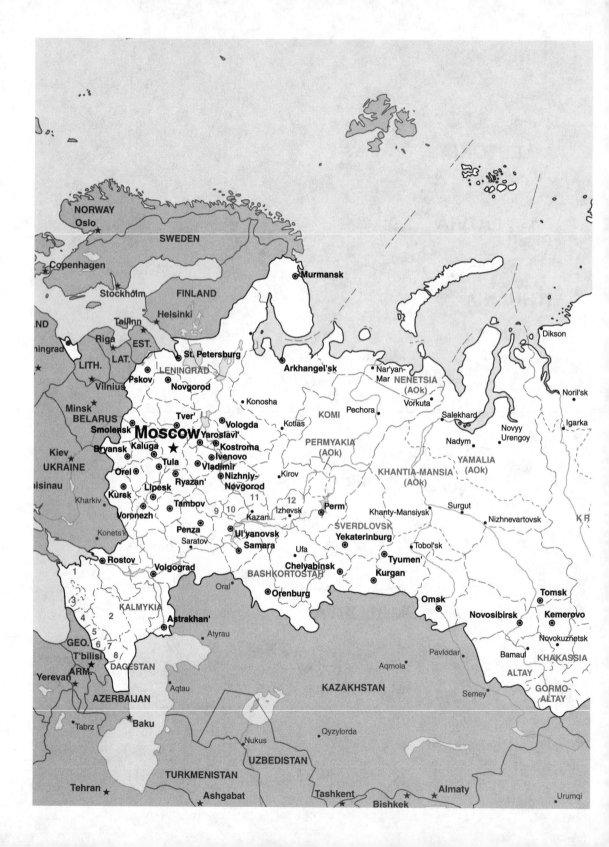

View from
Alexandrovsky
Convent to Spaso-
Evfimievsky Convent,
Suzdal, Russia

© Jim Steinhart of www.planetware.com

Communist-era complications aren't the only challenges you'll face as you seek out your family tree. Even basic questions, such as where your ancestors came from, might not have cut-and-dried answers. Before the USSR, the now-independent republics were part of the Russian Empire. So "Russian roots" encompasses far more than the present-day country. "Russian is often used as a generic term to describe people of widely varying ethnic backgrounds who have come to the United States from lands that were once part of the Russian Empire or ... the USSR," explains Eastern Europe scholar Paul Robert Magocsi. Ukrainians and Belarusians were often lumped in with Russians, for example. In fact, most immigrants from Russia weren't ethnic Russians: More than half were Jewish; another fifth were Poles and Germans.

These obstacles make tracing your roots tough—but not impossible. To uncover your family's history back in the former USSR, you'll need luck, expert help, and an understanding of the region's past.

TRACING RUSSIA'S ROOTS

The name Russia comes from the Rus', a nineth-century tribe of Scandinavian merchants and warriors. They built Kievan Rus', a state that encompassed Ukraine, Belarus, and European Russia. Kievan Rus' lasted through the thirteenth century, until

Tatar invasions reduced the empire to Moscovy, a duchy centered around Moscow. Moscovy's goal became reuniting the lands of Kievan Rus'.

By the fifteenth century, Moscovy was fending off not only the Tatars but also the Lithuanians. At its height, the powerful Lithuanian empire included Belarus, most of Ukraine, and part of Russia. A royal marriage united Lithuania and Poland in 1389; in 1569, the countries merged entirely, creating a Polish-Lithuanian commonwealth known as the Rzeczpospolita. Ivan "the Terrible" became Russia's first czar during the mid-sixteenth century; his rule was followed by the "Time of Troubles," a period of internal anarchy and foreign invasions.

After the famous Romanov dynasty took hold in 1613, Moscovy succeeded in expanding: It moved into Siberia, and then retook Ukraine in 1564. Sweden had pushed into the Baltic region, taking Estonia and Latvia, but after the Great Northern

GUM Department Store building on Red Square, Moscow

War (1700 to 1721), Russia folded both those areas into its realm. Peter the Great reorganized the government, proclaimed himself emperor, and renamed his empire Russia. The Rzeczpospolita fell in 1795, and Lithuania, too, was swallowed up by Russia. About the same time, Russia also gained Moldova, which had been controlled by the Ottomans. Russia continued to expand in the 1800s, taking Finland in 1809 and the rest of Poland in 1815. At that point, its empire covered one-sixth of the world's land.

As in the neighboring Austro-Hungarian and Ottoman empires, nineteenth-century imperial Russia was still entrenched in feudalism. Serfdom in Russia began in 1649; in Polish-Lithuanian lands, it hardened during the Rzeczpospolita. Feudalism endured longer here, with Russia not emancipating its serfs until 1861. The difficult transition from a medieval, agrarian society to a more modern, industrial one helped to spur emigration. "This led to the disruption of traditional agriculture

St. Basil's Church in Moscow, with towers and walls of the Kremlin at left

© Jim Steinhart of www.planetware.com

and the demise of the small-scale family economy," writes Ira A. Glazier, editor of *Migration from the Russian Empire* (Baltimore: Genealogical Publishing Co., 1997). Over-population, disease, and poverty led peasants to flee; "Russification" policies and forced conscription also pushed many out of the country.

Jewish people in the Russian Empire had other reasons to flee. Beginning in 1835, the government required Jews to live in only the "Pale of Settlement"—provinces on the western fringes of the empire, in what is now Poland, Lithuania, Belarus, and Ukraine. (The government also mandated vital-record-keeping.) A series of pogroms from the 1880s to 1914 fueled massive Jewish emigration.

The empire's social problems finally boiled into revolutions in 1905 and 1917. In the midst of World War I, Czar Nicholas abdicated, ending the three-century Romanov dynasty. Vladimir Lenin and the Bolsheviks seized power from the provisional government and attempted to create the first *soviet* (workers' council) state. The ensuing civil war of 1917 to 1921 pitted the Bolshevik "reds" against the anti-Bolshevik "whites." Lenin and the reds won, and Russia became the Union of Soviet Socialist Republics in 1922, setting the stage for the Cold War era.

MAKING WAVES

Small surges of Russian and Baltic emigrants crossed the Atlantic after the Bolshevik revolution and World War II, including waves of Jews who fled Europe during the Holocaust. But by the Soviet era emigration to the United States slowed due to stricter immigration laws, and those wishing to emigrate moved to other countries.

The earliest Russian immigrants to America were fur traders and hunters who settled in Alaska and California. This exploration grew out of the empire's eastward expansion through Siberia. Bering discovered the strait that bears his name in 1727 and landed on the Aleutian Islands in 1741. Beginning with Kodiak Island in 1784, Russian traders established dozens of Alaskan settlements. When Russia sold Alaska to the United States in 1867—at the bargain price of $7.2 million—half the settlers returned; others moved to California. In the early twentieth century, the West Coast again attracted Russians, primarily religious sects such as the Molokans, Dukhobors, and Old Believers.

The largest influx from Russia to North America came during the "great migration" of the late nineteenth and early twentieth centuries. More than 2.3 million immigrants from czarist Russia entered the United States between 1871 and 1910. Most came from the western areas of the empire—places outside Russia's current borders—including nearly three-quarters of a million Jews from the Pale.

This great migration brought an estimated 100,000 Belarusians and 250,000 Ukrainians to North America. Although the Russian-controlled provinces of Volhynia and Kiev supplied significant numbers of Ukrainian immigrants, the majority—85 percent—came from Galicia and Bukovina, which were then controlled by Austria-Hungary. From 1860 to 1914, 300,000 Lithuanians arrived, primarily from the provinces of Kaunas, Suvalkija, and Vilnius. Fewer immigrants came from the other modern Baltic countries: 5,000 Latvians entered the U.S. from 1905 to 1913, and an estimated 70,000 Estonians arrived by 1920.

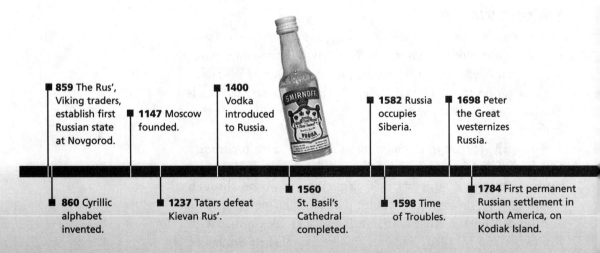

859 The Rus', Viking traders, establish first Russian state at Novgorod.

1147 Moscow founded.

1400 Vodka introduced to Russia.

1582 Russia occupies Siberia.

1698 Peter the Great westernizes Russia.

860 Cyrillic alphabet invented.

1237 Tatars defeat Kievan Rus'.

1560 St. Basil's Cathedral completed.

1598 Time of Troubles.

1784 First permanent Russian settlement in North America, on Kodiak Island.

These immigrants usually left from North Sea ports, especially Hamburg and Bremen in Germany. Although Bremen's pre-World War I emigration records were destroyed, Hamburg's records still exist. You can borrow microfilmed indexes and lists from the Family History Library (FHL)—check the catalog at <www.familysearch.org>—or access digitized copies through the Hamburg State Archive's fee-based database at <www.hamburg.de/fhh/behoerden/staatsarchiv/link_to_your_roots/English>, which currently covers 1890 to 1900.

SPEAKING THEIR LANGUAGE

Finding your immigrant ancestor, of course, is the key to extending your family tree to the old country. To have any hope of doing that, you'll need two clues: your immigrant's original name and hometown. These facts are crucial because they're the only way to find and identify your family in foreign records—but they can be tricky to determine because of foreign-language hurdles.

Names: Many immigrants to North America "Americanized" their names once they arrived in the United States. For example, they might have adopted the English equivalent, chosen a similar-sounding name, or made the spelling more American. For

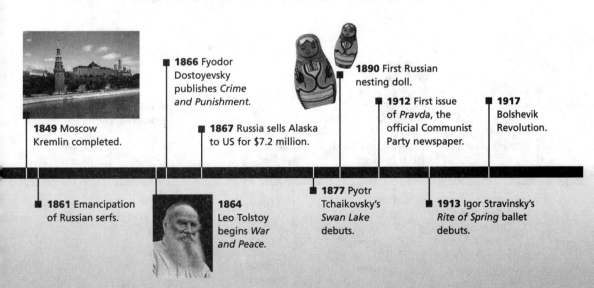

1849 Moscow Kremlin completed.

1861 Emancipation of Russian serfs.

1864 Leo Tolstoy begins *War and Peace.*

1866 Fyodor Dostoyevsky publishes *Crime and Punishment.*

1867 Russia sells Alaska to US for $7.2 million.

1877 Pyotr Tchaikovsky's *Swan Lake* debuts.

1890 First Russian nesting doll.

1912 First issue of *Pravda*, the official Communist Party newspaper.

1913 Igor Stravinsky's *Rite of Spring* ballet debuts.

1917 Bolshevik Revolution.

ancestors from the former Soviet Union or Russian Empire, new names were inevitable—Russians, Belarusians, and Ukrainians would at least have to transliterate their names from the Cyrillic to the Roman alphabet.

Keep in mind that Slavic and Baltic surname spellings often vary in grammatical context. Different suffixes denote gender and marital status. In Lithuanian, for instance, unmarried women's names end in -aite, -yte, -ute, or -te, while married women's surnames end in -iene. Russian female surnames end in -a. You'll need to pare down names to their "root" forms to track your ancestors.

Be aware of naming customs, too. In *Following the Paper Trail: A Multilingual Translation Guide* (Teaneck, N.J.: Avotaynu, 1994), Jonathan D. Shea and William F. Hoffman advise learning the Russian tradition. "Generally, Moscow has forced even non-Russians under its control to comply with Russian customs regarding names," they explain. The system works like this: Each person has a given name, patronymic, and surname. The patronymic usually ends in -ovich for men or -ovna for women.

Orthodox and Catholic families frequently named children for saints, selecting one whose feast day was close to the child's birthday. Jewish families named children after close deceased relatives.

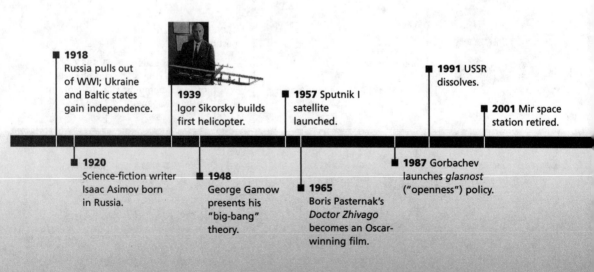

1918
Russia pulls out of WWI; Ukraine and Baltic states gain independence.

1920
Science-fiction writer Isaac Asimov born in Russia.

1939
Igor Sikorsky builds first helicopter.

1948
George Gamow presents his "big-bang" theory.

1957 Sputnik I satellite launched.

1965
Boris Pasternak's *Doctor Zhivago* becomes an Oscar-winning film.

1987 Gorbachev launches *glasnost* ("openness") policy.

1991 USSR dissolves.

2001 Mir space station retired.

Jews in the Russian Empire didn't adopt surnames until the government began requiring their use in the early nineteenth century.

Towns: As you search local sources for the place from which your ancestors came, you'll need a basic understanding of foreign geographical terms. Otherwise, you'll have trouble separating specific place names from more general descriptions. If you know that *gubernia* is Russian for province, you won't assume that Grandma came from the city Minsk if her naturalization papers give her birthplace as Minsk Gubernia. A list of terms for historical and present-day administrative districts is at <www.rtrfoundation.org/admindist.html>.

You should also become familiar with different names for your family's province and town—many places have names in multiple languages. Take L'viv, Ukraine: It's been known as Lvov in Russian, Lwów in Polish, Lvuv in Yiddish, and Lemburg in German. The city was the historical center of Galicia (Halychyna in Ukrainian), an area now split between Poland and Ukraine. Gazetteers will help you unpuzzle these name switches and locate defunct and tiny towns. Gary Mokotoff and Sallyann Amdur Sack's *Where Once We Walked* (Bergenfield, NJ: Avotaynu, 2002) is especially valuable for Jewish researchers because it identifies pre-Holocaust towns. Check the FHL catalog at <www.familysearch.org> for gazetteers that cover your ancestral country.

Ethnic organizations also may have resources and researchers for you to consult. The Balzekas Museum for Lithuanian Culture, for example, assists in town research. And don't forget online resources, such as the Jewish-Gen Shtetl Seeker at <www.jewishgen.org/ShtetlSeeker>. This place-name database is useful for all Eastern European researchers.

Once you've identified the name and town, you'll face a dizzying array of potential languages in European documents. Records from the USSR or Russian Empire are usually in Russian. Depending on the place and time, records may be in Polish, Hungarian, Romanian, Yiddish, German, or Latin, in addition to (or in place of) your ancestors' native language.

Don't panic—not even the most dedicated genealogist will master all those tongues. "You don't need to speak the language

© Jim Steinhart of www.planetware.com

Man fishing before
Winter Palace in St.
Petersburg

at all," assures Weiner. "You can work with a translator." Ethnic and professional genealogy groups can recommend translators, or you can consult the online directories for the Federation of East European Family History Societies <feefhs. org/frg/frg-pt.html> and the Association of Professional Genealogists <www.apgen.org/directory>.

So stick to learning basics such as foreign alphabets and key genealogical terms, and be able to recognize names and places. The Routes to Roots Foundation Web site, which Weiner created and maintains, has a key to Russian genealogical terms and downloadable alphabet charts for nine languages at <www.rtr foundation.org/archdta.html>. *Following the Paper Trail* offers genealogical word lists for Russian, Lithuanian, Polish, German, and Latin, plus sample records and their translations.

RECORDING YOUR PAST

Perhaps the greatest challenge of roots research in the former Soviet Union is limited access to records. Weiner has been conducting archive research there since 1991 and warns the work isn't easy: Records aren't fully microfilmed, organized, or digitized as they are elsewhere, and finding guides are scarce. "It's very often difficult to determine what records exist for a specific town," she says. Worse, some records have been destroyed, which means your family tree might be stunted by gaps in the archives' collections.

Record-keeping in the Russian Empire mostly resembled the practices elsewhere in Europe. Vital records were the purview of the church before the government stepped in. Older parish registers are usually held by an archive, while more recent ones (within the last seventy-five years) are in civil registration offices, says Kahlile Mehr, an FHL collection development specialist. The government took ten poll-tax censuses, referred to as revision lists (*revizskie skazki*), between 1719 and 1859. They're organized by place and then by social class, such as nobility (*dvorianstvo*), peasants (*krest'iane*), Cossacks (*kazaki*) and Jews (*yevreyski*). Surviving revision lists are in regional and historical archives, as are remaining copies of the 1897 census of the entire empire.

Some records have been microfilmed by the FHL. Its Estonian records represent the most complete film collection for any Eastern European country. But that's the exception—the library has several thousand church books for Belarus, Lithuania, and Moldova; close to 25,000 for Ukraine; and 45,000 for fewer than a dozen Russian provinces, plus assorted tax, census, and other records. To see exactly which records are available, try a place search of the FHL catalog. You'll also find a good rundown of available Jewish records at <www.jewishgen.org/infofiles/eefaq.html>.

Another option is to write to the archives—success on this front is increasing. Some national archives, including those in Belarus and Ukraine, have even put instructions and fees on their Web sites. But responses from the archives vary. Weiner says your level of success will depend on the archives' location, facilities, equipment, and communications. You also have to provide detailed information about the searches you want and send the fees (nonrefundable, of course) in advance. Your best bet, when possible, is to determine whether the records you want exist before you request archive research. You'll find some inventories on archives' Web sites and through the FHL.

Jewish researchers have an excellent resource in the Routes to Roots Foundation's Eastern European Archival Database

<www.rtrfoundation.org/archdta1.html>: It catalogs surviving archival records in Belarus, Lithuania, Poland, Moldova, and Ukraine.

When microfilmed records are unavailable and the archives' response is dubious, your wisest choice is probably to hire a professional. But Weiner urges caution. "It's like the Wild West with people setting up research services," she says. Some researchers are seizing a moneymaking opportunity, peddling services to foreigners regardless of the researchers' experience or qualifications. You should always get references from previous clients and a written agreement that outlines costs, the method of payment, a time frame for completing the research, and the format of the researcher's report.

The final option, now that the doors to your ancestral homeland are finally open, is traveling there to do the research yourself. If that's your plan, however, Weiner warns that you might not get the results you hope for. The archives' staff likely won't speak English, and they don't work at the speed we're accustomed to. You might travel those thousands of miles only to be told that the archives will send you an answer later.

But if you do decide to go, preparation is key. Contact the archives well in advance to find out the facility's hours, policies, and holdings. Bring a translator with you; it's tedious work, and you'll want to accomplish as much as possible in the time you have.

Still, these challenges are little cause for disappointment or discouragement. Today's maybe is better than yesterday's *nyet*. "Who ever dreamed we could even do this?" asks Weiner. Indeed, many people with roots in Russia, Ukraine, Belarus, Moldova, Estonia, Latvia, and Lithuania could barely imagine these new family history possibilities or the chance to walk in their ancestors' footsteps. The iron curtain is history—and you can finally reclaim your family's past for the future.

RESOURCES

RUSSIA

ORGANIZATIONS AND ARCHIVES

Central Historical Archive of Moscow (TsIAM)
117393, Moscow
ul. Profsoiuznaia
80, Russia
Tel: +7 (128) 67-86

Central State Historical Archive of St. Petersburg (TsGIA SPb)
190008, St. Petersburg
ul. Pskovskaia
18, Russia
Tel: +7 (219) 79-61

Federal Archival Service of Russia (ROSARKHIV)
103132, Moscow
ul. Il'inka
12, Russia
Tel: +7 (206) 27-85

State Archive of the Russian Federation (GARF)
119817, Moscow
ul. Bol'shaia Pirogovskaia
17, Russia
Tel: +7 (245) 81-41

BOOKS

Archives of Russia: A Directory and Bibliographic Guide to Holdings in Moscow and St. Petersburg
Patricia Kennedy Grimsted, ed. (Armonk, N.Y.: M.E. Sharpe, 2000)

Dictionary of Russian Personal Names
By Morton Benson
(Cambridge, N.Y.: Cambridge University Press, 1992)

Migration from the Russian Empire
series Ira A. Glazier, ed.
(Baltimore: Genealogical Publishing Co., 1995–)

The Russian Americans
By Paul Robert Magocsi
(New York: Chelsea House, 1989)

CD-ROMS

Russians to America, 1850–1896: Passenger and Immigration Lists
Genealogy.com, $39.99

WEB SITES

All Russia Family Tree
<www.vgd.ru/english.htm>

ArcheoBiblioBase: Archives in Russia
<www.iisg.nl/~abb>

BabelFish: Russian/English Translator
<babelfish.altavista.com>

A Dictionary of Period Russian Names
<www.sca.org/heraldry/paul>

Doukhobor Names
<users.accesscomm.ca/doukhobor.genealogy/Names.htm>

Molokan Home Page
<gecko.gc.maricopa.edu/clubs/russian/molokan>

Online English- Russian-English Dictionary
<www.freedict.com/onldict/rus.html>

Petersburg Genealogical Portal
<petergen.com/indexe.htm>

Researching Russian Roots
<www.mtu-net.ru/rrr>

Russia GenWeb
<www.rootsweb.com/~ruswgw>

Russia Message Boards
<boards.ancestry.com/mbexec/board/an/localities.asia.russia>

Russian Life **Magazine**
<www.rispubs.com>

Russia Nobility Genealogy
<www.geocities.com/~tfboettger/russian>

BELARUS

ORGANIZATIONS AND ARCHIVES

National Historical Archives of Belarus
55, Kropotkina St.
Minsk, 220002
Republic of Belarus
Tel: +375 (17) 268-65-22
<archives.gov.by/gosarchives/EArh/E_naz_ist.htm>

National Historical Archives of Belarus in Grodno
2, Tizengauza Sq.
Grodno, 230023
Republic of Belarus
Tel: +375 (15) 244-94-66
<archives.gov.by/gosarchives/EArh/E_Hist_grodno.htm>

BOOKS

*Belarusans
in the United States*
By Vitaut Kipel (Lanham,
Md.: University Press of
America, 1999)

*Historical Dictionary
of Belarus*
By Jan Zaprudnik (Lanham,
MD: Scarecrow Press, 1998)

WEB SITES

**Belarus: History
and Famous Personalities**
<www.ac.by/country/
history.html>

Belarusian Genealogy
<www.belarusguide.com/
genealogy1>

Belarus Message Boards
<boards.ancestry.com/
mbexec/board/an/localities.
eeurope.belarus>

Belarus Research
<maxpages.com/poland/
Belarus_Research>

**English-Belarusian
Dictionary**
<www.ceti.com.pl/~hajduk>

UKRAINE

ORGANIZATIONS
AND ARCHIVES

**Central State Historical
Archive of Ukraine in Kyiv**
Solomianska St., 24
03110 Kyiv-110 Ukraine
Tel: +380 (044) 277-30-02
<scarch.kiev.ua>

**Central State Historical
Archive of Ukraine in Lviv**
Soborna Sq., 3A
79008 Lviv-8 Ukraine
Tel: +380 (032) 272-30-63
<scarch.kiev.ua>

Ukrainian Museum-Archives
1202 Kenilworth Ave.
Cleveland, OH 44113 USA
Tel: (216) 781-4329
<www.umacleveland.org>

BOOKS

*Sources for Researching
Ukrainian Family History*
By Paul J. Himka (Edmonton:
Canadian Institute of
Ukrainian Studies, 1984)

The Ukrainian Americans
by Myron B. Kuropas
(Toronto: University of
Toronto Press, 1991)

Ukrainian Recipes
Joanne Asala, ed. (Iowa City,
Iowa: Penfield Books, 1996)

*Ukrainians in North
America: A Biographical
Directory of Noteworthy
Ukrainians in the United
States and Canada*
Dmytro M. Shtohryn, ed.
(Champagne, Ill.: Association
for the Advancement of
Ukrainian Studies, 1975)

WEB SITES

InfoUkes
<www.infoukes.com>

Ukraine Message Boards
<boards.ancestry.com/
mbexec/board/an/localities
.eeurope.ukraine>

Ukraine WorldGenWeb
<www.rootsweb.com/
~ukrwgw>

**Ukrainian
Linguistic Resources**
<lingresua.tripod.com/online>

MOLDOVA

ORGANIZATIONS
AND ARCHIVES

**Central State Archives
(Serviciul de Stat de Arhiva)**
67b Gheorghe Asachi St.
Kishinev 277028
Republic of Moldova
Tel: +373 (0422) 73-58-27

BOOKS

*Historical Dictionary
of the Republic of Moldova*
By Andrei Brezianu
(Lanham, Md.: Scarecrow
Press, 2000)

*Jewish Roots in Ukraine
and Moldova: Pages
from the Past and
Archival Inventories*
By Miriam Weiner (Secaucus,
N.J.: Routes to Roots
Foundation/YIVO Institute,
1999)

WEB SITES

Moldova GenWeb
<www.rootsweb.com/~
mdawgw>

Moldova Message Boards
<boards.ancestry.com/
mbexec/board/an/localities.
eeurope.moldova>

LITHUANIA

ORGANIZATIONS AND ARCHIVES

Balzekas Museum of Lithuanian Culture
6500 S. Pulaski Rd.
Chicago, IL 60629 USA
Tel: (773) 582-6500
<www.lithaz.org/museums/balzekas>

Historical State Archives of Lithuania (Lietuvos Valstybinis Istorijos Archyvas)
Gerosios Vilties 10
2015 Vilnius, Lithuania
Tel: +370 (2) 65 22 54

Lithuanian Archives Department (Lietuvos Archyvų Departamentas)
Mindaugo 8
2009 Vilnius, Lithuania
Tel: +370 (2) 65 11 37
<www.archyvai.lt/en/contact.htm>

Lithuanian Global Genealogical Society
Box 109
Redondo Beach, CA 90277
USA <www.lithuaniangenealogy.org>

Lithuanian State Parish Register Archives (Lietuvos Centrinis Metrika Archyvas)
Kalinausko 21
2009 Vilnius, Lithuania
Tel: +370 (2) 63 78 46

BOOKS

Address List of Roman Catholic Churches in Lithuania
Jonathan D. Shea, comp.
(New Milford, Conn.: Language and Lineage Press, 1995)

The Jews of Lithuania: A History of a Remarkable Community 1316–1945
By Masha Greenbaum
(Jerusalem: Gefen Books, 1995)

Lithuania: Past, Culture, Present
Saulius Zukas, ed. (Vilnus: Baltos Lankos, 1999)

Lithuanian Customs and Traditions
By Danuté Brazyté Bindokiené (Chicago: Pasaulio lietuviu bendruomene, 1989)

The Lithuanian Pioneers: A Study of Lithuanian Immigration to the United States Before World War I
By Jessie Ecker Daraska
(Chicago: JR Daraska, 2000)

Lithuanian Traditional Foods
Birute Imbrasiene, ed.
(Vilnus: Baltos Lankos, 1998)

WEB SITES

Contacting the Archives in Vilnius, Lithuania
<feefhs.org/frl/baltic/lt/ltarchiv.html>

How To Find Relatives in Lithuania
<www.lfcc.lt/howfind.html>

Lithuania Message Boards
<boards.ancestry.com/mbexec/board/an/localities.scan-balt.lithuania>

Lithuanian-American Genealogical Society
<feefhs.org/frg-lags.html>

Lithuanian Genealogical Research
<www.rootsweb.com/~ilwinneb/lithuani.htm>

Lithuanian Global Resources
<www.angelfire.com/ut/Luthuanian>

Lithuanian Heritage Magazine
<www.lithuanianheritage.com>

Lithuanian Place Name Changes
<www.rootsweb.com/~ilwinneb/placelit.htm>

Lithuanian Surnames
<www.lfcc.lt/publ/thelt/node9.html>

Lithuanian Terms for Document Translation
<lark.cc.ukans.edu/~raistlin/genealogy/terms.html>

Takas Telephone Directory
<www.infoplius.lt/en>

ESTONIA

ORGANIZATIONS AND ARCHIVES

Estonian American National Council
243 E. 34th St.
New York, NY 10016 USA
Tel: (212) 685-0776
<www.estosite.org/eng>

**Estonian
Genealogical Society**
Pk 4419
10511 Tallinn, Estonia
<www.genealoogia.ee/
English/english.html>

**Estonian Historical
Archives (Ajalooarhiiv)**
J. Liivi 4
50409 Tartu, Estonia
Tel: + 372 (7) 387 500
<www.eha.ee/english/
english.htm>

**National Archives
of Estonia (Riigiarhiiv)**
Maneézi 4
15019 Tallinn, Estonia
Tel: +372 (0) 693 8111
<www.riigi.arhiiv.ee>

National Library of Estonia
Tonismägi 2
15189 Tallinn, Estonia
Tel: +372 (0) 630 7611
<www.nlib.ee/inglise/
indexi.html>

BOOKS

Estonia and the Estonians
By Toivo U. Raun, 2nd ed.
(Stanford, Calif.: Hoover
Institution Press, 2001)

*Estonian Experience
and Roots: Ethnic Estonian
Genealogy with Historical
Perspective, Social
Influences and Possible
Family History Resources*
By Sigrid Renate Maldonado
(Fort Wayne, Ind.: As Was
Publishing, 1996)

*The Estonians in America,
1627–1975: A Chronology
and Fact Book*

Jaan Pennar, ed. (Dobbs
Ferry, N.Y.: Oceana
Publications, 1975)

*A Guide to Jewish
Genealogy in Latvia
and Estonia*
By Arlene Beare (London:
Jewish Genealogical Society
of Great Britain, 2001)

WEB SITES

English-Estonian Dictionary
<www.ibs.ee/dict>

Estonia Message Boards
<boards.ancestry.com/
mbexec/board/an/localities.
scan-balt.estonia>

Estonica
<www.estonica.org>

**How to Find Relatives
in Estonia**
<www.aai.ee/~urmas/urm/
vast.html>

LATVIA

ORGANIZATIONS
AND ARCHIVES

**American Latvian
Association**
400 Hurley Ave.
Rockville, MD 20850 USA
Tel: (301) 340-1914
<www.alausa.org>

**Historical Archives of Latvia
(Valsta Vestures Arhīvs)**
Slokas iela 16
Riga 1050, Latvia
Tel: +371 (2) 7612406
<www.arhivi.lv/engl/en-dep-
lvva.htm>

**State Archives of Latvia
(Valsts Arhīvs)**
Bezdeligu 1
Riga 1007, Latvia
<www.archiv.org.lv/LVA/
index2.html>

BOOKS

*The Latvians:
A Short History*
By Andrejs Plakans
(Stanford, Calif.: Hoover
Institution Press, 1995)

*The Latvians in America,
1640–1973: A Chronology
and Fact Book*
By Maruta Karklis (Dobbs
Ferry, N.Y.: Oceana
Publications, 1974)

A Taste of Latvia
By Siri Lise Doub (New York:
Hippocrene Books, 2000)

WEB SITES

Latvia Message Boards
<boards.ancestry.com/
mbexec/board/an/localities.
scan-balt.latvia>

Latvian-English Dictionary
<dictionary.site.lv/
dictionary>

**Latvian Genealogy
Hunting Hints**
<members.ozemail.com.au/
~skydives/gentips/1.htm>

Latvian GenWeb
<www.rootsweb.com/~
lvawgw>

The Latvian Language
<www.codefusion.com/
latvian>

Latvians.com
<www.latvians.com>

REGIONAL RESOURCES

ORGANIZATIONS AND ARCHIVES

East European Genealogical Society
Box 2536
Winnipeg, Manitoba
R3C 4A7 Canada
Tel: (204) 989-3292
<www.eegsociety.org>

Federation of East European Family History Societies
Box 510898
Salt Lake City, UT 84151 USA
<feefhs.org>

Immigration History Research Center
University of Minnesota
College of Liberal Arts
311 Andersen Library
222 21st Ave. S.
Minneapolis, MN 55455 USA
Tel: (612) 625-4800
<www1.umn.edu/ihrc/profiles.htm>

Interlink Bookshop & Genealogy Services
4687 Falaise Drive
Victoria, British Columbia
V8Y 1B4 Canada
Tel: (800) 747-4877
<www.genealogyunlimited.com>

Routes to Roots Foundation
136 Sandpiper Key
Secaucus, N.J. 07094 USA

Tel: (201) 601-9199
<www.rtrfoundation.org>

BOOKS

A Dictionary of Jewish Surnames from the Russian Empire
By Alexander Beider
(Teaneck, N.J.: Avotaynu, 1993)

Following the Paper Trail: A Multilingual Translation Guide
By Jonathan D. Shea and William F. Hoffman
(Teaneck, N.J.: Avotaynu, 1994)

In Search of Your European Roots: A Complete Guide to Tracing Your Ancestors in Every County in Europe
By Angus Baxter (Baltimore: Genealogical Publishing Co., 2001)

The Penguin Historical Atlas of Russia
By John Channon with Robert Hudson
(New York: Viking, 1995)

Where Once We Walked: A Guide to the Jewish Communities Destroyed in the Holocaust
By Gary Mokotoff and Sallyann Amdur Sack with Alexander Sharon. Rev. ed.
(Bergenfield, N.J.: Avotaynu, 2002)

WOWW Companion: A Guide to the Communities Surrounding Central and

Eastern European Towns
By Gary Mokotoff (Teaneck, N.J.: Avotaynu, 1995)

WEB SITES

E-Transcriptum: Free Russian and Lithuanian translations
<www.e-transcriptum.net/eng>

Family History Library Catalog
<www.familysearch.org/Eng/Library/FHLC/frameset_fhlc.asp>

FEEFHS Map Room: Russian Empire
<feefhs.org/maps/ruse/mapiruse.html>

GenForum: Countries Forums
<genforum.genealogy.com/regional/countries>

JewishGen
<www.jewishgen.org>

Mailing Lists
<www.rootsweb.com/~jfuller/gen_mail.html>

Petro Jacyk Resource Centre
<www.library.utoronto.ca/pjrc/pjrc.htm>

Italy

REGIONAL GUIDE
SHARON DEBARTOLO CARMACK

When you hear the word "Italian," what does it bring to mind? For many, it may conjure memories of sitting around the table after a fabulous spaghetti dinner on Sunday afternoons, drinking coffee, pushing crumbs, and hearing stories about *la famiglia*, friends, and neighbors. There's no better way to celebrate your roots than to gather again around the Italian dinner table and begin recording those precious stories. Like those of other ethnic groups, descendents of Italian immigrants risk losing their culture and traditions as they're assimilated into the culture of their new home. One way of keeping that ethnic heritage alive is to trace your family history and study the lives of your ancestors.

By the middle of the nineteenth century, Italy was one of the most overcrowded countries in Europe, and many began to consider the possibility of leaving their homeland to escape low wages, high taxes, illiteracy, and the political turmoil surrounding Italy's struggle to become an independent, unified state. To make matters worse, natural disasters, including the eruptions of both Mount Vesuvius and Mount Etna and an earthquake and tidal wave that swept through the Strait of Messina, devastated southern Italy during the early twentieth century. Later, the fascist rule of Benito Mussolini also caused a number of Italians to flee the country in the 1930s. Between 1876 and 1961, about 11,118,000 Italians took up residence elsewhere in Europe, and approximately 637,000 Italians immigrated to Canada. Between 1820 and

Venice waterway

1920, over 4,190,000 Italians crossed the Atlantic to the United States. And in the period between 1876 and 1976, some 460,000 Italians immigrated to Africa.

Because Italy wasn't unified until the 1860s, its people considered themselves citizens of a village or region, rather than a nation. In your country's records, you may find these early immigrants recorded by region—Genoese or Florentine, for example—rather than as "Italian." Those who emigrated in the late nineteenth and early twentieth centuries were mostly Italian peasants and unskilled laborers from rural communities in southern Italy—the regions of Abruzzi, Molise, Apulia, Basilicata, Calabria and Campania, parts of Latium, and the island of Sicily.

One of the most common mistakes researchers make when tracking their Italian origins is anxiously jumping the ocean too soon. No one wants to trace the wrong family line, which is entirely possible if you don't thoroughly research each genera-

The Coliseum, Rome

tion beforehand. Follow these ten steps to keep from "drowning" in the ocean and to make your Italian research more successful and fulfilling.

Step 1: Begin with home sources

To start your search, you need to know certain information—names, dates, and places—and sitting around the dinner table after a nice Italian meal with a glass of vino and some relatives is a good opportunity to get this information. (I've yet to meet an Italian family that doesn't love to talk about relatives who aren't present. You may get some of your best stories this way.) All research begins with the who, where, and when.

Venice alley
with woman

In order to successfully research your Italian immigrants and continue the search in Italian records, you need to learn your ancestors' full original names and the dates and places of their births. This information is usually obtained from oral family history or by scavenging through your home or relatives' homes (with their permission, of course) for documents such as passports, citizenship papers, alien registration cards, and birth, marriage, or death certificates.

Record all the statistical information you find on pedigree charts and family group sheets, noting where each piece of information came from. These forms may be downloaded from <www.familytreemagazine.com/forms/download.html>. Record the family stories in a notebook for now.

Step 2: Learn about genealogy in general

Next, read a basic how-to book on genealogical research methods and sources, such as Emily Anne Croom's *Unpuzzling Your Past: A Basic Guide to Genealogy*, 4th edition (Cincinnati, Ohio: Betterway Books, 2003), Desmond Walls Allen's *First Steps in Genealogy* (Cincinnati, Ohio: Betterway Books, 1998), or Christine Rose and Kay Ingalls' *The Complete Idiot's Guide to Genealogy* (New York: Alpha Books, 1997). Everyone has the same starting point, whether your ancestry is Italian, German, or Irish. Once you've looked at all the basic genealogical records,

Carnival, Venice

such as vital record certificates, censuses, and so on, you're ready to look for a naturalization record and passenger arrival list.

Step 3: Find naturalizations, passenger lists, or passports

From family stories, you may already know when your Italian ancestors arrived in their new homeland and by what means they traveled. If they arrived by ship, look for naturalization records first, since those may tell you the date of arrival and the name of the ship, depending on which country you live in and when your ancestors arrived. Next, try to find a passenger arrival list; however, this may be difficult.

During the 1800s and 1900s, most Italian emigrants left through the ports of Naples, Genoa, and Palermo, although some may have left from French ports, such as Le Havre, Marseilles, and Nice. Existing microfilmed passenger arrival records and some corresponding indexes from the 1820s forward for U.S. ports of arrival are in the custody of the National Archives, but they can be ordered through the Family History Library in Salt Lake City, Utah. The lists of the early 1900s give the most information, including each passenger's birthplace, the name of a relative left in the Old Country, and the name and address of the person the passenger was going to join in America.

If your Italian ancestor came through the Port of New York (Ellis Island) after 1892, you may be able to find the arrival on the Ellis Island database <www.ellisisland.org>. On this site, you'll find more than 22 million passengers and crew members who entered through the Port of New York between 1892 and 1924, the peak years of arrival. Be aware that you will need to know the name your ancestor used in Italy, as that will be the name recorded on the list when he purchased his ticket for departure. Italian women will be listed by their maiden names, not their married names, regardless of whether they are traveling with their husbands and children. If you do not know the wife's maiden name and she came after her husband, search for the children under their father's surname. (For more information on using the database, see my article "Ellis Island, Without Tears" in the December 2002 issue of *Family Tree Magazine*.)

Depending on the time of your ancestor's arrival, naturalization records can give you the precise date and port of arrival, as well as the name of the ship, the port of departure, and the immigrant's date and place of birth. Some records, however, may only give you the year when the immigrant arrived. Before 1906, an immigrant could go to any court of record and apply for citizenship. In fact, your ancestor could have initiated naturalization in one court and completed it in another court. To find naturalization records, check at various levels of courthouses—municipal, county, state, and federal—where the immigrant arrived and/or settled. After 1906, the records will be in the custody of the Bureau of Citizenship and Immigration Services (formerly known as the Immigration and Naturalization Service) in Washington, D.C., <www.bcis.gov/graphics/aboutus/history/index.htm>, although some of these records can be found in state archives and on microfilm through the Family History Library.

The Duomo Cathedral, Florence

If you can't find naturalization papers or passenger lists, you might have luck uncovering a passport. In 1869, the Italian government mandated that citizens obtain passports to move within their country. Because the Italian government used passports to make sure young men did not emigrate to avoid the military draft, the police were in charge of these records.

Venice café

Passports are still issued by the *questura* (head of the internal police) in each province. You may write to request passport information, but the archives where these records are kept are not public. Check with the *anagrafe* (registrar's office) in each comune; this office holds the records of residency changes and emigration along with dates and probable destinations. You may also generally find passports among the personal papers of the emigrant's family in his or her destination country. To learn more about these records, use handbooks, manuals, and guides for those resources.

Keep in mind that the United States and many other foreign countries did not require passports at the time, though, so many Italians emigrated without an official passport.

Step 4: Using Italian civil records

The civil records will be in Italian, of course, but armed with a good translation dictionary, you shouldn't have too much trouble. Cole's *Italian Genealogical Records* and Nelson's *A Genealogist's Guide to Discovering Your Italian Ancestors* are indispensable guides that show examples of the records and give English translations.

Like any group of records, each has its own obstacles and idiosyncrasies, such as gaps in records, ink bleed-through, and sporadic indexes, if any exist at all. Sometimes the index was filmed at the beginning of the volume, sometimes at the end, and sometimes in the middle when volumes were divided into two parts because more births (or whatever) occurred than expected, and it was necessary to begin a new volume. To add to the inconsistency, while most indexes were arranged alphabetically by the first letter of the last name, there were a few indexes that were arranged alphabetically by first name. Here is where you

NAMING PATTERNS

The traditional naming pattern of parents from southern Italy is to name the first son after the father's father; the second son after the mother's father; the third son after the father; the first daughter after the father's mother; the second daughter after the mother's mother; and the third daughter after the mother. If you don't know the names of your immigrant ancestors' parents, you can make an educated guess about their forenames based on this pattern.

For example, Salvatore and Angelina (Vallarelli) Ebetino named their children as follows:

1. Francesco	4. Stella	7. Michele
2. Fortunato	5. Isabella	8. Michele
3. Fortunato	6. Felice	9. Salvatore

From this, we can reasonably guess that Salvatore's parents' names were Francesco and Stella, because of the names of the first son and daughter, and that Angelina's parents were Fortunato and Isabella, because of the names of the second-born son and daughter. Further research confirmed this was exactly the case. Notice, also, that they named two children Fortunato and two Michele. This is because the first Fortunato and the first Michele died in infancy, and the names were used again (known as a "necronym") for the next child born of the same sex to preserve the naming pattern.

find out how popular the names Francesco and Maria really were. Many of the volumes I viewed for my ancestral village had either water damage or were damaged by worm infestation.

As with any record, reading the handwriting is sometimes more of a challenge, even more so than reading Italian. Numbers are frequently spelled out—milleottocentosessantotto (1868)—and when numerals are used, the numbers 5, 7, and 9 are often difficult to distinguish. Abbreviations used for September, October, November, and December were 7mber, 8mber, 9mber, and Xmber respectively, stemming from the ancient calendar

Lucca aerial view

when these are the seventh through tenth months of the year and thus named in Latin: septem is seven, octo is eight, and so on. Names might be abbreviated also: Ma for Maria, Anto for Antonio, and Franco for Francesco.

Despite these difficulties, Italian civil records are wonderful in the content of information they provide. Often there are two or three generations named within one document. For example, most of the birth records name the baby, the father and paternal grandfather, the mother's maiden name and mother's father, and sometimes there is additional marginal information about the child's marriage and death, giving the date and referencing the volume and record number where it was recorded. Marriage records give the couple's names, ages, and occupations, as well as parents' names (always mother's maiden name), and the dates the banns were posted. Death records provide the name of the deceased, the spouse, and parents. With the parents' names and mother's maiden name always provided, there is no problem in distinguishing the many Francesco Vallarellis from one another. Additionally, if a man or woman died leaving minor children, then the names and ages of the children may also appear on the death record. Unfortunately, causes of death were not recorded, which, given eighteenth- and nineteenth-century medical knowledge, would not be particularly helpful anyway unless the death had been accidental, such as from burns or drowning.

In Italian Catholic culture, women retained the use of their maiden names for all legal documents (including death records and passenger lists when coming to America), and with the father's name provided on all Italian documents, it is not difficult to trace female ancestors or distinguish one Maria from another.

BOOKS FOR BEGINNERS

There are several books to help you start learning about researching in Italian records:

- *A Genealogist's Guide to Discovering Your Italian Ancestors* by Lynn Nelson (Cincinnati, Ohio: Betterway Books, 1997). This guide shows you how to research your Italian ancestors using the microfilms of the Family History Library.
- *Finding Italian Roots: The Complete Guide for Americans* by John Philip Colletta (Baltimore: Genealogical Publishing Co., 2003). Colletta's guide takes you into records in America and Italy.
- *Italian-American Family History: A Guide to Researching and Writing About Your Heritage* by Sharon DeBartolo Carmack (Baltimore: Genealogical Publishing Co., 1997). My book focuses on researching Italians in America and how learning the folkways and customs of Italians can help your research.
- *Italian Genealogical Records: How to Use Italian Civil, Ecclesiastical, and Other Records in Family History Research* by Trafford R. Cole (Salt Lake City, Utah: Ancestry, 1995). This book provides an in-depth look at the records available in Italy and how to access them in person and from abroad.

Burano, canal, Venice

As with any record group—American or foreign—once you learn and understand the idiosyncrasies of the documents and how they were kept, researching in them becomes much easier.

Step 5: Study how your ancestors lived

While you're learning about records in Italy, start learning about your ancestors' lives. Keep in mind that you aren't just looking for names, dates, and places. Go beyond the skeletal pedigree chart and family group sheet—the who, where, and when—and seek the person behind the name—the why, how, and what was it like. Genealogical records don't ordinarily give us these answers.

You'll want to explore the broader, common experiences and trends, the day-

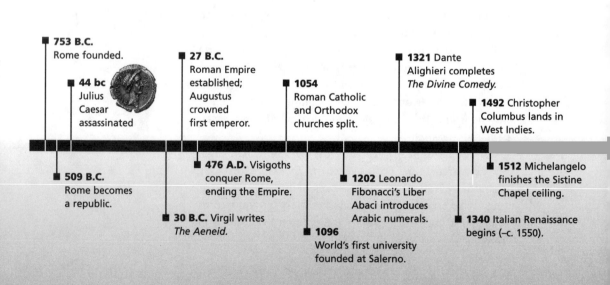

753 B.C. Rome founded.

44 bc Julius Caesar assassinated

27 B.C. Roman Empire established; Augustus crowned first emperor.

1054 Roman Catholic and Orthodox churches split.

1321 Dante Alighieri completes *The Divine Comedy*.

1492 Christopher Columbus lands in West Indies.

509 B.C. Rome becomes a republic.

476 A.D. Visigoths conquer Rome, ending the Empire.

30 B.C. Virgil writes *The Aeneid*.

1202 Leonardo Fibonacci's Liber Abaci introduces Arabic numerals.

1096 World's first university founded at Salerno.

1512 Michelangelo finishes the Sistine Chapel ceiling.

1340 Italian Renaissance begins (–c. 1550).

to-day activities, and the folkways of Italians, such as:

Food: Does anyone know an Italian who doesn't like to eat? Whenever possible, Italian immigrants prepared and ate food they were used to eating in Italy. Those growing up in Italian households probably remember that food was a crucial part of family celebrations and daily life. Food represented the family, being a product of the father who earned the money to buy food and the mother who prepared it.

So how will learning about your family's food habits help your genealogical research, besides adding some new recipes to your collection and a few inches to your waistline? Italian food is regional and may lead you to the area in Italy where your family came from, if you

San Giorgio, street lamp, Venice

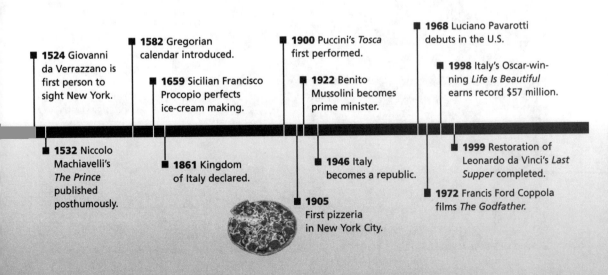

■ **1524** Giovanni da Verrazzano is first person to sight New York.

■ **1532** Niccolo Machiavelli's *The Prince* published posthumously.

■ **1582** Gregorian calendar introduced.

■ **1659** Sicilian Francisco Procopio perfects ice-cream making.

■ **1861** Kingdom of Italy declared.

■ **1900** Puccini's *Tosca* first performed.

■ **1922** Benito Mussolini becomes prime minister.

■ **1946** Italy becomes a republic.

■ **1905** First pizzeria in New York City.

■ **1968** Luciano Pavarotti debuts in the U.S.

■ **1998** Italy's Oscar-winning *Life Is Beautiful* earns record $57 million.

■ **1999** Restoration of Leonardo da Vinci's *Last Supper* completed.

■ **1972** Francis Ford Coppola films *The Godfather.*

don't already know this information. Or it may explain why your family ate certain foods and avoided others. When I interviewed my grandmother's cousin about the family's food habits, I learned they always had pasta at dinner meals, they only ate meat once a week—usually chicken, but they had a preference for eel—and pizza to them meant leftover bread dough topped with olive oil, onions, and some tomatoes (no cheese). When I read about food preferences in Waverley Root's *The Food of Italy* (New York: Vintage Books, 1992) for the region of Apulia where my family originally came from, I learned this is precisely how my ancestors had eaten while still in the Old Country.

"Birds of passage": By reading social histories of Italians, you may discover the reason your ancestor appeared on several passenger arrival lists to the United States. Many Italian men were "birds of passage"—immigrants who went back and forth between America and Italy several times before bringing their families over. This was the case with my great-grandfather, Albino DeBartolo, and it was puzzling to me at first. He origi-

The Vatican, Rome

nally came to America in 1905, went back to Italy a year or so later, came back to America in 1909, went back to Italy a year or so later, and finally returned to America for good in 1912. His wife and four children arrived the following year. Social histories gave me the probable reason for his behavior.

Southern Italians, in general, had a high rate of return migration from America—30 percent went back to Italy within five years of arrival in the new world—so always check for your male ancestors in more than one passenger arrival list. The goal for many Italian men was to earn enough money in the United States to be able to return to Italy and buy land. Some men traveled back and forth to Italy several times before deciding to settle in America and bring their families over. And since settling in America was not their original goal, birds of passage were also less likely to become naturalized citizens until after they'd lived in America for a number of years. My great-grandfather was a bird of passage who never became a U.S. citizen, despite more than thirty-five years in America.

Venice canal

These are just a few of the many Italian customs you may want to explore. Studying the social history will help you to better understand what you find in the genealogical records, to explain your ancestors' behaviors, and to give you great background material when you're ready for step ten.

Step 6: Check neighbors and relatives

Make sure you've done all of the research possible locally. By skipping generations and becoming too anxious to start research in Italy, you increase your chances of tracing the wrong ancestors. If you haven't found the name of your ancestors' home village by the time you've completed steps one through five, then

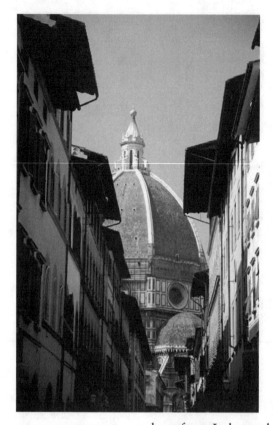

Duomo, Florence

your next step should be to research your ancestors' neighbors and relatives. Obtain the same types of records for these people as you did for your ancestors.

Italians tended to settle with friends and relatives from their homeland. In fact, the people from a particular Italian region, city, or village tended to settle in specific regions, cities, or even certain city blocks once in their new country. For example, in the 1890s in New York City, the area between Houston and Spring streets was occupied by Sicilians, while Italians from Genoa settled on Baxter Street.

Though Italy was unified by the time mass numbers of southern Italians began emigrating, these people still considered themselves primarily citizens of a town and were very regional. Language dialects varied from village to village and were incomprehensible to the residents of other regions; this is another reason why neighbors from Italy stuck together in their new countries. So discovering where neighbors and relatives came from may help you learn where your ancestors came from.

Step 7: Learn about your ancestors' village

Of course, visiting your ancestors' home village can't be surpassed, but if you can't make a trip to Italy, you can still learn something about the village from your country. Depending on the community's size, you may be able to find information about a village in travel guide books or on the Internet. Another good place to learn about a province or region is through Italian cookbooks: Look for ones that focus on a particular region of Italy, such as *Flavors of Puglia* by Nancy Harmon Jenkins (New York: Broadway Books, 1997). Besides giving you recipes, these books often offer some historical and cultural background of the area.

Step 8: Bridge the ocean

Now you're ready to bridge the ocean. You can do that several ways, most of which don't require a plane trip. Work your way across the Atlantic in this order:

Find and view the Italian microfilmed records available from the Family History Library or one of its worldwide Family History Centers. To find a center near you and to see what records are available for Italy, search the Family History Library Catalog online at <www.family-search.org/search/searchcatalog.asp>. The library has more than 28,000 rolls of microfilmed original documents from Italy alone. Most are of civil registration records—births, marriages, and deaths. Some span from 1809–1865, while others will span into the early 1900s. In the "Place" search, type in the name of your ancestor's city, town, or village to find out what records are available. Keep in mind, however, that while the Family History Library has an extensive collection, it doesn't have every record for every time period or locality. Microfilming is still ongoing in Italy, so keep checking the catalog if your area of interest hasn't been filmed yet. Also keep checking for new records being added to the collection. When I began research on my Terlizzi ancestors, the civil records spanned only 1809–1865. A few years later, the years 1866–1910 had been added.

Benedictine Abbey, Campanile, San Giorgio, Venice

Write to Italy to obtain records. The books listed in step four (except mine) will tell you how to write to Italian record repositories and even give you form letters translated into Italian that you can adapt to your family's specifics. The Italian postal system has a reputation for being the worst in the world, however, so if you don't get a response in about eight weeks, you might try sending your request again.

Temple of Concordia, Sicily

Hire someone in Italy to do research for you. Another new Web site can help you find a researcher in Italy: My Italian Family <www.myitalianfamily.com> provides research services for anyone who wants to explore the genealogy of their Italian families through a network of Italian and American researchers. But always be cautious of the researcher you hire—whether here or in Italy. Ask for the researcher's credentials and when you might expect a report. It's always better to get a referral from someone rather than hire someone unfamiliar to you. By networking with other genealogists in your country who are interested in Italian ancestry, you can learn who you should hire in Italy.

Make a trip to Italy to do the research yourself. While you may think this is obviously the best way to get records on your Italian ancestors, it may not be. Birth, marriage, and death records are usually kept at the village's civil registration office, and although one village may let you look through the ancient records until you're blue in the face, another may restrict access. For example, when I was in Terlizzi, Italy, population of about 2,500, I was given carte blanche to the civil vital records. In Potenza, just fifteen miles away and with a population of about 100,000, the clerk wouldn't even let me breathe on the record books. If you're in a situation where you can't look at the documents yourself, have specific goals in mind and a list of names and dates so the clerk can easily look things up for you, assuming that person is willing to do so. Remember, it's especially hard to sweet-talk the clerk into looking up records, or possibly allowing you to look at the records, if you don't speak the language.

Step 9: Find relatives in Italy

Not all of your ancestors' relatives emigrated—no doubt you have distant cousins still in the native village. Of course, one way to locate relatives in Italy is through the Internet, but remember that older family members in remote villages in Italy probably don't even have computers. The good old-fashioned telephone directory and a letter may be your best bet. You can access Italian telephone directories on the Web at <www. infobel.com/italy>.

Step 10: Write your Italian ancestors' stories

In this day and age when Italian families are often split by distance and there may be a loss of cultural heritage, it becomes all the more important to record your family's history. But don't just leave a collection of charts with names and dates. Write the stories of your Italian ancestors. If you combine family information with genealogical data and social history, future generations

Grand Canal,
Rialto Bridge

Venice clothesline

can gain an appreciation for what it took for their ancestors to leave their home in Italy and settle elsewhere.

And don't forget to preserve those gossipy family stories and food memories, too. For example, after one sumptuous dinner at Grandma's house, where the family "oohed" and "aahed" over her spaghetti sauce, we all insisted we wouldn't leave until we had her recipe. She shrugged her shoulders and said, "What recipe? You just open a jar of Ragu. Why spend all day making sauce when you can just buy it already made?" Of course, we were crushed, but today when I serve spaghetti made with Ragu, I proudly boast that it's my Italian grandmother's recipe. Tradition has to start somewhere!

CENSUS

The first Italian census was taken in 1871; successive censuses were once each decade.

The censuses taken from 1871–1901 are of limited use and are inconsistent in content. In most regions, the census named only the head of household, his occupation, and the number of persons in the house. However, after 1911, the censuses list the names, ages, occupations, birthplaces, and relationships to the head of the household for each resident.

Census records up to 1991 are held in the state archive of each province. Census records from 1911 or 1921 to 1991 are also usually found in each *comune's anagrafe* (register's office). The availability to the public differs from *comune* to *comune*.

RESOURCES

ARCHIVES AND ORGANIZATIONS

American Italian Heritage Association
P.O. Box 3136
Albany, NY 12203-3136 USA
<www.aiha-albany.org>

Italian Genealogical Group
7 Grayon Drive
Dix Hills, NY 11746 USA

Italian Genealogical Society of America
P.O. Box 3572
Peabody, MA 01961-3572
USA
<64.252.159.163/igsa/Default.htm>

Istituto genealogico italiano
Via Torta 14
50122 Firenze, Italia

National Italian American Foundation
1860 19th St., N.W.
Washington, DC 20009-5501
USA
<www.niaf.org>

POINT (Pursuing Our Italian Names Together)
Box 14966
Las Vegas, NV 89114 USA
<www.point-pointers.net/home.html>

BOOKS

Annuario delle Diocesi d'Italia, 1951
(Yearbook of the dioceses of Italy, 1951)
(Torino: Marietta, 1961)

Venice through a window

Archivio biografico italiano
(Italian biographical archive)
(München; New York: K.G. Saur, 1992) 1,046 microfiche

Archivio biografico italiano: Nuova serie
(Italian biographical archive: New Series)
(München: K.G. Saur, 1997) 690 microfiche

Archivio genealogico
(Genealogical studies)
(Firenze: Società Italiana di Studi Araldici e Genealogici, 1961–)

Cataloghi a stampa di periodici delle biblioteche italiane (1859–1967): bibliografia descrittiva
(Descriptive bibliography of periodicals in Italian libraries)
By Gertrude Nobile Stolp
(Firenze: Leo S. Olschki, 1968)

Enciclopedia storico-nobiliare italiana
(Historical encyclopedia of Italian nobility)
(Milano: Enciclopedia storico-nobiliare italiana, 1928)

Finding Italian Roots, 2d ed.
By John P. Colletta
(Baltimore: Genealogical Publishing, 2003)

A Genealogist's Guide to Discovering Your Italian Ancestors: How to Find and Record Your Unique Heritage
By Lynn Nelson (Cincinnati, Ohio: Betterway Books, 1997)

Genealogy in Italy
By Guelfo Guelfi Camajani
(Firenze: Istituto genealogico italiano, 1979)

Indice biografico italiano
(Italian biographical index)
4 vols. (München: K.G. Saur, 1993)

Indirizzi e numeri di telefono di tutta Italia (Addresses and telephone numbers of all of Italy) (Mannheim, Germany: Topware CD Service, 1996)

Internationaler biographis-cher Index (World biographical index) 3rd CD-ROM ed. (München: K.G. Saur, 1997)

The Italian American Experience: An Encyclopedia Salvatore J. LaGumina, Frank J. Cavaioli, Salvatore Primeggia, and Joseph A. Varacalli, eds. (New York: Garland Publishing Co., 2000)

Italian Genealogical Records: How to Use Italian Civil, Ecclesiastical, and Other Records in Family History Research By Trafford R. Cole (Salt Lake City, Utah: Ancestry, 1997)

Italian Repatriation from the United States, 1900—1914 By Betty Boyd Caroli (New York: Center for Migration Studies, 1973)

Italians to America, Lists of Passengers Arriving at U.S. Ports, 1880–1899 (Wilmington, Del.: Scholarly Resources, 1992–)

Italy and Associated Areas: Official Standard Names Approved by the U.S. Board on Geographic Names United States Board on Geographic Names

(Washington DC: US Government Printing Office, 1956)

La Storia: Five Centuries of the Italian American Experience By Jerre Mangione and Ben Morreale (New York: HarperCollins, 1992)

Libro d'Oro della Nobiltà italiana (Golden book of the Italian nobility) (Roma: Collegio Araldico, 1910–)

Our Italian Surnames By Joseph G. Fucilla (Baltimore: Genealogical Publishing Co., 1998)

South Italian Folkways in Europe and America: A Handbook for Social Workers, Visiting Nurses, School Teachers and Physicians By Phyllis H. Williams (New York: Russell & Russell, 1969)

The Unknown Internment: An Oral History of the Relocation of Italian Americans during World War II By Stephen Fox (Boston: Twayne Publishers, 1990)

PERIODICALS

Bolletino della Società di studi Valdese (Bulletin of the Society of Waldensian studies) [Torre Pellice, Italia]: Società` di Studi Valdesi, 1935–.

POINTers: The American Journal of Italian Genealogy Published by POINT (Pursuing Our Italian Names Together), P.O. Box 2977, Palos Verdes Penninsula, California, 90274 USA. 1987–.

WEB SITES

ARCHIVI: Italian Archive portal <www.archivi.beniculturali. it/sitoenglish.html>

D'addezio: Italian Genealogy Search Tools and Articles <www.daddezio.com/ italgen.html>

English-Italian Java Dictionary <www.freedict.com/onldict/ ita.html>

Genealogia Italiana <www.regalis.com/italgen .htm>

Italia Mia: Your guide to Italy and its products <www.italiamia.com/gene .html>

ItalianAncestry.com <www.italianancestry.com>

Italian Genealogical Group <www.italiangen.org/ default.stm>

Italian Genealogy Homepage <www.italgen.com>

Italian Genealogy Mailing Lists
<www.rootsweb.com/
~jfuller/ gen_mail_country-
ita.html>

Italian Genealogy Online and All Things Italian
<www.angelfire.com/ok3/
pearlsofwisdom>

Italy Genealogy Forum
<genforum.genealogy.com/
italy>

ItalyLink.com
<www.italylink.com/
genealogy.html>

Italy Maps
<www.lib.utexas.edu/Libs/
PCL/Map_collection/italy
.html>

Italy WorldGenWeb
<www.rootsweb.com/~
itawgw>

Joe's Italian Genealogy Page
<www.caropepe.com/italy>

Made in Italy
<www.made-in-italy.com>

My Italian Family
<www.myitalianfamily.com>

Professional Italian Genealogy Research
<www.italianfamilytree.com>

Radici: The Italian Genealogy Club
<www.initaly.com/gene>

R-O-Matic Italian-English Dictionary
<www.aromatic.com/itaeng>

Tricolore: The Home of Italians on the Net
<www.tricolore.net>

virtualitalia.com: genealogy
<www.virtualitalia.com/gene>

Greece and the Mediterranean

Greece
Cyprus
Malta

REGIONAL GUIDE

SUSAN WENNER JACKSON

Tracing your family tree back to the ancient isles of Greece may be an exciting notion, but it can also be a daunting one. Descendants with more common European ancestries—German, Irish, or Italian, for example—have it easy in comparison. Countless books, Web sites, professionals, organizations, specialized databases, and other resources exist to help them research their genealogies.

Greek genealogists don't have quite as many tools at their disposal.

But just because there's no magic Grecian genealogical formula to color in the leaves on your family tree, don't let that keep you from pursuing your ancestry. As with any country of descent, your genealogical journey to Greece should begin at home and travel backward in time, generation by generation. You may have heard stories of a great-great-grandfather who left his Grecian fishing village and set sail for the New World, made a religious pilgrimage to Rome and fell in love with it, or simply left his native country in search of adventure. But without knowing certain key facts about him (Greek name and exact place of origin), you won't get far—at least not accurately. And even knowing the name might not be enough.

Greece is one of the oldest and most innovative civilizations. From roughly 490 to 323 B.C., the Classical Age of Greece produced such major intellectual and cultural staples as Sophocles' *Oedipus Trilogy*, Socrates' development and exploration of logic, and the building of the Parthenon. The

Temple of Zeus ruins, Athens

Santorini village

Classical Age ended with the Peloponnesian Wars between Athens and Sparta, which left Greece vulnerable to the many invaders and occupiers that would come to rule the ancient civilization.

Philip of Macedon easily conquered the war-weary city-states after the Peloponnesian Wars, paving the way for his son, Alexander the Great, to stretch the rule of Macedonia into Egypt, Persia, and what are now parts of Afghanistan and India. However, by 146 B.C., Greece and Macedonia had fallen to another great ancient power and become Roman provinces.

In 395 A.D., the Roman Empire split into Eastern and Western kingdoms, and Greece became part of the opulent Byzantine Empire. But by the twelfth century, Byzantine power was undercut by invasions from Catalans, Franks, Genoese, Normans, and Venetians, leaving the empire open to a takeover.

In 1453, the Turks captured Constantinople, the Byzantine capital, and most of Greece came under Turkish control by 1500. In the late eighteenth century, a revival of Greek culture helped to begin the War of Independence against the Turks. In 1827, Russia, France, and Britain joined Greece in its quest for independence, but after it was achieved, the European powers decided that Greece should be a monarchy and installed a non-Greek ruler. The monarchy lasted until 1967, when a group of army colonels staged a coup d'etat. Military rule collapsed in 1974, and a democratic republic was established the following year—the first for Greece in roughly 2,400 years.

Unfortunately, as a result of all the invasions, wars, and foreign rule imposed on Greece, many genealogical records have been destroyed. The main archives are the State General Archives (Genika Archeia Tou Kratous, Theatrou 6, 10552 Athens), where records are available for research after fifty years. You may also want to check out the Historical Archives of Crete (Historika Archeia Kritis, Odos I. Sfakianaki 20, Khanea, Kriti) or the headquarters of the Orthodox Church (Aghais Filotheis 21, 10556 Athens).

Street, Skiathos

EMIGRATION TO AMERICA

The majority of Greek emigrants to America arrived in the late nineteenth and early twentieth centuries, mostly settling in the northeastern and central northern states and working as farmers or, in some cases, skilled laborers. They left the Balkans and surrounding lands because of economic hardship and regional conflict. Their ports of departure in Greece were likely Patras or Piraeus (near Athens). From these towns, according to the RootsWeb Guide's Greek "lesson" <www.rootsweb.com/~rwguide/lesson27.htm?sourceid=00392187256283445490#Greeks>, emigrants went to Naples, Italy, or another European port to change ships for the trip to America; there was

Lindos, pathway
Rhodes

no direct steamship line from Greece to the United States until 1907. Once they arrived, organizations such as the Panhellenic Union and Greek American Progressive Association helped Greek immigrants make their way in the United States.

If your Greek ancestor immigrated to America, names are a tricky business. Many Greek immigrants changed their names upon arrival in the United States, which helped them fit into their new home country but doesn't necessarily help you trace their paths back to the old country. If your ancestor's American first name was John, his Greek first name may have been Ioannis. (Try plugging names into the First Name Translator at Daddezio.com's Greek Genealogy site <www.daddezio.com/grekgen.html>.) An American middle name is often the equiv-

776 B.C. First Olympic Games are held.

c. 750–500 B.C. City-states are formed throughout the Mediterranean that function as political units or polis, each ruled by a king and council.

461–446 B.C. First of the Peloponnesian Wars begins between Sparta and Athens.

356 B.C. Alexander the Great is born.

286 Emperor Diocletian divides the Roman Empire in two, forming modern Greece (the Byzantine Empire).

641 Slavs overrun Greece.

c. 750–700 B.C. Homer writes *The Iliad* and *The Odyssey*.

490–479 B.C. Greek Persian Wars.

399 B.C. Socrates is tried and executed for his opposition to the Thirty Tyrants.

267 A.D. Goths ruin Athens, Sparta, and Korinth.

1147 Roger II of Sicily takes Corfu from the Byzantines and pillages Corinth, Athens, and Thebes.

alent of a Greek middle initial, which stands for the father's first name.

Women took the first letter of their father's first name as their middle initial but changed it to the first letter of their husband's first name upon marriage. Last names also need to be "translated" from their American version to the original Greek name. Even if an immigrant wanted to keep his Greek name, it may not have been recorded correctly when he first arrived or it may have been misspelled later by a clerk who wasn't familiar with the language and incorrectly interpreted handwritten documents.

Names can also be clues to previous generations. It was traditional for Greeks to name their first son after his paternal grandfather and their first daughter after her paternal grandmother.

PLACES OF ORIGIN

On her Web site <www.licacatsakis.com>, Greek genealogy expert Lica Catsakis places heavy emphasis on knowing precisely where an ancestor came from in Greece. Besides the name of the town itself, you also need to learn which district (*eparhia*) and county (*nomos*) the town is in. District capitals are where you'll find older documents, kept in General Archives (*Genika*

1205 The duchy of Athens is founded by the crusader Othon de la Roche.

1458 The Turks occupy Athens.

1770 At the instigation of Russian agents, the inhabitants of the Peloponnese rise up against Ottoman rule. The revolt is put down by the Turks with Albanian support.

1822 Nationalist rebels proclaim the independence of Greece and draw up a constitution.

1830 Independence guaranteed by London Conference.

1430 Sultan Murat II captures the Thessalonica, held by Venice since 1423.

1303 Mercenaries employed by the Byzantine emperor, Andronicus II, defeat the Ottomans but then turn against the empire.

1821 Archbishop Germanos of Patras calls for a Greek uprising against the Ottomans. The Ottomans begin a campaign of repression following a Greek massacre of Turks in the Peloponnese. Greek rebels capture Tripolitza, the main Turkish fort in the Peloponnese.

1863 Prince William of Denmark becomes King George of Greece.

1823 Turks withdraw.

Arheia tou Kratous). You should find out which municipality (*dimos*) the town belongs to, since this is where the records are found, or in the case of a smaller town, which community (*koinotis* or *koinotita*) it is part of.

VITAL RECORDS

Vital records will be crucial to your search. Birth, death, and marriage records in Greece are called *lixiarheion* and were recorded by church and (later) government officials. Often, Greek Orthodox priests recorded these important events in their parishioners' lives, but the details varied. You'll likely find older Greek diocese registers at the diocese in larger cities (*Iera Mitropolis*). Typical diocese birth or baptism records contain the child's name, date of birth, parents' names, and the godparent's name. Death records should include the name of the deceased, father's name, date of death, age, marital status, cause of death, and place of burial. Marriage certificates reveal the date they were issued, as well as the couple's names, birthplaces, residence, parents' names, and whether it was the first or subsequent marriage for either person.

Beginning in 1925, the national government required civil registration of births, deaths, and marriages by the mayor's office in smaller towns (*Dimotika Arheia*) and by special offices

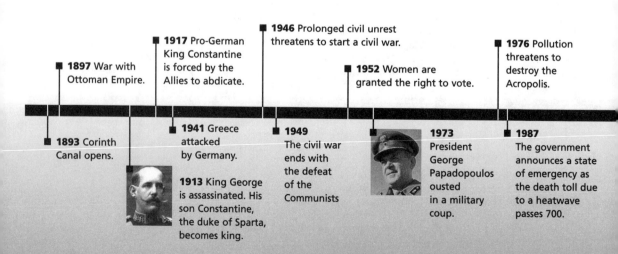

1897 War with Ottoman Empire.

1917 Pro-German King Constantine is forced by the Allies to abdicate.

1946 Prolonged civil unrest threatens to start a civil war.

1952 Women are granted the right to vote.

1976 Pollution threatens to destroy the Acropolis.

1893 Corinth Canal opens.

1941 Greece attacked by Germany.

1913 King George is assassinated. His son Constantine, the duke of Sparta, becomes king.

1949 The civil war ends with the defeat of the Communists

1973 President George Papadopoulos ousted in a military coup.

1987 The government announces a state of emergency as the death toll due to a heatwave passes 700.

Porch overlooking the
sea, Santorini Islands

in larger cities. Compared to diocese records, these civil registers
are much more revealing, genealogically speaking. In addition to
the usual facts (names, dates), Greek civil birth records also list
more information about the parents, such as occupation, citizenship, residence, and religion. Civil death records include the
name of the deceased; date, time, cause, and place of death; marital status, residence, birthplace, age, occupation, citizenship,
religion, parents' names, and date recorded. Marriage records
add the citizenship and religion of the married couple to the
usual information provided by church marriage certificates.

Some communities kept additional vital records, such as male
registers, or *mitroon arrenon* (similar to today's Selective Service
registration in the United States), and resident registers, or *dimi-
tologion* (lists of family groups). Also, notary offices
(*symvolaiografeion*) may contain legal records about your ancestors, including land transfers, wills, and dowry contracts.

Temple of Poseidon
ruins, Sounion

CENSUS

Greece's first government census (*apografai*) was taken in 1828, and again in 1830. Prior to this, other countries that ruled the Greek population took such accounts. In 1834, the department of national statistics was formed, and it conducted annual censuses from 1836 to 1845. From 1848 to 1951, the government periodically took a full census and local officials maintained the records in between, recording births, deaths, and residency changes. After 1951, Greece conducted censuses every ten years. These records list the names of heads of household, spouses, and children, along with ages, sex, birthplaces, occupations, and length of residency.

OTHER INFORMATION SOURCES

Whether or not you're able to find your family in the record books, don't stop looking. Your search can span beyond the usual sources to learn more about who your ancestors were and where they came from. Lica Catsakis recommends:

- searching for books about your ancestral town's history.
- skimming newspapers which may list current or former residents and "government gazettes" listing new laws, drafting, and voting lists.
- looking at the backs of family icons, or pictures of patron saints, where family members often recorded birthdates.

Check out the Balch Institute for Ethnic Studies of the Historical Society of Pennsylvania's Greek Manuscript Collections <www.balchinstitute.org/manuscript_guide/html/greek.html> for historical Greek newspapers, photographs, Greek-American association records, and more.

Santorini church

Also, the Greek American Collection at the University of Minnesota's Immigration History Research Center contains a variety of archival and published material documenting Greek settlement and activity throughout the United States.

The Hellenic Library and Historical Archive in Athens, Greece, contains archives dating back to the sixteenth century, but mostly covering the nineteenth and twentieth centuries. Search the archives for information about personalities, families, institutions, and organizations that played a role in Greek political and economic developments. In California, the Speros Basil Vryonis Center for the Study of Hellenism is a nonprofit research institute dedicated to fostering a better understanding of Greek civilization and its interaction with other cultures. The center emphasizes the modern Greek world, the Greek-American community, and the Greek diaspora in English-speaking countries such as Canada, Australia, England, and South Africa.

SET YOUR SAILS

One final challenge you'll have to overcome as a Greek genealogist is the Greek language. Unlike German or Italian, Greek has a completely different alphabet from English, so not only will you have to struggle over foreign words in your research (often in old-fashioned handwriting), you will also have to decipher the letters themselves. It would be worthwhile for you to learn the Greek alphabet and at least some key words for your research. A list of genealogically significant Greek words and their English meanings is included in Catsakis' *Greek Genealogical Research* (Salt Lake City, Utah: The Section, 1988). With a little knowledge and the best resources as your "crew," you'll soon be the captain of a ship sailing smoothly toward your Greek homeland roots.

RESOURCES

ORGANIZATIONS AND ARCHIVES

The Balch Institute for Ethnic Studies of the Historical Society of Pennsylvania: Greek Manuscript Collections
<www.balchinstitute.org/manuscript_guide/html/greek.html>

Hellenic and Historical Genealogical Association
<www.helleniccomserve.com/genealogy.html>
Tel: (603) 431-7030
E-mail: HellasGenealogy @aol.com

The Hellenic Library and Historical Archive
5 Aghiou Andreou St.
10556 Athens, Greece
Tel: +301 321 1149
Fax: +301 3667
<www.elia.org.gr/english/default.htm>

Immigration History Research Center Guide to Collections: Greek American Collection
<www1.umn.edu/ihrc/greek.htm#top>

The Speros Basil Vryonis Center for the Study of Hellenism
3140 Gold Camp Dr.
Suite 50

Rancho Cordova, CA 95670-6023 USA

State General Archives
Theatrou 6
TK 105 52 Athens
Tel: +3 210 321 9601
<gak.att.sch.gr/en/depart.html>

BOOKS

A Bibliographic Guide on Greeks in the United States, 1890–1968
By Michael N. Cutsumbis
(Staten Island, N.Y.: Center for Migration Studies, 1970)

Greek Gazetteer:
A Dictionary of Towns,
Volumes 1 and 2
By Lica Catsakis (Salt Lake
City, Utah: LHC Bywater,
2000–)

Greek Genealogical
Research
By Lica Catsakis (Salt Lake
City, Utah: The Section,
1988)

Greek Immigrant
Passengers, 1885–1910: A
Guide and Index to
Researching Early Greek
Immigrants
By Mary Voultsos (Worcester,
Mass.: Mary Voultsos, 1992)

Greek Immigrants,
1890–1920
By Rosemary Wallner
(Mankato, Minn.: Blue Earth
Books, 2003)

Studies in Greek Genealogy.
By Molly Broadbent (Leiden:
E.J. Brill, 1968)

WEB SITES

GREECE

Cyndi's List: Greece
<www.cyndislist.com/greece.
htm>

D'Addezio.com:
Greek Genealogy
<www.daddezio.com/
grekgen.html>

Ellines.com:
The Greek Connection
<www.ellines.com>

GoGreece.com
<www.gogreece.com/society
_culture/genealogy.html>

Greece Genealogy Forum
<http://genforum.
genealogy.com/greece>

Greece GenWeb Project
<www.rootsweb.com/
~grcwgw>

Greece Research List
<www.feefhs.org/gr/grrl/
grrl.html>

Greek Alphabet
<www.physlink.com/
Reference/GreekAlphabet.cfm>

Greek-English/
English-Greek Dictionary
<www.kypros.org/
cgi-bin/lexicon>

GreekFamilies.com
<www.greekfamilies.com>

Hellenistic Resources
Network
<www.hri.org>

Lica Catsakis' Web Site
<www.licacatsakis.com>

CYPRUS

Cyprus Genealogy Forum
<genforum.genealogy.com/
cyprus>

The Republic of Cyprus
on the Web
<www.pio.gov.cy>

MALTA

Certifikati: Public Registry
<www.certifikati.gov.mt/
?lng=en>

MaltaGenealogy.com
<fast.net.au/tancarville/
contents.htm>

Malta Genealogy Forum
<genforum.genealogy.com/
malta>

Maltese Genealogy Services
<sites.waldonet.net.mt/
sultan/gene.htm>

Maltese Nobility
<www.geocities.com/
maltesenobility>

Search Malta
<www.searchmalta.com/dir/
Society_And_Culture/
Genealogy/more2.shtml>

Spain and Portugal

Spain
Portugal
Andorra

REGIONAL GUIDE
DAVID A. FRYXELL

The "discovery" of the New World in the fifteenth century and the expulsion of Jews and Moors from Spain changed Spanish history forever. This age of migration and conquest inspired countless explorers, missionaries, religious fugitives, and fortune seekers to leave the Iberian Peninsula (today known as Spain and Portugal) for a chance to make their mark on North, Central, and South America. Once the transatlantic connection was made, emigrants continued to cross the sea in waves—even as late as the 1950s, when many left Spain to escape economic and political turmoil associated with the rule of Francisco Franco. In addition to those who immigrated to the Western Hemisphere, many Spaniards also set out for the neighboring European countries of France and Italy. For obvious geographical reasons, their cultural ties remained a bit more true to those of the Old World than for those immigrants who chose to cross the ocean.

Although Hispanics constitute an increasingly significant group of the world's population, many who reside in Canada, the Americas, and the Caribbean don't take the time to trace their ancestry back to Spain. Modern Hispanic culture often combines a variety of native heritages with that of the traditional Spanish, and their roots wind through the many Spanish-speaking countries around the globe. So once you've researched your family tree in your own country, it's time to head right to the source.

Those of Portuguese ancestry often have a more direct

Harbor,
Las Palmas,
Canary Islands

Dancer, Spain

genealogical link to the old country than their Spanish neighbors. They celebrate their heritage in Portuguese enclaves, which exist in places ranging from California, where the Portuguese Historical Museum in San Jose <www.serve.com/phsc> preserves their past, to the islands of the Azores.

The fifteenth century was also Portugal's age of discovery; the nation's explorers planted flags in Madeira Island, the Azores, Cape Bojador, and Cape Verde. Not long afterward, the Portuguese reached Africa and rounded the Cape of Good Hope—establishing trading posts in Africa and giving Portugal it's own route to India. Vasco de Gama reached India and established Portuguese colonies there, and Pedro Cabral claimed what is now Brazil. Other Portuguese explorers reached the Far East, China, and Japan. For that brief moment in time, Portugal was the richest country in Europe.

Emigration on a massive scale began in the latter part of the nineteenth century and continued into the 1980s. The main motive for recent emigration was economic. Despite it's illustrious history of conquest and discovery, modern Portugal has long been among the poorest countries in Europe. With the countryside unable to support generation after generation of farmers and few opportunities existing in the manufacturing sector, many Portuguese had to go abroad to find work.

In some periods, Portuguese emigrated to avoid military service. In your research, you will notice that emigration increased during World War I and during the 1960s and early 1970s, when Portugal waged a series of wars in an attempt to retain its African colonies.

During the last few centuries, the greatest number of emigrants moved to the Western Hemisphere, particularly Brazil, Venezuela, and Argentina. The Americas were seen as a New

Volcano,
Pico del Teide,
Isla De Tenerife,
Canary Islands

World offering hope, jobs, land, and a chance to start fresh. Between 1864 and 1974, the Americas received approximately 50 percent of all Portuguese emigration. However, it's important to note that Western Europe began to experience an economic boom in the 1950s that lasted until the first oil crisis of 1973. The boom created millions of jobs, and Portuguese migrants opted to forego their transatlantic ship tickets to fill them. France was the most popular destination, with the Federal Republic of Germany (West Germany), Switzerland, Belgium, Britain, and the Netherlands also attracting large groups of Portuguese.

Other ethnic groups have found their way from the Iberian Peninsula to the Western Hemisphere, notably the Basques. The Basque Museum and Cultural Center in Boise, Idaho, <www.basquemuseum.com> and the Center for Basque Studies at the University of Nevada-Reno <basque.unr.edu> in the United States have helped to preserve this rich heritage.

LEAPING THE LANGUAGE BARRIER

To begin tracing your Spanish, Portuguese, or other Iberian roots, you may first want to take a crash course in your ancestors' language. Unlike the fortunate descendants of English-speaking European countries—and even unlike those with such common ancestries as German and Italian, where active genealogical groups have created many resources in English—Portuguese and especially Spanish researchers will hit a language barrier. Even many of the most useful sites on the Web, that English-dominated global resource, are entirely in Spanish or Portuguese. Where other ancestries have World GenWeb sites <www.worldgenweb.org> in English, the site for Spain <www.genealogia-es.com> "speaks" only Spanish; Portugal doesn't currently have a site, though there is an extremely helpful site for the Azores <home.pacifier.com/~kcardoz/azoresindex.html>, which includes useful Portuguese information—and it's in English.

Beyond the Web, you'll need at least a smattering of your ancestral language to make sense of the records you find and to write away for records. You can compose a serviceable records request by cobbling together the phrases in the Spanish and Portuguese Letter-Writing Guides from the Family History Library (click on "S" or "P" at <www.familysearch.org/Eng/Search/RG/frameset_rhelps.asp>). The same FHL page also contains helpful Genealogical Word Lists for both languages. Also take advantage of free online translation services and dictionaries.

Bullfighting ring, Ronda

It helps to keep in mind a few key language differences from English. The Spanish alphabet actually contains twenty-eight letters, with the *ñ* and the combinations *ch* and *ll* considered separate characters; the letter *w* is not considered part of the Spanish alphabet, though it may be found in names and terms of foreign origin. Spanish also uses acute accent marks (´) over the vowels *a, e, i, o,* and *u,* though these don't affect alphabetization. Portuguese, which is very similar to Spanish, sticks with the English alphabet, although the letters *k* and *w* are used only in words of foreign origin. But Portuguese also uses a blizzard of accent and diacritical marks (not affecting alphabetical order): *á, é, í, ó, ú, ç, ê, ô, à, è,* and *ü,* as well as the tilde (~) over the letters *a, e, o,* and *u,* which you'll discover can't always even be typed on U.S. computer keyboards.

Both Spanish and Portuguese allowed a variety of spellings in documents before the mid-1700s, when spelling was standardized. The FHL's Genealogical Word Lists include a brief guide to common spelling variations and letter substitutions.

You should also remember that people in both countries write dates much the way genealogists are trained to do—but differently than most of us grew up writing them. The standard order is day, month (which is lower-cased), year; in between the date and month and the month and year goes "de," meaning "of." So, for example, if your Spanish great-grandfather was born March 8, 1870, you would write: *8 de marzo de 1870.* In Portuguese, the same date would be *8 de março de 1870.*

SURNAME SECRETS

Spanish and Portuguese surnames can be tricky, but they can also give you important clues. It's common to add prefixes such as "de la" to surnames—remember Zorro's alter ego, Don Diego de la Vega? These may trip you up when scanning alphabetized lists, since the prefix is often ignored. Don Diego might look for his Spanish ancestors under *Vega, de la* as well as *De la Vega*— check both, to be safe.

On the plus side, from a genealogical standpoint, is the tradition of women keeping their maiden names after marriage. Every genealogist who's ever despaired of finding a female ancestor's maiden name must wish for Spanish ancestry! Another helpful Spanish tradition is for a child to take on both the father's and mother's last names, using the father's surname as his or her family name. So, for example, when Julia Jimenez Montero gets married to Alejandro Ignacio Perez, she remains Julia Jimenez

Montero; she might also tack on her husband's family name, becoming Julia Jimenez Montero de Perez. When Julia and Alejandro have a daughter, Marta, the girl would take Perez as her surname from her father, then add her mother's surname (in the woman's case, the name immediately after her Christian name) to be Marta Perez Jimenez. The Portuguese variation on this theme is that the second surname, not the first, is the man's family name, so she would be Marta Jimenez Perez.

This pattern can be invaluable in tracing your Spanish and Portuguese ancestors. Not only will you know the last names of your grandfather, great-grandfather, and so forth, but you should also know the maiden names of your grandmother, great-grandmother, and so on. You may want to look for a missing male ancestor under his mother's surname as well as his father's.

Castelo da Pena, Sintra

PUZZLING OUT PLACES

As in any other genealogical quest, once you have a sense of the surnames you're seeking, the next key ingredient for success is geography: Where did your ancestors come from in the old country? Even once you know the answer, finding that exact place—so you can start to search for records there—may be a challenge. You'll want to "drill down" to the smallest geographic unit possible, but you'll also need to know what larger jurisdiction that town or parish is part of.

In northern Spain, towns are grouped together in municipalities; towns in southern Spain are more likely to be independent municipalities themselves. You can find an Alphabetic Listing of Spanish Municipalities online at <www.ldelpino.com/listamun.html>. Luis del Pino, who created that listing, recommends turning to your library if the town you're looking for

Paio de los Leones
at the Alhambra,
Granada

doesn't make his list; ask if the reference department has a copy of *Diccionario Geográfico*, compiled about 1850 by Pascual Madoz. Spain's municipalities, in turn, are part of provinces. Spain has fifty provinces, though these are often grouped under the original fifteen kingdoms that make up today's Spain. You can find a list of provinces and kingdoms under "Spain" at <home.att.net/~Alsosa/his orgs.htm>.

Portugal's basic unit of geography is the town or *freguesia*, which in turn are grouped into a council, similar to counties in the U.S. Multiple councils make up a district, and records are generally kept on the district level, whether at a Civil Registry or filed away in libraries and archives (*Bibliotecas e Arquivos*). Portugal proper has eighteen district archives, with another three in the Azores and one in Madeira; the administrative districts are named for their most important towns. You can find an online, interactive atlas of Portugal (in Portuguese, but the search is straightforward) at <atlas.isegi.unl.pt/website/atlas/din/viewer.htm>.

CHURCH RECORDS

Once you've found the right place, you may want to turn to the church there first. Because both Spain and Portugal are overwhelmingly Catholic countries, many of their older records were kept by the local church. Not until the nineteenth century did civil authorities begin to get into the record-keeping business.

Spanish parishes kept records of christenings, confirmations, marriages, and deaths generally beginning between 1550 and 1650, depending on the locale; parishes also took censuses, called *padrones*, on an irregular basis. According to del Pino, you may find a few parishes with records as far back as 1500, whereas others have no records before 1800. These records may still be kept at the original parish, or they may have been transferred to a central Bishopric Archive. In general, parish books in which the most recent record dates back ninety years or more have been transferred to a provincial-level archive. (Though that's not universally true, del Pino warns: In the province of Toledo, for example, most church records are still kept in the town parishes.) You can write to the bishop's office (using the guidelines in the FHL's letter-writing guide) by addressing:

Excmo. Sr. Obispo de (name of diocese)
(postal code) (city), (state)
España/Spain

You can find the appropriate postal code online at <www.correos.es/13/04/index.asp>. If the records are still at the parish level, you can find the address using an Internet "phone book" and searching for *parroquia* in the appropriate city; consult <www.infobel.com/teldir> for foreign phone books online.

Similarly, Portuguese churches kept records of baptisms (*batismos*), marriages (*casamentos*), and deaths (*obitos*). These records typically date to the 1600s—the oldest still surviving dates from 1529—though the information recorded changed over the years. Records from the 1800s are particularly complete and include many details. Much as in Spain, record books with no entries more recent than ninety years ago will generally be found in district archives rather than individual parishes. You can write to a bishop's office by addressing:

Exmo. Sr. Bispo da (name of diocese)
(postal code), (city), (state)
Portugal

Portuguese postal codes can be found online at <www.ctt.pt/CodigoPostal/CodigoPostal.jsp>.

When writing to a local parish in either country, you'll get better results if you include a small donation—$5 or $10—with your request. The FHL's letter-writing guide advises that U.S. currency is most convenient for the recipient. Or you could send a cashier's check payable to "Parroquia de (locality)."

Many church records from Spain and Portugal have been microfilmed by the FHL. You can search the library's holdings at

<www.familysearch.org/Eng/Library/FHLC/frameset_fhlc.asp>, and then borrow the microfilm for a small fee from your local Family History Center.

GOVERNMENT RECORDS

Spain began its official Civil Register of vital records about 1870. If the records for your ancestors have not been microfilmed by the FHL, you'll need to write to the Civil Register of your family's town:

> Oficina del Registro Civil
> (postal code) (city), (state)
> España/Spain

You may be able to find out what records—of all sorts—have been archived for your ancestral town in Spain by searching an ongoing online catalog from the Spanish Ministry of Culture at <www.mcu.es>. You can also try the ministry's CIDA database at <www.cultura.mecd.es/archivos/jsp/plantillaAncho.jsp?id= 25&contenido=/archivos/gfd/formulario.jsp>, which lets you actually search for documents containing, say, a particular surname. You can also search by town or by a particular archive. The CIDA database covers not only Spain but also many archives in Latin America. You can find the addresses of Spanish archives to write for the documents you've found with the links at <www.cultura.mecd.es/archivos>.

1143: Portugal becomes independent; Alfonso I becomes first king.

1478: Spanish Inquisition established.

1494: Treaty of Tordesillas divides New World between Spain and Portugal.

1519–22: Ferdinand Magellan of Portugal leads first circumnavigation of the globe.

1533: Pizarro conquers the Incas.

1420: Portuguese ships sent by Prince Henry the Navigator begin voyages.

1492: Spain expels Moors; Columbus makes landfall in the New World.

1479: Ferdinand and Isabella unite Spain.

1497-99: Vasco da Gama of Portugal becomes first European to sail to India.

1521: Cortés conquers Aztec Mexico.

1532: Portugal establishes first settlement in Brazil.

1534: Ignatius Loyola founds The Society of Jesus in Spain.

Portugal began voluntary civil registration for non-Catholics as early as 1832, though official records don't really start until 1878. Civil registration became mandatory in 1911. You can write the Civil Registration Office in your ancestral town by addressing:

> Conservatória do Registo Civil
> (postal code), (city), (state)
> Portugal

IMMIGRATION RECORDS

Fortunately for American researchers, most early emigrants from Spain to the Americas left from a single port, Seville, and the archives there are quite complete. Seville's *Archivo General de Indias* maintains all the information about people traveling to America from 1500 to 1800. Its *List of Passengers to America (1509-1701)* includes crucial genealogical data about each passenger: name, place of birth, parents' names, destination in America, departure date, and often the parents' place of birth and the passenger's occupation. The archive is also home to the *Informaciones y Licencias*, the records of each passenger's application for a license to leave for America. Potential emigrants were thoroughly investigated, and the information that was compiled could be a research gold mine.

The list of passengers has been converted to electronic format,

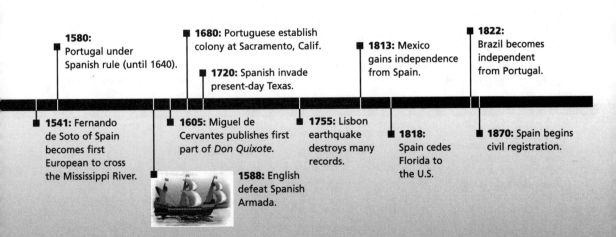

1580: Portugal under Spanish rule (until 1640).

1680: Portuguese establish colony at Sacramento, Calif.

1720: Spanish invade present-day Texas.

1813: Mexico gains independence from Spain.

1822: Brazil becomes independent from Portugal.

1541: Fernando de Soto of Spain becomes first European to cross the Mississippi River.

1605: Miguel de Cervantes publishes first part of *Don Quixote.*

1755: Lisbon earthquake destroys many records.

1818: Spain cedes Florida to the U.S.

1870: Spain begins civil registration.

1588: English defeat Spanish Armada.

so it's easy for the archive staff to do a search on your behalf. The license records, unfortunately, are too vast to have been made easily searchable, so you'll need to travel to Seville or hire a researcher there to access them. You can find out more about the archives at <www.cultura.mecd.es/archivos/jsp/plantillaAncho.jsp?id=61> and contact it by writing, phoning, faxing, or e-mailing:

> Archivo General de Indias
> Avda. de la Constitución, 3
> 41071 Sevilla - España/Spain
> Tel.: 954 500 530 and 954 500 528
> Fax: 954 219 485
> E-mail: agi1@cult.mec.es

Portugal created similar records, *passaportes*, on all emigrants beginning in 1757. Much like American passenger records, these became more detailed as time went on, and later records contain a wealth of details about Portuguese emigrants. Passport records are kept in the district archives; for a list, see <home.att.net/~Alsosa/hisorgs.htm> and scroll down to Portugal. Some are also at the National Archives in Lisbon. A number of passport records—for Madeira, for example—have been microfilmed and are available through the FHL.

Opposite page:
Founder's Chapel,
Batalha

1878: Portugal begins civil registration.

1907: Spaniard Pablo Picasso and Frenchman Georges Braque begin to establish Cubism.

1928: António de Oliveira Salazar becomes dictator of Portugal.

1951: Spain lifts ban on Basque language in schools.

1936: Spanish Civil War begins.

1975: Juan Carlos restores Spanish monarchy.

1904: Spanish surrealist artist Salvador Dalí born.

1910: Portugal abolishes monarchy and establishes republic.

1898: Spanish-American War.

1939: Francisco Franco becomes dictator of Spain.

1976: New Portuguese constitution created and multiparty elections held.

Painted ceramic artwork, Sintra, Portugal

OTHER RESOURCES

Still running into roadblocks in searching for your Spanish and Portuguese ancestors? Fortunately, there are a variety of other types of records you can try. Explore Spain's military archives in Segovia for records of any of your male ancestors who may have served. If you think you may have noble blood, consult Spain's Royal Chancilaries for proof and for family histories. Spain also has a mix of civil censuses that may be of help. Notary records have historically been of great importance in Spain, as in Latin America, as notaries were involved in certifying almost every major life event (including emigration, until the mid-nineteenth century); these can be challenging to search, as they are distributed among all levels of archives. Portugal has excellent will records, which are kept (after thirty years) in its district archives. And of course there are the records of the Inquisition in both countries.

If you're still stumped, try joining several mailing lists and connecting with ethnic genealogical organizations. You may even want to consider visiting Spain or Portugal in person. Even if you don't find every answer about your ancestors there, you'll still have the pleasure of exploring a beautiful part of the world—the place your family once called home.

RESOURCES

SPAIN

ORGANIZATIONS AND ARCHIVES

Archivo de la Corona de Aragon
Calle Almogávares, 77
08018 Barcelona
Palacio de los Virreyes
Conde de Barcelona, 2
Tel: 934 854 318
or 934 854 285
Fax: 933 001 252
E-mail: aca@cult.mec.es

Archivo General de la Administración
C/ Paseo de Aguadores, 2
28871 Alcalá de Henares
Tel: 918 892 950
Fax: 918 822 435
E-mail: aga@cult.mec.es

Archivo General de Indias
Avda. de la Constitución, 3
41071 Sevilla
Tel: 954 500 530
or 954 500 528
Fax: 954 219 485
Email: agi1@cult.mec.es

Archivo General Militar de Segovia
Plaza Reina Victoria
Eugenia, s/n.
40071 Segovia
Tel: 921 460 758
Fax: 921 460 757
E-mail: archivosg@ext.mde.es

Archivo General del Patrimonio Nacional-Real Casa
Bailen, s/n
(Palacio Real) 28013
Madrid

Archivo General de Simancas
C/ Miravete, 8
47130 Simancas
(Valladolid)
Tel: 983 590 003
or 983 590 750
Fax: 983 590 311
E-mail: ags@cult.mec.es

Archivo Histórico Nacional
Serrano 115
28006 Madrid
Tel: 917 688 500
Fax: 915 631 199
E-mail: ahn@cult.mec.es

Archivo de la Real Chancillería de Granada
Plaza del Padre Suárez, 1
18009 Granada
Tel: 958 22 23 38

Archivo de la Real Chancillería de Valladolid
C/. Chancillería, 4
47071 Valladolid
Tel: 983 250 232
or 983 245 746
Fax: 983 267 802
E-mail: arch@cult.mec.es

Asociacion de Diplomados en Genealogia, Heraldica y Nobiliaria
Alcala, 20-2a Oficina 7-B
Edificio Teatro "Alcazar"
28014 Madrid, Spain

Asociacion de Hidalgos a Fuero de España
Aniceto Marinas, 114
28008 Madrid, Spain

Genealogical Society of Hispanic America
Box 9606
Denver, CO 80209 USA

The Hispanic Genealogical Society
Box 231271
Houston, TX 77223 USA
<www.hispanicgs.com>

The Society of Hispanic Historical and Ancestral Research
Box 490
Midway City, CA 92655 USA
<members.aol.com/shhar>

Spanish American Genealogical Association
Box 794
Corpus Christi, TX 78403 USA
<members.aol.com/sagacorpus/saga.htm>

BOOKS AND AUDIOTAPES

"The Best in the World: Catholic Church Records of Spain, Portugal, and France"
Lecture by Peggy Ryskamp
(Audiotapes.com, 1995)

"Catholic Marriage Dispensations in the Diocesan Archives of Spain & Mexico"
Lecture by George R. Ryskamp
(Audiotapes.com, 1994)

Finding Your Hispanic Roots
By George R. Ryskamp
(Baltimore: Genealogical Publishing Co., 1997)

"Genealogical Research in the Archives of Spain"
Lecture by George R. Ryskamp
(Audiotapes.com, 1996)

*Historical Dictionary
of Spain*
By Angel Smith
(Lanham, Md.: Scarecrow
Press, 1996)

"Inquisitions and
Archival Resources of
Late Medieval/Early
Modern Spain"
Lecture by
Lawrence H. Feldman
(Audiotapes.com, 1999)

"Las Islans Canarias, Spain's
Stepping Stone to the
New World: Its Geography,
History, and Genealogical
Significance For America"
Lecture by Paul Newfield III
(Audiotapes.com, 1994)

*Mexican and Spanish
Family Research*
By J. Konrad (Munroe Falls,
Ohio: Ohio Summit
Publications, 1987)

"Natural de España:
Connecting Your
Ancestors with Spain"
Lecture by
George R. Ryskamp
(Audiotapes.com, 1992)

"Notaries and Notarial
Records in Northern
New Spain"
Lecture by
George R. Ryskamp
(Audiotapes.com, 1996)

"The Province of Texas
and Available Records in
the Archivo General de
Indias in Sevilla, Spain"
Lecture by Peter E. Carr
(Audiotapes.com, 1994)

"Researching Spanish
Archives Without
Going to Spain"
Lecture by Alfred E. Lemmon
(Audiotapes.com, 1988)

"Spanish Colonial Records
of Northern New Spain
(Northern Mexico,
Southwestern United
States, Florida, and
Louisiana)"
Lecture by
George R. Ryskamp
(Audiotapes.com, 1992)

*Tracing Your
Hispanic Heritage*
By George R. Ryskamp
(Riverside, Calif.: Hispanic
Family History Research,
1984)

WEB SITES

**Biblioteca Nacional
(in English)**
<www.bne.es/ingles/
derecha.htm>

CIDA Database
<www.cultura.mecd.es/
archivos/jsp/plantillaAncho
.jsp?id=15&contenido=/
archivos/ba/formulario.jsp>

Hispanic Genealogy Sources
<home.att.net/~Alsosa/
hisorgs.htm>

**Perry Castañeda Library
Map Collection—Spain**
<www.lib.utexas.edu/maps/
spain.html>

Royal House of Bourbon
<www.geocities.com/
Heartland/Hills/1150>

Sí, Spain
<www.sispain.org>

Spain Mailing Lists
<www.rootsweb.com/~
jfuller/gen_mail_country-
spa.html>

Spanish Archives
<www.cultura.mecd.es/
archivos>

Spanish-English Dictionary
<www.freedict.com/onldict/
spa.html>

Spanish Genealogy
<www.ldelpino.com/geneal.
html>

Spanish GenWeb
<www.genealogia-es.com>

**Spanish Ministry of
Culture Archives Catalog**
<www.cultura.mecd.es/
archives/jsp/plantillaAncho.
jsp?id=6>

Spanish Postal Codes
<www.correos.es/13/04/
index.asp>

BASQUE
GENEALOGY &
HISTORY

**The Basque
Genealogy Home Page**
<home.earthlink.net/
~fybarra>

Center for Basque Studies
University
of Nevada-Reno/322
Reno, NV 89557 USA
Tel: (775) 784-4854 ext. 254
E-mail: basque@unr.edu

The Etxeto Basque Family Genealogy Home Page
<www.etxeto.com>

Euskal Herria: The Basque Country
<www.ee.ed.ac.uk/~ja/index1.html>

Larry Trask's Basque Page
<www.cogs.susx.ac.uk/users/larryt/basque.html>

PORTUGAL

ORGANIZATIONS AND ARCHIVES

American-Portuguese Genealogical Society
Box 644
Taunton, MA 02780 USA
<www.tauntonma.com/apghs>

Arquivo Nacional da Torre do Tombo
Largo de S. Bento
200 Lisbon, Portugal

Arquivo Regional da Acores
Palacio Betancourt, Rua Conseilheiro
Angra do Heroismo, Azores

Arquivo Regional da Madeira
Palacio de S. Pedro
9000 Funchal, Madeira

Instituto Portugues de Heraldica
Avenida da Republica 20
1000 Lisbon, Portugal

J.A. Freitas Library
Portuguese Union

of the State of California
1120 E. 14th St.
San Leandro, CA 94577 USA
Tel: (510) 483-7676
E-mail: upec@upec.org
<www.upec.org/html/body_freitas.html>

Portuguese Historical and Cultural Society
Box 161990
Sacramento, CA 95816 USA
<www.sacramentophcs.com>

Portuguese Historical Museum
Box 18277
San Jose, CA 95158 USA
<www.serve.com/phsc/index.shtml>

BOOKS

Historical Dictionary of Portugal
By Douglas K. Wheeler
(Lanham, Md.: Scarecrow Press, 2002)

The Portuguese Making of America : Melungeons and Early Settlers of America
By Manuel Mira (Franklin, N.C.: Portuguese-American Historical Research Foundation, 2001)

WEB SITES

Azores GenWeb
<home.pacifier.com/~kcardoz/azoresindex.html>

Azores: Source of Immigration to the Americas
<www.lusaweb.com/azores>

Finding Your Portuguese Roots
<www.lusaweb.com/genealogy/html/searching.cfm>

Perry Castañeda Library Map Collection—Portugal
<www.lib.utexas.edu/maps/europe/portugal.jpg>

Portugal Atlas
<atlas.isegi.unl.pt/website/atlas/din/viewer.htm>

Portugal Mailing Lists
<www.rootsweb.com/~jfuller/gen_mail_country-por.html>

Portuguese-English Dictionary
<www.freedict.com/onldict/por.html>

Portuguese Genealogy Links
<www.well.com/user/ideamen/pgeneal.html>

Portuguese Genealogy Resources
<www.lusaweb.com/genealogy>

Portuguese Passenger Ship Master List
<www.dholmes.com/ships.html>

Portuguese Postal Codes
<www.ctt.pt/CodigoPostal/CodigoPostal.jsp>

Ship List Database
<www.lusaweb.com/genealogy/gendata/shiplist.cfm>

Your European Jewish Ancestors

HOW-TO GUIDE
DENA EBEN

"You are my brother," the Moroccan vendor proclaimed to my father. All his life, my father's olive complexion, unlike that of any close relative, had drawn stares and comments. His parents fled Germany for America in the 1930s, but his dark skin, coupled with a thick, black beard, told a different story. That day in the Jerusalem marketplace was no exception.

Until my father's bone marrow closely matched a boy of Portuguese descent, we'd only speculated that his skin tone signaled Arabic roots. Finding out that he had genetic ties to the Iberian peninsula revised the story: Not only had our ancestors escaped Hitler, but also the Inquisition.

Donating bone marrow—although it can save a life—is not the best route to finding your Jewish roots. While all Jews are genetically linked, millennia of migration in the Diaspora and the scattering of Jews after the Babylonian Exile in 597 B.C. make the chances of being a potential donor slim to none. Instead, the best advice mirrors other forays into genealogy: Go with what you know and work your way into the past.

Jewish genealogy is about discovering culture, not necessarily religion, although it helps if you have a small amount of basic theological knowledge. When you delve into a rich and well-documented 5,761-year history, sometimes the line between culture and religion blurs. A working knowledge of key terms, such as *shtetl* (small Jewish community in Eastern Europe), *ketubah* (marriage contract), or *get* (divorce contract), may be invaluable to your research.

IN THE BEGINNING

Vera Weizmann, wife of Israel's first president, Chaim Weizmann, once noted, "We Jews are a strange people: We remember Moses, the Kings David and Solomon, but we know next to nothing about our own forefathers besides our parents and occasionally our grandparents."

But those recent relatives are the best place to start your research. Chances are pretty good that you may have a living first- or second-generation relative who can shed light on your family's arrival in your country.

Present-day Jews generally have origins in one of three groups. The largest and most influential culture comes from Eastern Europe. Broadly known as Ashkenazim, they immigrated to countries such as North and South America, England, South Africa, Australia, and Denmark en masse during the Russian pogroms, from 1881 through 1914. Waves continued to arrive throughout the twentieth century, particularly as Jews fled many European countries during World War II.

A second Ashkenazic segment migrated from Western assimilated cultures such as France and Germany. The German Jews, for example, established communities in the Americas starting in the 1840s. The third segment, called Sepharadim, originated in Spanish, Portuguese, Arab, and African nations, as well as Dutch and English colonies. They arrived in the United States at various points dating back to the Marranos, who came to the Americas with Columbus.

Since your ancestors most likely migrated with the most recent Ashkenazic group, collecting family stories and interviews to document your experience may involve dealing with a very manageable one hundred years. Trace your family's immigration and fill in as many blanks as possible: Why did your ancestors leave their native country? Where did they come from? Where did they settle? How did they maintain their Jewish identity?

For specific genealogical guidance, contact one of the more than seventy-five worldwide Jewish Genealogial Societies. Look for the JGS in your area at JewishGen <www.jewishgen.org>. This site also lists many other resources, including groups specializing in a particular region. If you know approximately where

your family settled and its area of origin, a local society or interest group will be a great resource.

BEYOND THE BEGATS

If you're still stumped, traditional Jewish naming patterns might turn partial information into breakthroughs, since they provide clues about other family members. Traditionally, Ashkenazic Jews are named after a close deceased relative, so a birth date could signify the approximate death date of an ancestor sharing that name.

If several male children within an extended family born in the same year were given the name Abraham, for example, this is a strong indicator that some common relative with the given name Abraham died shortly before the birth of the children. Ashkenazic Jewish genealogists who suspect they might be related will often go through the ritual of comparing given names in their families, looking for a pattern of similar given names.

Unfortunately, Israelis of Ashkenazic descent have virtually abandoned this naming practice, and it is becoming less common among Ashkenazic Jews in the Diaspora. But for persons who were born before 1950, these naming rules usually apply. Also note that, today, practicing Ashenazic Jews usually have a Hebrew name, which references the parents' Hebrew names, and an American name.

Sephardic Jews have a different tradition and name their children according to the following pattern: The firstborn son is named after the father's father; the firstborn daughter is named after the mother's mother; second son after the mother's father; and the second daughter after the father's mother.

CROSSING THE SEA

Ask your living relatives for clues to your ancestors' immigrant origins. Finding your family's home country, province, and ideally, village is crucial to tracing your roots to the other side of the Atlantic. You can also consult passenger arrival lists, immigration records, and naturalization records; for more on these records, see *A Genealogist's Guide to Discovering Your Immigrant & Ethnic Ancestors* by Sharon DeBartolo Carmack (Cincinnati, Ohio: Betterway Books, 2000).

Once you've identified a country or region of origin, you can often acquire records by contacting specific foreign state archives. On average, an inquiry will be a pricey $300 to $500, but the information gleaned could be more valuable than the cost to obtain it. It could also substitute for or better prepare you for a heritage trip. Moldova, however, will not process information requests and accepts such inquiries only through Routes to Roots <www.routestoroots.com>.

Research firms, like the New Jersey-based Routes to Roots, often shed light on a dark past. Some have research contacts in Europe; others have branch offices in those countries. Individual genealogists in Europe, the United States, and Canada also hire out their services; the Federation of Eastern European Family

1492 Jews are expelled from Spain. Columbus, with conversos Jews aboard, reaches the New World.

1648-49 Chmielnicki cossack massacres in Poland.

1650 Twelve Jewish families granted permission to settle in Curacao. Jews settle in Jamaica, permitted to own land and practice their religion.

1700s Rise of Hasidism in Russia and Poland.

1732 Congregation Mickve Israel, oldest synagogue in Western Hemisphere, built in Curacao.

1820s Rise of Reform Judaism in Germany.

1858 Edgardo Mortara, a little boy, is abducted in Italy after forced conversion, creating worldwide protests.

1628 First Jews settle in Barbados, an English colony. By 1710 there are two synagogues on the island.

1500s Rise of Kabbalah in Safed, Palestine.

1655 Jews allowed to resettle in England, from which they had been barred since 1290.

1654 Jews expelled from Brazil; twenty-three land in New Amsterdam.

1791 Jews granted citizenship in France. Beginning of Jewish Emancipation in Europe.

1760 Jewish merchants and their families settle in New Orleans.

1840 Jews in Damascus, Syria, are accused of blood libel, arousing world reaction.

1868 Benjamin Disraeli becomes English prime minister. Queen Victoria makes him Earl of Beaconsfield.

Historical Societies maintains a list at <feefhs.org/frg/frg-pg.html>.

Another source for European records is the Family History Library in Salt Lake City, Utah <www.familysearch.org>, most of whose holdings can be borrowed from your local Family History Center. "They have incredible collections of Jewish vital records for Germany, Poland, and Hungary," Mokotoff notes, "and they are slowly acquiring records in such countries as Lithuania, Belarus, and the Ukraine." If the FHL doesn't have the records you need, however, you may be in for a long wait: The opening of government records in post-Communist Eastern Europe has led to a flood of information that still needs to be transferred to microfilm.

Cemeteries also may have clues to your ancestral origins. Many immigrants organized in *landsmanshaftn*, denoting a common town of origin, and Jewish cemeteries often belong to congregations that drew members from the same Old World community. Congregational or *landsmanshaft* plots, like those of my great-grandparents, list an immigrant's birthplace on the tombstone. (There is also a tradition of leaving rocks on top of the gravestone, which may indicate to a visitor that another relative or friend of the deceased is available to make more genealogical connections.)

■ **1894** French staff officer Alfred Dreyfus is convicted of treason and imprisoned on Devil's Island in the Caribbean. He is later exonerated.

■ **1917** Balfour Declaration pledges British support for Jewish national homeland. United States enters World War I against Germany. Russian Revolution.

■ **1919** Jewish delegations to the Paris Peace Conference after World War I seek minority rights for European Jews.

■ **1931** Three million Jews live in Poland, making it the largest Jewish population outside the U.S.

■ **1881** Czar Alexander II assassinated in St. Petersburg, Russia. Pogroms and persecution of Jews follows, and immigration to America is accelerated. Two million Eastern European Jews will emigrate to America through 1914.

■ **1896** Theodore Herzl founds political Zionism; First World Zionist Congress is held.

■ **1929** Arab rioters kill sixty-seven Jewish settlers in Hebron, British Mandate Palestine.

■ **1922** British Mandate on Palestine (Land of Israel) approved by League of Nations.

■ **1933** Rise of Adolph Hitler. German Nazis proclaim general boycott of all Jewish businesses.

Once you obtain even partial information, such as port of entry, limited vital statistics, and most importantly, region or town of origin, you can start unlocking your overseas roots. All it takes is a lot of patience and a bit of *chutzpah*—nerve, or in this case, perseverance—an intrinsic quality that has helped Jews survive throughout history.

BEARING WITNESS

You might think that the migratory nature of the Jewish people and the purging of communities by the Cossacks during the pogroms and the Nazis during the Holocaust means many Jews have no concrete evidence of their past. This popular misconception can hinder successful research. "While most things Jewish were destroyed, birth and death records exist in government archives," Mokotoff says.

Many also believe that a heritage trip to the old country would turn up very little information, since most vestiges of *shtetl* life have been erased by tyranny and time. On a recent trip to the Ukraine, I found plenty of evidence to the contrary. The famous Brodsky Synagogue in Kiev, long used as a puppet theater by the Communists, now functions as a house of prayer; sawdust from new floorboards filled the air during my visit. Formerly repressed or partially destroyed communities find

1935 Germans pass Nuremberg Laws restricting legal and civil rights of German Jews.

1941 Einsatzgruppen (special units) follow German troops into Soviet Union, perpetuating systematic murder.

1942 Nazi leaders refine the "Final Solution"—the genocide of the Jewish people—at Wannsee Conference.

1945 Nuremberg War Crimes Tribunal estimates that 6,000,000 Jews have been murdered by the Nazis.

1950s Hundreds of thousands of Jews from Europe and Arab lands come to Israel.

1956 Sinai campaign by Israel, France, and England.

1940 Nazis establish ghettos in Poland.

1948 Israel is founded as a nation and is recognized by the United States.

1960 Adolph Eichmann stands trial in Israel for crimes against the Jews and humanity during World War II.

1939 Germany invades Poland, starting World War II. Steamship St. Louis, carrying 907 Jewish German refugees, is turned back by U.S. and Cuba. U.S. Jewish population estimated at 4,770,000.

1947 Ancient scrolls, some dating from 22 B.C.E., are discovered at Qumram near the Dead Sea. UN approves partition of British Mandate Palestine into Jewish and Arab states.

renewal today, though they're struggling. In fact, one way to encourage these communities' rebirth is by planning a heritage trip that will give hope and provide volunteers, supplies, or funds.

If you're searching for survivors or victims of the Holocaust, heritage museums and Holocaust centers may have the records you need. Fortunately, the atrocities were well documented. Yad Vashem <www.yadvashem.org.il>, Israel's national Holocaust records archive and museum, keeps a names registry, as does the United States Holocaust Memorial Museum <www.ushmm.org> in Washington, DC. Holocaust "remembrance centers" in major cities also may contain archives and directory books. The Museum of Jewish Heritage <www.mjh-nyc.org> in New York City is currently developing a Family History Center and has a collection of 15,000 objects, photographs, and films relating to specific families and communities dating from the 1880s to the present.

TEACH YOUR CHILDREN'S CHILDREN

For many Jewish genealogists, researching the past brings them closer to the present. "Most claim that they feel more Jewish since they've started," Mokotoff says. "I think it's because you immerse yourself in Jewish history."

1969 Golda Meir elected Prime Minister of Israel.

1978 Israel-Egypt Peace Treaty.

1989 Soviet Union permits Jews to emigrate on their first application for visa.

1991 Breakup of Soviet Union leads to rise of nationalism and outbreaks of anti-Semitism.

1993 Israel signs Agreement with the PLO.

1967 Israel is victorious over Egypt, Jordan, Syria, and Iraq in Six Day War.

1973 Egypt and Syria attack Israel on the Day of Atonement, starting the Yom Kippur War, which Israel wins.

1987 Uprising of Palestinian Arabs, known as the Intifada, begins on Judea, Samaria (West Bank) and Gaza.

1994 Israel-Jordanian Peace Treaty.

1992 Operation Solomon brings almost all Ethiopian Jews to Israel.

1970 Soviet Jews agitate for right to emigrate.

1985 Operation Moses, airlift of Ethiopian Jews to Israel.

The connection to history fuels a need to sustain that legacy. Present-day researchers combat centuries of persecution by passing on stories about generations past. You may find surprises, like my father's Arabic-Iberian roots, or inspiring moments like my visit to the Brodsky Synagogue. Even something as small as a recipe can be significant. Perhaps look into adopting Israeli customs that will bring you closer to a vibrant and inherently Jewish culture.

Don't forget to document your own family's life. By preserving your daily life and customs, your own children and grandchildren will be able to carry the mantle of your 5,761-year-old heritage.

RESOURCES

ORGANIZATIONS AND ARCHIVES

American Jewish Historical Society
<www.ajhs.org>

Center for Jewish History
15 W. 16th St.
New York, NY 10011 USA
Tel: (212) 294-6160
<www.cjh.org>

Central Archives for the History of the Jewish People
Sprinzak Building, Givat Ram
Hebrew University
Box 1149
91010 Jerusalem, Israel
Tel: +972 (2) 563-5716
<sites.huji.ac.il/archives>

The Jacob Rader Marcus Center of the American Jewish Archives
3101 Clifton Ave.
Cincinnati, OH 45220 USA
Tel: (513) 221-1875
<www.huc.edu/aja>

Jewish Genealogy Society of New York
<www.jgsny.org>

Leo Baeck Institute
(German Jewry)
<www.lbi.org>

Routes to Roots
136 Sandpiper Key
Seacaucus, NJ 07094 USA
Tel: (201) 866-4075
<www.routestoroots.com>

The Sephardi Federation
(Iberian, Arabic, African Jewry)
<www.sephardichouse.org>

Yad Vashem
Box 3477
91034 Jerusalem, Israel
Tel: +972 (2) 644-3400
<www.yadvashem.org.il>

YIVO Institute for Jewish Research
(East European Jewry)
<www.yivoinstitute.org>

BOOKS

The Cross and the Pear Tree: A Sephardic Journey
By Victor Perera (Berkeley: University of California Press, 1996)

A Dictionary of Jewish Names and Their History
By Benzion C. Kaganoff (Northvale, N.J.: Jason Aronson Publishers, 1996)

The Encyclopedia of Jewish Genealogy, Volume I: Sources in the United States and Canada
Arthur Kurzweil and Miriam Weiner, eds. (Northvale, N.J.: Jason Aronson Publishers, 1991–)

Getting Started in Jewish Genealogy
By Gary Mokotoff and Warren Blatt (Bergenfield, N.J.: Avotaynu, 1999)

How to Document Victims and Locate Survivors of the Holocaust
By Gary Mokotoff and Benjamin Meed (Teaneck, N.J.: Avotaynu, 1995)

Jewish Literacy: The Most Important Things to Know About the Jewish Religion, Its People and Its History
By Joseph Telushkin (New York: William Morrow & Co., 1991)

Jewish Roots in Poland: Pages from the Past and Archival Inventories
By Miriam Weiner (Seacaucus, N.J.: Routes to Roots Foundation, 1997)

Scattered Seeds: A Guide to Jewish Genealogy
By Mona Freedman-Morris (Boca Raton, Fla.: RJ Press, 1998)

Sourcebook for Jewish Genealogies and Family Histories
By David S. Zubatsky and

Irwin M. Berent (Teaneck, N.J.: Avotaynu, 1996)

A Travel Guide to Jewish Russia & Ukraine
By Ben G. Frank (Gretna, La.: Pelican, 2000)

Where Once We Walked
By Gary Mokotoff and Sallyann Amdur Sack. Rev. ed. (Teaneck, N.J.: Avotaynu, 2002.)

WEB SITES

Avotaynu: The International Review of Jewish Genealogy
<www.avotaynu.com>

Beth Hatefutsoth: Museum of the Jewish Diaspora
<www.bh.org.il>

Cyndi's List: Jewish
<www.cyndislist.com/jewish.htm>

DoroTree
<www.dorotree.com>

Genealogy Resources on the Internet: Jewish Mailing Lists
<www.rootsweb.com/~jfuller/gen_mail_jewish.html>

Ilanot
<www.bh.org.il/shop/ilanot.asp>

JewishGen
<www.jewishgen.org>

Jewish Web Index
<jewishwebindex.com>

Judaism and Jewish Resources
<shamash.org/trb/judaism.html>

Museum of Jewish Heritage
<www.mjhnyc.org>

US Holocaust Memorial Museum
<www.ushmm.org>

Appendix A

To find a Family History Center near you in the United States, see <www.familysearch.org/Eng/Library/FHC/frameset_fhc.asp> and enter the state of your choosing or see The Family Tree Guide Book (Cincinnati, Ohio: Betterway Books, 2002).

EUROPEAN FAMILY HISTORY CENTERS

AUSTRIA

Graz Austria
Eckertstrasse 136
Graz, Steiermark, Austria
Tel: 43 316 585657

Innsbruck Austria
Phillipine-Welser-Strasse 16
Innsbruck, Tirol, Austria
Tel: 43-512-342464

Klagenfurt Austria
Hirschenwirt Strasse 17
Klagenfurt, Karnten, Austria
Tel: 43-463-21130

Linz Austria
Spaunstrasse 83
Linz, Oberosterreich, Austria
Tel: 43-732-342610

Salzburg Austria
Andreas-Rohracherstrasse 20
Salzburg, Salzburg, Austria
Tel: 43-662-825785

Salzburg Flachau Austria
Bahnhof Strasse 20
A-5202 Neumarkt, Austria
Tel: 43-62 164898

Vienna Austria
Böcklinstrasse 55
A-1020 Wien
Wien, Niederosterreich, Austria
Tel: 43-1-720-798517

Wels Austria
Camillo-Schulz-Strasse 30
Wels, Oberosterreich, Austria
Tel: 43-7242-63718

BELGIUM

Antwerp Belgium
Bergen op Zoom Laan 20
Merksem
Antwerpen (Merksem), Belgium
Tel: 32-3-6460859

Breda Netherlands
Mgr. De Vethstraat 112
Breda, Noord Brabant, Belgium
Tel: 31-76-5213141

Brugge Belgium
Predikherenstraat 25
Brugge, West Vlaanderen,
Belgium

Bruxelles Belgium
108 Avenue Henri Jaspar
B-1060 Bruxelles, Brabant,
Belgium
Tel: 32-2-5392137

Charleroi Belgium
160, Rue de la Tombe
Mont-sur-Marchienne, Hainaut,
Belgium
Tel: 32-71-436657

Eindhoven Netherlands
De Koppele 1 A
Eindhoven, Noord Brabant,
Belgium
Tel: 31-40-2423526

Gent Belgium
Kortrijkse Steenweg 1060
St. Denijs Westrem, Oost-
Vlaanderen, Belgium

Heerlen Netherlands
Servicemens
Burgemeester D.
Hesseleplein 26 A
Heerlen, Limburg, Belgium
Tel: 31-45-5717863

Liege Belgium
67, Rue de la Grande Rotisse
Grivegnee-Liege, Liege,
Belgium
Tel: 32-43-433463

Mechelen Belgium
Leopold Straat 87
Mechelen, Antwerpen,
Belgium

Namur Belgium
45, rue du Grand Tige
Erptent, Namur, Belgium
Tel: 32-8130-1513

Nivelles Belgium
66, Chaussée de Braine Le
Comte
Nivelles, Brabant, Belgium
Tel: 32-67-219385

St. Niklaas Belgium
Tuinlaan 102
Belsele-Waas, Oost-
Vlaanderen, Belgium

Vlissingen Netherlands
Badhuissstraat 161
Vlissingen, Zeeland, Belgium

DENMARK

Aalborg Denmark
Riishøjsvej 20
DK-9000
Aalborg, Nordjylland
County, Denmark
Tel: 45-98131157

Aarhus Denmark
Langenæs Alle 31
DK-8000
Aarhus, Aarhus County,
Denmark
Tel: +45-86141584

Esbjerg Denmark
Spangsbjerg Mollevej 34
DK-6700
Esbjerg, Ribe County,
Denmark
Tel: +45-75457725

Fredericia Denmark
Kaltoftevej 27
DK-7000
Fredericia, Vejle County,
Denmark
Tel: +45-75912672

Frederikshavn Denmark
Nils Juelsvej 51
DK-9900
Frederikshavn, Nordjylland
County, Denmark
Tel: +45-98427733

Odense Denmark
Lahnsgade 58
Odense C, Fyn County,
Denmark
Tel: +45-66178674

Slagelse Denmark
Skovvejen 50
DK-4200
Slagelse, Vestsjaelland
County, Vestsjaelland,

Denmark
Phone: +45-53526837

ENGLAND

Aldershot England
St. Georges Road
Aldershot, Hampshire
County, England
Tel: 1252 321460

Ashton England
Patterdale Road
Crowhill Estate
Ashton-under-Lyne,
Lancashire County, England
Tel: 161 330 3453

Barrow England
Abbey Road
Barrow-in-Furness, Cumbria
County, England
Tel: 1229 820050

Billingham England
The Linkway
Billingham, Cleveland
County, England
Tel: 1642 563162

Birkenhead England
2 Reservoir Road
Prenton, Merseyside,
England
Tel: 151 608 0157

Blackpool England
Warren Drive
Blackpool, Lancashire
County, England
Tel: 1253 858218

Bristol England
721 Wells Road
Whitchurch
Bristol, Somerset County,
England
Tel: 1275 838326

Cambridge England
670 Cherry Hinton Road
Cambridge, Cambridgeshire,
England
Tel: 1223 247010

Canterbury England
Forty-Acre Road
Canterbury, Kent County,
England
Tel: 1227 765431

Carlisle England
Langrigg Road
Morton Park
Carlisle, Cumbria County,
England
Tel: 1228 526767

Cheltenham England
Thirlestaine Road
Cheltenham, Gloucesteshire
County, England
Tel: 1242 523433

Coventry England
Riverside Close
Whitley
Coventry, West Midlands
County, England
Tel: 24 7630 3316

Crawley England
Old Horsham Road
Crawley, West Sussex
County, England
Tel: 1293 516151

Douglas Isle of Man
Woodside-Woodburn Road
Douglas, England
Tel: 1624 675834

Exeter England
Wonford Road
Exeter, Devon County,
England
Tel: 1392 250723

Forest of Dean England
Wynols Hill
Queensway
Colesford, Gloucestershire
County, England
Tel: 1594 832904

Gillingham England
2 Twydall Lane
Gillingham, Kent County,
England
Tel: 1634 388900

Grimsby England
Linwood Avenue
Waltham Road
Grimsby, Lincolnshire
County, England
Tel: 1472 828876

Harborne England
38 Lordswood Road
Harborne
Birmingham, West Midlands,
England
Tel: 121 427 6858

Hastings England
2 Ledsham Avenue
St. Leonards-on-Sea, East
Sussex County, England
Tel: 1424 754563

Helston England
Clodgey Lane
Helston, Cornwall County,
England
Tel: 1326 564503

High Wycombe England
743 London Road
High Wycombe,
Buckinghamshire County,
England
Tel: 1494 459979

Huddersfield England
12 Halifax Road
Birchencliffe
Huddersfield, West Yorkshire
County, England
Tel: 1484 454573

Hull England
725 Holderness Road
Hull, Yorkshire County,
England
Tel: 1482 701439

Ipswich England
42 Sidegate Lane West
Ipswich, Suffolk, England
Tel: 1473 723182

Kings Lynn England
Reffley Lane
Kings Lynn, Norfolk County,
England
Tel: 1553 670000

Lancaster England
Overangle Road
Morecambe, Lancashire
County, England
Tel: 1524 33571

Leeds England
Vesper Road
Leeds, West Yorkshire
County, England
Tel: 113 258 5297

Leicester England
Wakerley Road
Leicester, Leicestershire
County, England
Tel: 116 249 0099

Lichfield England
Purcell Avenue
Lichfield, Staffordshire,
England
Tel: 1543 414843

Lincoln England
Skellingthorpe Road
Lincoln, Lincolnshire County,
England
Tel: 1522 680117

Liverpool England
4 Mill Bank
Liverpool, Merseyside
County, England
Tel: 151 252 0614

London England Hyde Park
64-68 Exhibition Road
South Kensington
London, England
Tel: 20 7589 8561

**London England
Wandsworth**
149 Nightingale Lane
Balham
London, England
Tel: 20 8673 6741

Lowestoft England
165 Yarmouth Road
Lowestoft, Suffolk, England
Tel: 1502 573851

Macclesfield England
Victoria Road
Macclesfield, Cheshire
County, England
Tel: 1625 427236

Maidstone England
76B London Road
Maidstone, Kent County,
England
Tel: 1622 757811

Manchester England
Altrincham Road
Wythenshawe
Manchester, England
Tel: 0161 902 9279

Mansfield England
Southridge Drive
Mansfield, Nottinghamshire
County, England
Tel: 1623 626729

**Newcastle-Under-Lyme
England**
The Brampton
Newcastle-Under-Lyme,
Staffordshire County,
England
Tel: 1782 630178

Newchapel England
The London Temple
West Park Road
Newchapel
Nr Lingfield, Surrey County,
England

Newport England
Chestnut Close
Shide Road
Newport, Isle of Wight
County, England
Tel: 1983 532833

Northampton England
137 Harlstone Road
Northampton,
Northamptonshire County,
England
Tel: 160 458 7630

Norwich England
19 Greenways
Eaton
Norwich, Norfolk County,
England
Tel: 1603 452440

Nottingham England
Stanhome Square
West Bridgford
Nottingham,
Nottinghamshire County,
England
Tel: 115 914 4255

Orpington England
Station Approach
Orpington, Kent County,
England
Tel: 1689 837342

Peterborough England
Cottesmore Close, off
Atherstone Ave
Netherton Estate
Peterborough,
Cambridgeshire County,
England
Tel: 1733 263374

Plymouth England
Mannamead Road
Plymouth, Devon County,
England
Tel: 1752 668666

Pontefract England
Park Villas Drive
Pontefract, West Yorkshire
County, England
Tel: 1977 600308

Poole England
8 Mount Road
Parkstone
Poole, Dorset County,
England
Tel: 1202 730646

Portsmouth England
Kingston Crescent
Portsmouth, Hampshire,
England
Tel: 23 9269 6243

Preston England
Reception Building
Temple Way
Chorley, Lancashire County,
England
Tel: 1257 226145

Rawtenstall England
Haslingden Road
Rawtenstall, Lancashire
County, England
Tel: 1706 213460

Reading England
280 The Meadway
Tilehurst
Reading, Berkshre County,
England
Tel: 1189 410211

Redditch England
321 Evesham Road
Crabbs Cross
Redditch, Worcestershire
County, England
Tel: 1527 401543

Scarborough England
Stepheny Drive at Whitby
Road
Scarborough, North
Yorkshire County, England
Tel: 1723 501026

Sheffield England
Wheel Lane
Grenoside
Sheffield, Yorkshire County,
England
Tel: 114 245 3124

St. Helier England
Rue de la Vallee
St Mary, Jersey County,
Channel Islands, England
Tel: 1534 482171

St. Albans England
London Road at Cutenhoe
Road
Luton, Bedfordshire County,
England
Tel: 1582 482234

St. Austell England
Kingfisher Drive
St. Austell, Cornwall County,
England
Tel: 1726 69912

Staines England
41 Kingston Road

Staines, Middlesex County,
England
Tel: 1784 462627

Stevenage England
Buckthorne Avenue
Stevenage, Hertfordshire
County, England
Tel: 1438 351553

Sunderland England
Linden Road, off Queen
Alexander Road
Sunderland, Tyne & Wear
County, England
Tel: 191 528 5787

Sutton Coldfield England
185 Penns Lane
Sutton Coldfield, West
Midlands County, England
Tel: 121 386 1690

Telford England
72 Glebe Street
Wellington, Shropshire
County, England
Tel: 1952 257443

Thetford England
Station Road
Thetford, Norfolk County,
England
Tel: 1842 755472

Trowbridge England
Brook Road
Trowbridge, Wiltshire
County, England
Tel: 1225 777097

Watford England
Hempstead Road
Watford, Hertfordshire
County, England
Tel: 1923 251471

Wednesfield England
Linthouse Lane

Wednesfield
Wolverhampton, England
Tel: 1902 724097

Weymouth England
396 Chickerell Road
Weymouth, Dorset County,
England

Worcester England
Canada Way
Lower Wick
Worcester, Worcestershire
County, England
Tel: 1432 352751

Worthing England
Goring Street
Worthing, West Sussex
County, England
Tel: 1903 765790

Yate England
Wellington Road
Yate, Avon County, England
Tel: 1454 323004

Yeovil England
Forest Hill
Yeovil, Somerset County,
England
Tel: 1935 426817

York England
West Bank
Acomb
York, Yorkshire County,
England
Tel: 1904 786784

FRANCE

Angers France
169, Rue de Letenduere
F-49000
Angers, Loire-Atlantique,
France
Tel: 33-2-41802866

Arras France
64 Bis, Rue Winston Churchill
Arras F-62000, Pas-de-Calais,
France
Tel: 33-21-500217

Bayonne France
3, Allee Bonne Fontaine
Lotissement de l'Union
Anglet F-64600, Pyrenees-
Atlantiques, France
Tel: 33-5-59521372

Bergerac France
24, Rue Saint Louis
Bergerac F-24100,
Dordogne, France
Tel: 33-5-53583633

Bordeaux France
10, Rue Pierre Romain
Talence
TALENCE F-33400, Gironde,
France
Tel: 33-5-56374636

Brest France
1, Place de Strasbourg
Brest F-29200, Finistere,
France
Tel: 33-2-98417242

Caen France
2, Rue Pierre Anne
Caen F-14000, Calvados,
France
Tel: 33-231-830988

Calais France
1, Quai de l'Yser
Calais F62100, Pas-de-Calais,
France
Tel: 33-3-21974468

Cannes France
80, Boulevard du Perier
Le Cannet F-06110, Alpes-
Maritimes, France
Tel: 33-4-92181567

Carcassonne France
17, Rue Henri Gout
Carcassonne F-11000, Aude,
France
Tel: 33-568-723284

Cergy-Pontoise
1, Rue des Merites
Cergy Pontoisse, Val-d'Oise,
France
Tel: 33-1-34248538

Chambery France
75, Avenue du General
Leclerc
Chambery, Savoie, France
Tel: 33-4-79629948

Charleville-Meziere France
31, Avenue du Marechal
Leclerc
Charleville-Meziere,
Ardennes, France
Tel: 33-3-24561634

Clermont-Ferrand France
298, Rue de L'Oradou
Clermont-Ferrand, Puy-de-
Dome, France
Tel: 33-4-73275036

Compiegne France
37 quai du close des Roses
60200 Compiegne, France
Tel: 33-3-44860285

Dijon France
15, Rue Pere Ch. du Foucault
Dijon, Cote-d'Or, France
Tel: 33-3-80421833

Dunkerque France
Rue De Bruxelles, ZAC de
Boermhol
Coudekerque-Branche,
Nord, France
Tel: 33-3-28605136

Evry France
20, Boulevard Louise Michel
Evry, Essonne, France
Tel: 33-1-69911365

Grenoble France
74, Cours de la Liberation
Grenoble, Isere, France
Tel: 33-4-76841596

Le Havre France
130 Boulevard de Strasbourg
Le Havre, Seine-Maritime,
France
Tel: 33-2-35412959

Le Mans France
91, Rue d'Isaac
Chemin Departemental
Le Mans, Sarthe, France
Tel: 33-2-43814180

Lille France
1 rue Breve-Pont-de-Boise
F 59650 Villeneuve d'Ascq,
Nord, France
Tel: 33-320-611117

Limoges France
45, Rue Gaston Charlet
Limoges, Haute-Vienne,
France
Tel: 33-5-55500534

Lyon France
10 avenue de Verdun
F 69130 Ecully, Rhone,
France
Tel: 33-4-78330074

Marseille Borely France
7, avenue du Parc Borely
Marseille, Bouches-du-
Rhone, France
Tel: 33-4-91766785

Meaux France
1, Voie Gallo-Romaine
Quincy Voisins, Seine-et-

Marne, France
Tel: 33-160-092566

Melun France
545, Rue des Freres Thibault
Dammarie les Lys, Seine-et-
Marne, France

Metz France
11, Rue Maurice Bompard
Metz, Moselle, France
Tel: 33-387-368235
{LCHD]Montpellier France
66, Rue Daunou
Montpellier, Herault, France
Tel: 33-4-67079319

Mulhouse France
29, Rue Robert Meyer
Pfastatt, Haut-Rhin, France
Tel: 33-389-503782

Nancy France
69, Rue de Badonviller
Nancy, Meurthe-et-Moselle,
France
Tel: 33-383-964001

Nantes France
123, Route de Sainte Luce
Nantes, Loire-Atlantique,
France
Tel: 33-2-40 50 68 45

Nice France
5, Avenue Therese
Nice, Alpes-Maritimes,
France
Tel: 33-4-93530078

Nimes France
55, Chemin du Mas de
Vignolles
Nimes, Gard, France
Tel: 33-4-66297482

Nogent France
2, bis Rue Lepoutre
Nogent-sur-Marne, Val-de-

Marne, France
Tel: 33-148-63164

Orleans France
45, Avenue de la Petite
Espere
St-Jean-de-la-Ruelle, Loiret,
France
Tel: 33-2-38437509

Paris France Lilas
64, Rue Romainville
Paris, Ville-de-Paris, France
Tel: 33-142-452929

Pau France
47 rue Clement Ader
Pau, Pyrenees-Atlantiques,
France
Tel: 33-5-59320540

Perigueux France
148, Rue des Combes
Perigueux, Dordogne,
France
Tel: 33-5-53039865

Perpignan France
25, Rue Philippe Lebon
Perpignan, Pyrenees-
Orientales, France
Tel: 33-4-68508727

Reims France
5, Rue Bazin
Reims, Marne, France
Tel: 33-3-26091180

Rennes France
53, Rue de Rennes
Cesson-Sevigne, Ille-et-
Vilaine, France
Tel: 33-2-99836622

Rouen France
38, Rue Saint-Romain
Rouen, Seine-Maritime,
France
Tel: 33-235-897460

Saint Die France
224, Rue du Haut d'Arnold
Saint Die, Vosges, France
Tel: 33-329-553781

Saint Etienne France
4, Rue de Robinson
Saint Etienne, Loire, France
Tel: 33-4-77339426

Saint Quentin France
15 Bis, Boulevard Victor
Hugo 15
Saint Quentin, Aisne, France
Tel: 33-3-23052381

Strasbourg France
100, Route du General de
Gaulle
Schiltigheim, Bas-Rhin,
France
Tel: 33-388-836265

Toul France
Rue Robert Schumann
Ecrouves, Meurthe-et-
Moselle, France
Tel: 33-383-632896

Toulon France
Bat. L'Eglantine A
Toulon, Var, France
Tel: 33-4-94611400

Toulouse France
10, Avenue de Levaur
Toulouse, Haut-Garonne,
France
Tel: 33-5-61119281

Tours France
70, Boulevard de Chinon
Joue les Tours, Indre-et-
Loire, France
Tel: 33-2-47746647

Troyes France
49 Bis, Rue Jean Nesmy

Troyes, Aube, France
Tel: 33-325-812171

Valence France
8, Rue Baudin
Valence, Drome, France
Tel: 33-4-75429038

Valenciennes France
98, Avenue Anatole France
Anzin, Nord, France
Tel: 33-3-27299454

Versailles France
5, Rond-Point de l'Alliance
Versailles, Yvelines, France
Tel: 33-1-34221589
{LAHD}Germany
Aachen Germany
Hammerweg 4
Aachen, Nordrhein-
Westfalen, Germany
Tel: 49-241-76494

GERMANY

Annaberg-Buchholz Germany
Bahnhofstrasse 19
Annaberg-Buchholz,
Sachsen, Germany
Tel: 49-3733-3416

Augsburg Germany
Agnes-Bernauer-Strasse 32
Augsburg, Bayern, Germany
Tel: 49-821-5899068

Bad Kreuznach Germany
Am Kapellenberg 9
Bad Kreuznach, Rheinland
Pfalz, Germany
Tel: 49-0671-46347

Baumholder Germany
Gewerbegebiet 8
Baumholder, Rheinland
Pfalz, Germany
Tel: 49-6783-980565

Berlin Germany
Klingelhoefer Strasse 24
Berlin, Berlin, Germany
Tel: 49-30-25794336

Bielefeld Germany
Hainteich Strasse 80
Bielefeld, Nordrhein-
Westfalen, Germany
Tel: 49-521-881966

Bitburg Germany
Thilmanystrasse 8
Bitburg, Rheinland Pfalz,
Germany
Tel: 49-6561-5873

Bonn Germany
Rene-Schickele-Strasse 8
Bonn, Nordrhein-Westfalen,
Germany
Tel: 49-228-645978

Brandenburg Germany
Baeckerstrasse 16
Brandenburg, Brandenburg,
Germany
Tel: 49-3381-224379

Braunschweig Germany
Triftweg 55
Braunschweig,
Niedersachsen, Germany
Tel: 49-531-55322

Bremen Germany
Emmastrasse / Ottilie-
Hoffmann-Strasse 2
Bremen, Bremen, Germany
Tel: 49-421-2238557

Bremerhaven Germany
Parkstrasse 28
Bremerhaven,
Niedersachsen, Germany
Tel: 49-471-88937

Celle Germany
Waldweg 2

Celle, Niedersachsen,
Germany
Tel: 49-5141-23447

Coburg Germany
Eupenstrasse 1
Coburg, Bayern, Germany
Tel: 49-9561-10643

Darmstadt Germany
Richard Wagner Weg 78
Darmstadt, Hessen, Germany
Tel: 49-6151-718429

Dortmund Germany
Carl-von-Ossietzky-Strasse 5
Dortmund, Nordrhein-
Westfalen, Germany
Tel: 49-231-718256

Dresden Germany
Tiergartenstrasse 40
Dresden, Sachsen, Germany
Tel: 49-351-4716391

Duisburg Germany
Essenberger Strasse 251
Duisburg, Nordrhein-
Westfalen, Germany
Tel: 49-203-315950

Dusseldorf Germany
Morsenbroicher Weg 184 A
Dusseldorf, Nordrhein-
Westfalen, Germany
Tel: 49-211-625846

Ellwangen Germany
Dr. Adolf Schneider Strasse 9
Ellwangen, Baden-
Wurttemberg, Germany
Tel: 49-7961-52357

Erfurt Germany
Hochheimer Strasse 14
Erfurt, Thuringen, Germany
Tel: 49-361-2252741

Esslingen Germany
Hegensbergerstrasse 32
Esslingen, Baden-
Wurttemberg, Germany
Tel: 49-711-311428

Forst Germany
Spremberger Strasse 52
Forst, Brandenburg,
Germany
Tel: 49-3562-984081

Frankfurt Germany
Eckenheimer Landstrasse
262-264
Frankfurt, Hessen, Germany
Tel: 49-69-54806899

Freiberg Germany
Hainichener Strasse 64
Freiberg, Sachsen, Germany
Tel: 49-3731-359620

Friedrichsdorf Germany
Taunusstrasse 15
Friedrichsdorf, Hessen,
Germany
Tel: 49-6172-72096

Gorlitz Germany
Julius-Motterlerstrasse 29
Gorlitz, Sachsen, Germany
Tel: 49-3581-855565

Gottingen Germany
Godehardstrasse 26
Gottingen, Niedersachsen,
Germany
Tel: 49-551-63918

Halberstadt Germany
Mozart Strasse 7
Halberstadt, Sachsen Anhalt,
Germany
Tel: 49-3941-21858

Halle Germany
Rennbahnring 9

D-06124 Halle, Sachsen,
Germany
Tel: 49-345-6950039

Hamburg Germany
Wartenau 20
Hamburg, Hamburg,
Germany
Tel: 49-40-2504573

Hamm Germany
Hammer Strasse 215
Hamm, Nordrhein-
Westfalen, Germany
Tel: 49-2381-599193

Hanau Germany
Donaustrasse 38
Hanau, Hessen, Germany
Tel: 49-6181-12280

Hannover Germany
Hildesheimer Strasse 344
Hannover, Niedersachsen,
Germany
Tel: 49-511-8699724

Heidelberg Germany
Schroderstrasse 94
Heidelberg, Baden-
Wurttemberg, Germany
Tel: 49 6221 401884

Heilbronn Germany
Romerstrasse 151
Heilbronn, Baden-
Wurttemberg, Germany
Tel: 49-7131-44520

Ingolstadt Germany
Durer Weg 8
Kaufbeuren, Bayern,
Germany
Tel: 49-8341-68510

Kaiserslautern Germany
Servicemens
Lauter Strasse 1
Kaiserslautern, Rheinland

Pfalz, Germany
Tel: 49-(0) 631-95245

Karlsruhe Germany
Ernst-Frey-Strasse 7
Karlsruhe, Baden-
Wurttemberg, Germany
Tel: 49-721-815798

Kassel Germany
Tischbein Strasse 61
Kassel, Hessen, Germany
Tel: 49-561-26543

Kiel Germany
Kieler weg 160
Kiel, Schleswig-Holstein,
Germany
Tel: 49-431-91733

Koblenz Germany
Moltkestrasse 3
Koblenz, Rheinland Pfalz,
Germany
Tel: 49-0261-17747

Koln Germany
Forststrasse 130
Koln, Nordrhein-Westfalen,
Germany
Tel: 49-221-9792055

Kothen Germany
Wathelosring 27
Gewerbegebeit
Kothen, Sachsen-Anhalt,
Germany
Tel: 49-3496-510223

Krefeld Germany
Untergath 25
Krefeld-Fischeln, Nordrhein-
Westfalen, Germany
Tel: 49-2151-399227

Landshut Germany
Ahornstrasse 115
Ergolding, Bayern, Germany
Tel: 49-871-78541

Langen Germany
Birkenstrasse 22
Langen, Hessen, Germany
Tel: 49-6103-22649

Langenhorn Germany
Eberhofweg 90
Hamburg, Hamburg,
Germany
Tel: 49-40-5207273

Leer Germany
Friesenstrasse 80
Leer, Niedersachsen,
Germany
Tel: 49-491-67870

Leipzig Germany
Oeserstrasse 39
Leipzig, Sachsen, Germany
Tel: 49-341-4793949

Lubeck Germany
Rabenstrasse 5
Lubeck, Schleswig-Holstein,
Germany
Tel: 49-451-343556

Ludwigsburg Germany
Riedstrasse 20
Freiberg, Baden-
Wurttemberg, Germany
Tel: 49-7141-75877

Mannheim Germany
Lampertheimer Strasse 98
Mannheim, Baden-
Wurttemberg, Germany
Tel: 49-621-745080

Marburg Germany
Marburger Strasse 90
Marburg, Hessen, Germany
Tel: 49-6441-81219

Michelstadt Germany
Kreuzweg 10
Michelstadt, Rheinland Pfalz,

Germany
Tel: 49-6061-73757

Minden Germany
Derfflinger Strasse 52
Minden, Nordrhein-
Westfalen, Germany
Tel: 49-571-46784

Monchengladbach Germany
An der Landwehr 51
Monchengladbach,
Nordrhein-Westfalen,
Germany
Tel: 49-2161-206402

Munich Germany
Ruckertstrasse 2
Munchen, Bayern, Germany
Tel: 49-089-53 80 873

Neubrandenburg Germany
Seestrasse 4
Neubrandenburg,
Mecklenburg-Vorpommern,
Germany
Tel: 49-395-5841790

Neumunster Germany
Kieler Strasse 333
Neumunster, Schleswig-
Holstein, Germany
Tel: 49-432-939887

Nurnberg Germany
Kesslerplatz 8
Nurnberg, Bayern, Germany
Tel: 49-911-581367

Offenburg Germany
Hildastrasse 55
Offenburg, Baden-
Wurttemberg, Germany
Tel: 49-0781-36523

Oldenburg Germany
Friedhofsweg 21
Oldenburg, Niedersachsen,

Germany
Tel: 49-441-776991

Osnabruck Germany
Siebensternstrasse 65
Osnabruck, Niedersachsen,
Germany
Tel: 49-541-803293

Paderborn Germany
Schultze-Delitzsch-Strasse 19
Paderborn, Nordrhein-
Westfalen, Germany
Tel: 49-5251-61850

Passau Germany
Neubergerstrasse 123
Passau, Bayern, Germany
Tel: 49-851-7561036

Pinneberg Germany
Saarlandstrasse 11
Pinneberg, Schleswig-
Holstein, Germany
Tel: 49-4101-29809

Plauen Germany
Loberingstrasse 25
Plauen, Thuringen, Germany
Tel: 49-3741-441031

Rahlstedt Germany
Saseler Strasse 1
Hamburg, Hamburg,
Germany
Tel: 49-40-6791444

Regensburg Germany
Domplatz 6
Regensburg, Bayern,
Germany
Tel: 49-941-560831

Rheinpfalz Gemany
Karl-Raeder-Strasse 4
Limburgerhof, Rheinland
Pfalz, Germany
Tel: 49-6236-61927

Rosenheim Germany
Finsterwalder Strasse 46
Rosenheim, Bayern,
Germany
Tel: 49-8031-42763

Rostock Germany
Budapester Strasse 80 A
Rostock, Mecklenburg-
Vorpommern, Germany
Tel: 49-381-2005880

Saarbrucken Germany
Kalmanstrasse 88
Saarbrucken, Saarland,
Germany
Tel: 49-681-44837

Schwenningen Germany
Beim Schutzenwiesle 10
Villingen-Schwenningen,
Baden-Wurttemberg,
Germany
Tel: 49-7720-5655

Schwerin Germany
Schlossgartenallee 18 A
Schwerin, Mecklenburg-
Vorpommern, Germany
Tel: 49-385-568361

Spandau Germany
Hugelschanze 10-12
Spandau
Berlin, Berlin, Germany
Tel: 49-30-3752194

Stadthagen Germany
Ecke Schachtstrasse /
Jahnstrasse
Stadthagen, Niedersachsen,
Germany
Tel: 49-5721-3130

Stuttgart Germany
Birkenwaldstrasse 46
Stuttgart, Baden-
Wurttemberg, Germany
Tel: 49-711-2572281

Stuttgart Germany II
Deidesheimer Strasse 39
Stuttgart, Baden-
Wurttemberg, Germany
Tel: 49-711-8893910

Tubingen Germany
Mohlstrasse 26
Tubingen, Baden-
Wurttemberg, Germany
Tel: 49-7071-26674

Ulm Germany
Baumgartenstrasse 5
Neu Ulm, Baden-
Wurttemberg, Germany
Tel: 49-731-87602

Waiblingen Germany
Fronackerstrasse 70
Waiblingen, Baden-
Wurttemberg, Germany
Tel: 49-7151-18674

Wesel Germany
Schermbecker Landstrasse
34-36
Wesel, Nordrhein-Westfalen,
Germany
Tel: 49-281-8110576

Wetzlar Germany
Im Amtmann 2
Wetzlar-Blankenfeld,
Hessen, Germany
Tel: 49-6441-77770

Wiesbaden Germany
Genealogische
Forschungsstelle
Erich Ollenhauer Strasse 36
Wiesbaden, Hessen,
Germany
Tel: 0049-0611-841833

Wilhelmshaven Germany
Herbart Strasse 83
Wilhelmshaven,

Niedersachsen, Germany
Tel: 49-4421-37250

Wolfsburg Germany
Hesslinger Strasse 15
Wolfsburg, Niedersachsen,
Germany
Tel: 49-5361-291504

Wolgast Germany
Tannenkampweg 81
Wolgast, Mecklenburg-
Vorpommern, Germany
Tel: 49-3836-600444

Worms Germany
Karthaeuserstrasse 25
Trier, Rheinland Pfalz,
Germany
Tel: 49-6501-74577

Wuppertal Germany
Martin-Luther-Strasse 6
Wuppertal, Nordrhein-
Westfalen, Germany
Tel: 49-202-87207

Wurzburg Germany
Frauenhofer Strasse 8
Wurzburg, Bayern, Germany
Tel: 49 931 284866

Zwickau Germany
Gellertstrasse 1A
Zwickau, Sachsen, Germany
Tel: 49-375-785282

HUNGARY

Budapest Hungary
Huvosvolgyi Ut 94 B
Budapest, Hungary
Tel: 36-1-1353698

ICELAND

Reykjavik Iceland
Asabraut 2
I-210

Gardabaer, Iceland
Tel: +354-5547103Reykjavik
Iceland

IRELAND

Cork Ireland
Scarsfield Road
Wilton
Cork, Co Cork County,
Ireland
Tel: 353 21 4341737

Dublin Ireland
Finglas Road
Glasnevin
Dublin 9, Ireland

Limerick Ireland
Doradoyle Road
Limerick, Limerick County,
Ireland

ITALY

Agrigento Italy
Via Catania 132
Agrigento, Sicilia, Italy
Tel: 39-91-341001

Alessandria Italy
Via XXIV Maggio 12
Alessandria, Piemonte, Italy
Tel: 39-131-264302

Bari Italy Puglia
Via Cancello Rotto 30
Bari, Puglia, Italy
Tel: 39-80-5010380

Bergamo Italy
Via Carducci 142/168
Bergamo, Lombardia, Italy
Tel: 39-35-401772

Bolzano Italy
Via Druso 339
Bolzano, Trentino-Alto

Adige, Italy
Tel: 39-0471-930780

Brescia Italy
Via Milano 138
Brescia, Lombardia, Italy
Tel: 39-030-312156

Cagliari Italy
Via Peretti (fronte Osp.
Brotzu)
Pirri, Sardegna, Italy
Tel: 39-70-530043

Catania Italy
Via Giuseppe Laino 10 s/n
Localita Fuedo Grande
I-95126 Catania, Sicilia, Italy
Tel: 39-95-7125128

Como Italy
Via Varesina 175 A
Como, Lombardia, Italy
Tel: 39-31-505032

Cosenza Italy
Corso D'Italia 142
Cosenza, Calabria, Italy

Crotone Italy
Via Venezia 99
Crotone, Calabria, Italy

Firenze Italy
Via Becciolini 9
Firenze, Toscana, Italy
Tel: 39-55-4222403

Foggia Italy
Via Napoli 12
Foggia, Puglia, Italy
Tel: 39-881-742582

Genova Italy
Via R. Ceccardi 4/2
Genova, Liguria, Italy
Tel: 39-10-532741

La Spezia Italy
Via Del Molo 64 A
La Spezia, Liguria, Italy
Tel: 39-187-517893

Livorno Italy
Via Giuseppe Coen
Livorno, Toscana, Italy
Tel: 39-586-857554

Messina Sicily
Via San Giacomo Isolato, 11E
Isolato 1/
I-98122 Messina, Sicilia, Italy
Tel: 39-90-718029

Milano Italy
Viale Don Orione 10
Milano, Lombardia, Italy
Tel: 39-2-2847416

Modena Italy
Via Cilea 36
Modena, Emilia-Romagna,
Italy
Tel: 39-059-370745

Napoli Italy
Corso Vittorio Emanuele
494C
Villa del Pino Fabb. C
Napoli, Campania, Italy
Tel: 39-81-5490012

Novara Italy
Via Michelangelo
Buonarrotti 22A
Novara, Piemonte, Italy
Tel: 39-321-611185

Palermo Italy
Via Catania 132
Palermo, Sicilia, Italy
Tel: 39-91-341001

Pescara Italy
Via Trilussa 20
Pescara, Ambruzzo, Italy
Tel: 39-85-377107

Piacenza Italy
Via Felice Frasi 4
Piacenza, Emilia-Romagna,
Italy
Tel: 39-523-388408

Pisa Italy
Via Achille Grandi-Localita
Barbaricina 1
Pisa, Toscana, Italy
Tel: 39-50-520136

Pordenone Italy
Via San Quirino 62
Pordenone, Friuli-Venezia,
Italy
Tel: 39-434-361727

Ragusa Italy
Viale Europa 167
Ragusa, Sicilia, Italy
Tel: 39-932-642004

Rimini Italy
{LISTlVia del Capriolo 12
Rimini, Emilia-Romagna,
Italy
Tel: 39-541-753075

Roma Italy
Piazza Carnaro 20
I-00141 Roma, Lazio, Italy
Tel: 39-68-7182113

Sassari Italy
Via Adelasia 1
Sassari, Sardegna, Italy
Tel: 39-79-237805

Siracusa Italy
Via M. Politi Lauden 10
Siracusa, Sicilia, Italy
Tel: 39-931-69980

Taranto Italy
Via Lorenzo Snow (contrada
Rahu)
Taranto, Puglia, Italy
Tel: 39-99-7796738

Torino Italy
Corso Grosseto 53/7
Torino, Piemonte, Italy
Tel: 39-11-251669

Trapani Italy
Via Della Provincia 5/7
Casa Santa, Sicilia, Italy
Tel: 39-923-563622

Trieste Italy
Gorizia, Friuli-Venezia, Italy
Tel: 39-481-522366

Venezia Italy
Via Castellana 124 C
Zelarino, Zelarino, Italy
Tel: 39-041-908181

Verona Italy
Via Luzzatti 41
Verona, Veneto, Italy
Tel: 39-45-521088

LITHUANIA
Tallinn Estonia
Dala 6
Tallinn, Lithuania

LUXEMBOURG
Luxembourg Branch
57, Rue de Beggen
Luxembourg, Luxembourg
Tel: 352-423561

NETHERLANDS
Amsterdam Netherlands
Zaaiersweg 17
Amsterdam, Noord-Holland,
Netherlands
Tel: 31-20-6944990

Apeldoorn Netherlands
Boerhaave Straat 62
Apeldoorn, Gelderland,

Netherlands
Tel: 31-55-5211179

Den Bosch Netherlands
Boschveldweg 17
5211 VG 's-Hertogenbosch,
Zuid Holland, Netherlands
Tel: (31) 78-6141903

Den Helder Netherlands
Texelstroomlaan 4
Den Helder, Noord-Holland,
Netherlands
Tel: 31-223-623074

Dordrecht Netherlands
Singel 312
Dordrecht, Zuid Holland,
Netherlands
Tel: 31-78-6135537

Groningen Netherlands
Paterswoldse Weg 531
Groningen, Groningen,
Netherlands
Tel: 31-50-5256271

Leeuwarden Netherlands
Sophialaan 3
Leeuwarden, Friesland,
Netherlands
Tel: 31-58-2135361

Rotterdam Netherlands
Oosteinde 73
Rotterdam, Zuid Holland,
Netherlands
Tel: 31-10-2142578

Utrecht Netherlands
Prinses Irenelaan 51 A
Utrecht, Utrecht,
Netherlands
Tel: 31-30-2444218

Zoetermeer Netherlands
Westwaarts 56
Zoetermeer, Zuid Holland,

Netherlands
Tel: 31-79-3312643

NORTHERN IRELAND

Belfast Northern Ireland
403 Holywood Road
Belfast, Co Down County,
Northern Ireland
Tel: 28 9076 8250

Coleraine Northern Ireland
8 Sandelfield
Coleraine, Co Londonderry
County, Northern Ireland
Tel: 2870 321214

**Londonderry Northern
Ireland**
Racecourse Road
Belmont Estate
Londonderry, Londonderry
County, Northern Ireland

NORWAY

Bergen Norway
Asbakken 14
N-5032
Minde, Bergen, Hordaland
County, Norway
Tel: +47-55910510

Bodo Norway
Gamle Riksvei 112
N-8013
Bodo, Norway

Drammen Norway
Ellings Holts Gate 15
N-3022
Drammen, Buskerud County,
Norway
Tel: +47-32822943

Fredrikstad Norway
Rosenlund 20
N-1617

Fredrikstad, Ostfold County,
Norway
Tel: +47-69397285

Kristiansand Norway
Slettheiveien 80
Kristiansand, Vest-Agder
County, Norway
Tel: +47-38026455

Moss Norway
Nesveien 29
N-1500
Moss, Ostfold County,
Norway
Tel: +47-69275455

Oslo Norway
Hekkveien 9
N-0571
Oslo, Akershus County,
Norway
Tel: +47-22384314

Skien Norway
Sverresgatan 19
N-3921
Portsgrunn, Telemark
County, Norway
Tel: +47-35554101

Stavanger Norway
Box 308
N-4000
Stavanger, Rogaland County,
Norway
Tel: +47-51589977

PORTUGAL

Alverca Portugal
Rua do Acougue Velho
Alverca do Ribatejo, Lisboa,
Portugal
Tel: 351-019584919

Angra do Heroismo Portugal
Rua Professor Monjardino 45

Angra do Heroismo, Acores,
Portugal
Tel: 351-95628477

Barreiro Portugal
Rua 1o de Dezembro 51
Barreiro, Setubal, Portugal
Tel: 351-12156603

Beja Portugal
Rua Dom Manuel I, no. 9
Beja, Beja, Portugal

Benfica Portugal
Rua Jorge Barradas 14-B
Lisboa, Lisboa, Portugal

Coimbra Portugal
Rua Pedro Nunes
Quinta Vale das Flores
Coimbra, Coimbra, Portugal
Tel: 351-39-718437

Faro Portugal
Rua Pintor Artur Costa
Antiga
Faro, Faro, Portugal
Tel: 351-89801488

Foz Portugal
Avenida Marechal Gomes da
Costa 774
Porto, Porto, Portugal
Tel: 351-122-6172850

Funchal Portugal
Rua Tenente Coronel
Sarmento 25
P-9000-020Funchal, Madeira,
Portugal
Tel: 351-91236860

Guimaraes Portugal
Rua Dom Joao IV
Guimaraes, Braga, Portugal

Leiria Portugal
Leiria, Leiria, Portugal
Tel: 351-044823617

Lisboa Portugal
Avenida Almirante Gago
Coutinho 93
Lisboa, Lisboa, Portugal
Tel: 351-18463067

Miratejo Portugal
Rua Ferreira de Castro 10-A
Miratejo
P-2855 Corroios, Setubal,
Portugal
Tel: 351-1-2552222

Oeiras Portugal
Avenida da Republica 47
Nova Oeiras, Lisboa,
Portugal
Tel: 351-14437727

Ovar Portugal
Rua Gomes Freire 1
Ovar, Aveiro, Portugal
Tel: 351-56575470

Ponta Delgada Portugal
Rua Manuel Augusto
Amaral 18
Ponta Delgada, Acores,
Portugal
Tel: 351-9626409

Portimao Portugal
Rua Dr. Adelino Amaro da
Costa s/n
(junto ao Hotel Tropimar)
Portimao, Faro, Portugal
Tel: 351-8284544

Porto Portugal
Rua Agostinho de Campos
166
Porto, Porto, Portugal
Tel: 351-2520748

Povoa do Varzim Portugal
Rua Bocal da Gandara
Povoa do Varzim, Porto,
Portugal
Tel: 351-252626072

Setubal Portugal
Av. General Daniel de
Sousa,48-50
P-2900 Setubal, Setubal,
Portugal
Tel: 351-65772693

Viseu Portugal
Rua Candido dos Reis 81
Viseu, Viseu, Portugal
Tel: 351-32425559
{LAHD}Scotland
Aberdeen Scotland
North Anderson Drive
Aberdeen, Grampian
County, Scotland
Tel: 1224 692206

SCOTLAND

Alloa Scotland
Grange Road
Westend Park
Alloa, Scotland
Tel: 1259 211148

Alness Scotland
Kilmonivaig
Seafield
Portmahomack, Ross-shire
County, Scotland
Tel: 1862 871631

Dumfries Scotland
36 Edinburgh Road
Albanybank
Dumfries, Dumfies-shire
County, Scotland
Tel: 1387 254865

Dundee Scotland
Bingham Terrace
Dundee, Tayside County,
Scotland
Tel: 1382 451247

Edinburgh Scotland
30A Colinton Road

Edinburgh, Midlothian
County, Scotland
Tel: 131 337 3049

Elgin Scotland
Pansport Road
Elgin, Morayshire County,
Scotland
Tel: 1343 546429

Glasgow Scotland
Julian Avenue
Glasgow, Strathclyde
County, Scotland
Tel: 141 357 1024

Inverness Scotland
13 Ness Walk
Inverness, Inverness-shire
County, Scotland
Tel: 1463 231220

Kilmarnock Scotland
1 Whatriggs Road
Kilmarnock, Ayrshire,
Scotland
Tel: 1563 526560

Kirkcaldy Scotland
Winifred Crescent
Forth Park
Kirkcaldy, Fifeshire County,
Scotland
Tel: 1592 640041

Lerwick Scotland
South Road
Lerwick, Zer Orq, Shetland
Islands, Scotland
Tel: 1595 695732

Paisley Scotland
Glenburn Road
Paisley, Renfrewshire
County, Scotland
Tel: 141 884 2780

Stornoway Scotland
Newton Street

Stornoway, Isle of Lewis
County, Scotland
Tel: 1851 870972

SPAIN

Albacete Spain
Calle Vicente Aleixandre 1
esq. Martinez de la Osa
Albacete, Albacete, Spain
Tel: 34-96-7247630

Alcala de Henares Spain
Calle Cuenca esq. San
Sebastian
28804
Alcala de Henares, Madrid,
Spain
Tel: 34-91-8812953

Alcoy Spain
Calle Oliver 27, bajo
3880
Alcoy, Alicante, Spain
Tel: 34-96-7247630

Algeciras Spain
Calle Sevilla 43
11201
Algeciras, Cadiz, Spain
Tel: 34-95-6604618

Alicante Spain
Calle El Aiun s/n
03010
Alicante, Alicante, Spain
Tel: 34-96-5247008

Aviles Spain
Gonzales Abarca 43-47
Aviles, Asturias, Spain
Tel: 34-98-5563581

Badajoz Spain
Avenida Ramon y Cajal 13
06001
Badajoz, Badajoz, Spain
Tel: 34-92-4221664

Badalona Spain
Calle Antiqua de Valencia
49-51
08913
Badalona, Barcelona, Spain
Tel: 34-93-3990751

Barcelona Spain
Avenida Virgen de
Montserrat 60
08024
Barcelona, Barcelona, Spain
Tel: 34-93-2108353

Bilbao Spain
Henao 52
48009
Bilboa, Vizcaya, Spain
Tel: 34-94-4240181

Burgos Spain
Calle Bartolome Ordonez 1,
bajo
09006
Burgos, Burgos, Spain

Cadiz Spain
C/Hibiscos 4
E-11007 Cadiz, Cadiz, Spain
Tel: 0034 956 264771

Cartagena Spain
Calle Jacinto Benavente 1
30290
Cartagena, Murcia, Spain
Tel: 34-968-503834

Cartarroja Spain
Patronato Pablo IV
Catarroja, Valencia, Spain

Cornella Spain
Calle Maladeta 61
08950
Espluges de Llobregat,
Barcelona, Spain
Tel: 34-93-4733148

El Ferrol Spain
Venezuela 7-9
15404
E-15404 El Ferrol, La Coruna,
Spain

Elche Spain
Camino de la Almazara s/n
03203
Elche, Alicante, Spain
Tel: 34-96-5421141

Fuerteventura Spain
Calle Maria Estada 36
35600
Puerto del Rosario, Las
Palmas, Spain

Gandia Spain
Carrer 2 de Mayo
c/v Jacinto Benavende y
Reyes Catolicos
46700
Gandia, Valencia, Spain

Jaen Spain
Calle Santa Maria del Valle
23009
Jaen, Jaen, Spain
Tel: 34-95-3275149

La Coruna Spain
Calle Bugallal Marchesi 5 BD
E-15008 La Coruna, La
Coruna, Spain
Tel: 34-98-1152746

**La Palmas de Gran
Canaria Spain**
Calle Luis Doreste Silva 50
35004
Las Palmas de Gran Canaria,
Las Palmas, Spain
Tel: 34-92-8242735

Leon Spain
Maximo Cayon Waldaliso 12
24005
Leon, Leon, Spain

Logrono Spain
6 Plaza de las Chiribitas s/n
(junto a la Escuela
de Turismo)
26004
Logrona, La Rioja, Spain

Lorca Spain
Calle Jeronimo Santa Fe
30800
Lorca, Murcia, Spain

Madrid Spain
Avenida Pablo Iglesias 22
28003
Madrid, Madrid, Spain
Tel: 34-91-5343416

Madrid Spain (Templo)
Calle del Templo nr.2
28030
Madrid, Madrid, Spain
Tel: 34-91-3017600

Malaga Spain
Calle Plaza de Babel 1
29005
Malaga, Malaga, Spain
Tel: 34-95-2240515

Mostoles Spain
Calle Pintor Miro 12, bloque
28 bis
28933
Mostoles, Madrid, Spain
Tel: 34-91-6642712

Murcia Spain
Calle Miguel de Unamuno
Santa Maria de Garcia
E-30009 Murcia, Murcia,
Spain
Tel: 34-968-503834

Oviedo Spain
Silla del Rey 3
33006
Oviedo, Asturias, Spain
Tel: 34-98-5275667

Pamplona Spain
Ronda de Ermitagana 16
(Parc 20 Sec 1)
31008
Pamplona, Navarra, Spain
Tel: 34-94-8175887

Ponferrada Spain
Calle Gomez Nunez 34,
entreplanta
24400
Ponferrada, Leon, Spain

Pontevedra Spain
Calle Avenida de Vigo, 15
entreplanta
36003
Pontevedra, Pontevedra,
Spain
Tel: 34-98-6862117

Sabadell Spain
Ronda de Poniente 179-181
Sabadell, Barcelona, Spain
Tel: 34-93-7268161

San Fernando Spain
Calle Isaac Peral 31
11100
San Fernando, Cadiz, Spain
Tel: 34-95-6594029

San Sebastian Spain
Catalina de Erauso 21
20010
San Sebastian, Guipuzcoa,
Spain

Santa Cruz de Tenerife Spain
Calle Poeta Hernandez
Amador 27
Santa Cruz de Tenerife,
Santa Cruz de Tenerife,
Spain
Tel: 34-92-2240387

Sevilla Spain
Santo Domingo de la
Calzada 14

Sevilla, Sevilla, Spain
Tel: 34-95-4377753

Tarragona Spain
Avenida Marques de
Montoliu 16
43022
Tarragona, Tarragona, Spain
Tel: 34-97-7241920

Terrassa Spain
Calle Pau Marsal 12
E-08222 Tarrasa, Tarragona,
Spain
Tel: 34-93-7853086

Torrejon de Ardoz Spain
Avenida Constitucion 155
28850
Torrejon de Ardoz, Madrid,
Spain
Tel: 34-91-6773091
{LCHD]Valencia Spain
Calle Polo y Peyrolon 17,
bajo
Valencia, Valencia, Spain
Tel: 34-96-3934803

Valladolid Spain
Calle de Leon 3, bajo
Valladolid, Valladolid, Spain
Tel: 34-98-3374657

Vilafranca Spain
Amalia Soler 7, primero
Vilafranca del Penedes,
Barcelona, Spain
Tel: 34-93-8171124

Vitoria Spain
Calle Pedro Asua 6
Vitoria, Alava, Spain
Tel: 34-94-5262193

Zaragoza Spain
Calle de Jesus Grazia
Zaragoza, Zaragoza, Spain
Tel: 34-97-6389806

SWEDEN

Alingsas Sweden
Safirgatan 2
N-44145
Alingsas, Alvsborg County,
Sweden
Tel: +46-16-322-14918

Boras Sweden
Kvibergsgatan 81
S-50263
Boras, Alvsborg County,
Sweden
Tel: 033-129744

Borlaenge Sweden
Vasagatan 8
S-78432
Borlaenge, Kopparberg
County, Sweden
Tel: +46- 243-15119

Jonkoping Sweden
Hagalundsgatan 2
S-55265
Jonkoping, Jonkoping
County, Sweden
Tel: +4636-710781

Lulea Sweden
Blomgatan 5
S-95154
Lulea, Norrbotten County,
Sweden
Tel: +46-920-225154

Malmoe Sweden
Vikingagatan 90
S-21774
Malmoe, Malmohus County,
Sweden
Tel: +46-40-263375

Orebro Sweden
Lingonstigen 2 A

S-70360
Orebro, Orebro County,
Sweden
Tel: +46-19 254870

Skelleftea Sweden
Nygatan 74
S-93134
Skelleftea, Vasterbotten
County, Sweden
Tel: +46-910-53046

Skovde Sweden
Niklasbergagatan 1
S-54136
Skovde, Skaraborg County,
Sweden
Tel: +46-500-85528

Sundsvall Sweden
Umeaevaegen 2
S-85266
Sundsvall, Vasternorrland
County, Sweden
Tel: +46-60-500350

Umeae Sweden
Glimmervaegen 9
S-90740
Umeae, Vasterbotten
County, Sweden
Tel: +46-90-196021

Uppsala Sweden
S:t Johannesgatan 41
S-75264
Uppsala, Sweden
Tel: +46-18-516574

Vastra Froelunda Sweden
Gnistgatan 6
S-42143
Vastra Froelunda, Goteborg
och Bohus County, Sweden
Tel: +46-31-456692

WALES

Cardiff Wales
Heol Y Deri
Rhiwbina
Cardiff, South Glamorgan
County, Wales
Tel: 29 2062 5342

Gaerwen Wales
Holyhead Road
Gaerwen, Anglesey County,
Wales
Tel: 1248 421894

Merthyr Tydfil Wales
Nanty Gwenith Street
George Town
Merthyr Tydfil, Mid glamor-
gan County, Wales
Tel: 1685 722455

Newcastle Emlyn Wales
Cardigan Road
Newcastle Emlyn, Dyfed
County, Wales
Tel: 1239 711472

Rhyl Wales
Rhuddlan Road
Rhyl, Clwyd County, Wales
Tel: 1745 331172

Swansea Wales
Cockett Road
Swansea, West Glamorgan
County, Wales
Tel: 1792 585792

Contributors

S. Chris Anderson is the author of eleven books and two manuals; a reviewer for the *National Genealogical Society Quarterly*; guest editor of *The Palatine Immigrant*; a retired university professor; a speaker for national, state, and county societies; and currently both a title examiner for a law firm and an archival consultant for a government agency.

Kyle J. Betit is a professional genealogist, author, lecturer, columnist, and former coeditor of *The Irish At Home and Abroad* journal. He makes frequent trips to Ireland for research and works in applying genealogy research to medical genetics studies. Kyle is also master of ceremonies and codirector of the Good Samaritan Program at the Cathedral of the Madeleine in Salt Lake City.

Sharon DeBartolo Carmack is a Certified Genealogist, the author of scholarly and popular books and articles including the book *You Can Write Your Family History* (Cincinnati, Ohio: Betterway Books, 2003), the editor of Betterway Genealogy Books, and a contributing editor for *Family Tree Magazine*. Sharon writes commissioned family histories and offers editorial services for genealogists.

Rick Crume is a contributing editor for *Family Tree Magazine*. A sixth-generation Minnesotan, he has actively researched his own family history since age 14. He created the Genealogical Library Master Catalog, the largest bibliography of genealogical and local history books ever published. He belongs to genealogical societies in the U.S., Canada, England, Scotland, Wales, and Germany.

Dena Eben is a former assistant editor for *Family Tree Magazine*.

David A. Fryxell is founder and former editor-in-chief of *Family Tree Magazine* and is also former editor-in-chief of Betterway Books.

Lise Hull is an American freelance writer and researcher specializing in British heritage. In 1985, she was stationed in Pembrokeshire, Wales, as a commissioned officer in the U.S. Navy and became enamored with Britain. Since then Hull has extensively explored the UK and its heritage, both as a resident and as a returning visitor. Her interest in Welsh history and heritage naturally led her to study Welsh genealogy. In 2001, she received a Master of Arts with distinction from University of Wales, Aberystwyth, obtaining a degree in Heritage Studies from the Department of History and Welsh History. In 2002, she received the first ever Faculty of Arts award for best dissertation. Hull also has a Master of Public Affairs, specializing in Historic Preservation, from Indiana University (Bloomington, Indiana); another Master of Arts with distinction in Counseling Psychology, from National University (Sacramento, California); and a Bachelor of Arts in Anthropology (minor in archaeology) from Franklin and Marshall College (Lancaster, Pennsylvania). In 1994, shortly after her retirement from the Navy, she began working as a freelance writer and researcher specializing in British heritage. Her book, *Countries of the World: Scotland*, was published by Times Media in 2000. In recognition of that book, Thomson/Gale publishers recently selected Hull for inclusion in their reference book, *Something About The Author*, which highlights talented children's writers. Another book, *Castles of Wales: Glamorgan*, is scheduled for publication by Wales Books in late 2003. Hull has just completed a guide to studying in the UK, written for international students, and is presently working on a book about tracing family history for a publisher in the United Kingdom. She writes the "Wales Off the Beaten Track" column for *Ninnau*, the North American Welsh newspaper, and is on the staff of *Renaissance Magazine*, writing their "Castles Lore" and "Digging Up the Past" columns. Her work has been published by *Everton's Family History* and *Genealogical Helper* magazines, *Celtic Heritage*, *Military History Quarterly*, *History Today*, *Pembrokeshire Life*, *Activity Wales*, *Faces*, *Scottish Journal*, *US Scots*, *AntiqueWeek*, and other print and online publications. Details on Hull's research and travel business, Castles Unlimited, may be viewed at <www.castles-of-britain.com>.

Susan Wenner Jackson is a former managing editor of *Family Tree Magazine*.

Linda Jonas is the past president of the British Isles Family History Society-U.S.A. Linda has been a full-time family historian for more than twenty years and has focused on helping Americans find their British Isles ancestry. She has been supervisor, staff trainer, and instructor at the Los Angeles Family History Center, which holds the largest British Isles resource collection outside of Salt Lake City. She is a popular lecturer and writer on all aspects of U.S. and British Isles research. Linda is now director of the McLean [Virginia] Family History Center, which specializes in Scottish research.

Rhonda R. McClure is a professional genealogist specializing in New England research and computerized genealogy. She has been involved in online genealogy for fifteen years. She was the Data Manager of the Genealogy RoundTable on Genie® for seven years and the forum manager for the Genealogy Forum on MSN® for eighteen months. Her recent endeavors involve the researching of the famous and infamous. She is a contributing editor to *Biography Magazine* with her "Celebrity Roots" column and a contributing writer to *The History Channel Magazine* with her "Heritage" column, both dealing with the unique ancestral or familial relationships of the famous and celebrated. She has compiled approximately 120 celebrity trees of those in entertainment, sports, literature, and politics. She has authored articles in *Ancestry Magazine*, *Genealogical Computing*, *Everton's Genealogical Helper*, and *Family Tree Magazine*. She is author of the award-winning *The Complete Idiot's Guide to Online Genealogy*, now in its second edition and The Official Family Tree Maker fast & easy series for versions 7 through 10 of the program. Her latest book is *Finding Your Famous and Infamous Ancestors*, published by Betterway Books, and it is her second with them. Her first was *The Genealogist's Computer Companion*. As a lecturer, she has spoken at national conferences, including NGS, FGS, and GenTech, as well as participating in the Brigham Young University Computerized Genealogy Conference for a number of years. She has upcoming speaking engagements across the country. She is the current President of the Genealogical Speakers Guild and a member of the National Genealogical Society, the New England Historic Genealogical Society, the International Society of Family History Writers and Editors, and the National Writers Union.

Paul Milner is a native of northern England. He is a professional genealogical researcher who has specialized in British Isles research for more than twenty years. He is a past president of the British Interest Group of Wisconsin and Illinois (BIG-WILL). Since 1992, he has written and edited the society newsletter. He writes book reviews for *FORUM*, the Federation of Genealogical Societies' quarterly journal. Paul is a nationally known and popular speaker at genealogical conferences and seminars and typically draws audiences of several hundred genealogists for his lectures.

Dwight A. Radford is a native of Ooltewah, Tennessee. He resides in Salt Lake City, Utah, where he has been doing genealogy professionally since 1986. He specializes in Irish and Irish immigrant research and travels to the Republic of Ireland and Northern Ireland yearly to con-

duct on-site research for his clients. He can be contacted at radfordut@att.net.

Melanie Rigney is the former editor of *Writer's Digest* magazine and former contributing editor of *Family Tree Magazine*.

Allison Stacy is the editor of *Family Tree Magazine*.

Maureen A. Taylor is the author of *Scrapbooking Your Family History* (Betterway Books, 2003), *Preserving Your Family Photographs* (Betterway Books, 2003), and *Uncovering Your Ancestry through Family Photographs* (Betterway Books, 2000). She is also a contributing editor of *Family Tree Magazine*.

Ernest Thode is the manager of the local history and genealogy department of the Washington County Public Library in Marietta, Ohio. He is the author of nine books including *German-English Genealogical Dictionary* (2d edition, GPC, 2000) and *Address Book for Germanic Genealogy* (6th edition, GPC, 2000). He is an officer in his local genealogical society.

Index